MANAGING MEDIA CONVERGENCE

Pathways to Journalistic Cooperation

T0337952

Other Titles in the
Media and Technology Series:

MANAGING MEDIA CONVERGENCE

Pathways to Journalistic Cooperation

Kenneth C. Killebrew

Media and Technology Series
Alan B. Albarran, Series Editor

Blackwell
Publishing

Media and Technology
A Blackwell Publishing Series

Kenneth C. Killebrew is Assistant Professor and Director of Graduate Studies in the School of Mass Communications, University of South Florida, Tampa. He has worked extensively in both television and print news for more than two decades.

©2005 Blackwell Publishing

Blackwell Publishing Professional
2121 State Avenue, Ames, Iowa 50014, USA

Orders: 1-800-862-6657
Office: 1-515-292-0140
Fax: 1-515-292-3348
Web site: www.blackwellprofessional.com

Blackwell Publishing Ltd
9600 Garsington Road, Oxford OX4 2DQ, UK
Tel.: +44 (0)1865 776868

Blackwell Publishing Asia
550 Swanston Street, Carlton, Victoria 3053, Australia
Tel.: +61 (0)3 8359 1011

Authorization to photocopy items for internal or personal use, or the internal or personal use of specific clients, is granted by Blackwell Publishing, provided that the base fee of $.10 per copy is paid directly to the Copyright Clearance Center, 222 Rosewood Drive, Danvers, MA 01923. For those organizations that have been granted a photocopy license by CCC, a separate system of payments has been arranged. The fee code for users of the Transactional Reporting Service is 0-8138-1108-2/2005 $.10.

Printed on acid-free paper in the United States of America

First edition, 2005

Library of Congress Cataloging-in-Publication Data

Killebrew, Kenneth C.
  Managing media convergence : pathways to journalistic cooperation / by Kenneth C. Killebrew.—1st ed.
      p. cm.—(Media and technology series)
  Includes bibliographical references and index.
  ISBN 0-8138-1108-2 (alk. paper)
  1. Journalism—Management. 2. Journalism—Technological innovations. I. Title. II. Series.

  PN4784.M34K55 2005
  070.4'068—dc22
                                                                    2004011198
The last digit is the print number: 9 8 7 6 5 4 3 2 1

Contents

Foreword

In *Managing Media Convergence: Pathways to Journalistic Coopera-tion,* author Kenneth C. Killebrew approaches the evolving topic of media convergence from a management perspective and offers new and insight-ful information that will be of use to students, professors and industry practitioners. While much has been written on convergence, Killebrew is the first author to look at this topic through a managerial lens.

Focusing on management within journalistic enterprises, the author first provides an understanding of convergence through three introductory chapters, detailing concepts frequently associated with media convergence by illustrating how ownership, technology and globalization form our ideas on convergence. The next two chapters detail theoretical aspects of traditional management science and organizational communication and how they evolve in a convergence atmosphere.

Killebrew then enlightens the reader by detailing the role of creativity and change and its impact on the journalistic process, and models that have been used to help understand convergence issues. The author follows with discussions on the role of power and risk among journalists; the in-fluence of convergence on the regulatory process; aspects of convergence impacting advertising and public relations; and a summary chapter that tries to objectively look at convergence by asking if this is simply the lat-est trend or the beginning a new era of fully integrated media?

Managing Media Convergence: Pathways to Journalistic Cooperation will generate new thinking on managing journalists in a converging envi-ronment, and challenge our contemporary assumptions regarding media management practices. As the newest member of the Blackwell Series on Media and Technology, *Managing Media Convergence* joins a group of other distinguished titles helping to promote greater understanding of the interplay of media and technology and its impact on individuals, society and the globe.

Alan B. Albarran, Ph. D.
The University of North Texas
Series Editor, Media and Technology

Preface

"…truth between candid minds, can never do harm."
Thomas Jefferson
to John Adams
(July, 1891)

Depending on whom you talk to, you will hear at least four definitions of convergence. Some will base their definition on the changing technology, others will base it on economic models or advertising, and some will examine it from the audience's perspective. Still others believe that convergence itself is shifting too rapidly for a single definition. In reality, it is likely the factors are not shifting at all and that in some ways, the definition "creators" (and that perhaps includes me) are making it all too complex.

Convergence is, above all else, about information and how we prepare, post and transfer that information from one place to another. The complexity comes after this point, not before, and often has more to do with people, perceptions and their "reality" than with fact; that is the focus of this book.

Before moving further, it should be noted that I understand that convergence is already controversial. Whether blamed for stifling media and social voices, wreaking havoc in the battle over ending cross-ownership rules, or a ploy for further excessive media concentration, sides are lining up. It is hitting hardest those who hold to the deepest traditions of journalism, in which the expectation is that every voice has a right to be heard. This book will attempt to tackle some of those issues. The alternatives pointed out here will be applauded by some, hated by others and looked upon with aggravation by still others.

As media managers, it is essential that we understand both where the complexity takes place and how it should be defined for those who work or will work daily in converged environments. In the context of news as information, this obviously requires an emphasis on journalism and journalistic training. It also should be noted that throughout this book, the term "journalist" is used holistically to talk about the work of information gatherers and disseminators.

From journalists' standpoint, convergence is really about understanding that they will be asked to write stories in ways unlike their traditional training or in their current job. Although convergence is still about "doing" the traditional journalistic activities of gathering information and arranging information into a sensible story, it forces journalists and editors to turn from their historical functions and apply their skills in new ways. They ultimately must be prepared to place information on more than one stage and must understand that the story will look different from one stage (or platform) to another.

Unfortunately, technological change isn't just driving the media marketplace today; it is defining that marketplace. Many media organizations are placing the emphasis on the technology, largely ignoring what journalists do best: reporting and presenting information. Consequently, while the changes appear uncomplicated, i.e. learn more than one writing style and more than one method of presentation, there has been a great deal of resistance to these innovations. The resistance should have been anticipated, and in many ways was part of the calculations of owners, but the depth of the resistance was misjudged. Attempts to "fix" the resistance have met with limited success.

The breadth of the resistance also may have caught observers and owners off guard. Critics have called upon Congress to stop the process of cross-ownership of broadcast and print outlets. They cite the strangling of voices in the media marketplace by callous and absentee owners. The outcry against "convergence" has led some to begin to back away from the concept altogether, turning instead to the notion of "collaboration."

This book is about identifying and meeting these new journalistic challenges. It is about bringing together a variety of management elements and applying them to the field of journalism. It will examine the concerns of the marketplace and the practices of regulators. It also will examine the social consequences of poor ownership decisions and pose solutions to those problems. Along the way we will endeavor to examine the face of media management and present students, scholars and practitioners with practical and useful tools to enable them to do their jobs better in the new marketplace media.

Whatever the powers of media ownership eventually come to call this new journalistic endeavor, it is likely that the days of independent and highly competitive journalism in singly-owned and operated print, broadcast and internet platforms are fast fading. We'll stick with calling this occurrence convergence.

In this volume, I have attempted to look for the best answers in the world we face today. Those answers may change quickly. That is the nature of media. We cannot go backward, at least not too far, so we must struggle to find answers in the present.

This is but one perspective, and it should be understood that what is laid forth here is being forwarded less from a desire to create a new model for journalism than to move discussion from the continuing space of churn into a pragmatic dialog for change. Issues of fairness, openness, the workplace and society are all touched on here. How we ultimately answer these questions and still hold on to ethics, diversity, localism and profitability all in the face of ownership concentration and globalization is more of a challenge than one book can answer. Convergence is the beginning of change, not its endpoint. When we realize that, we will be able to take at least a few steps forward.

As you read these chapters, you should understand that no single theoretical or management frame is expressly supported. The key is to examine all approaches and glean from what is available to bring it to application in convergence management. Neither should this book's approach be viewed as exhaustive. Many excellent approaches to management have been excluded from the discussion but may be fodder for future writing.

Chapters 1 and 2 are written to set forth the issues influencing the adoption of convergence and the political and social circumstances currently surrounding news room adaptation to convergence. Chapter 1 will review issues from a global perspective with a great deal of discussion on the nature of voices, global media concentration, and the impact on convergence. Chapter 2 will attempt to bring these issues "home" to the United States with discussions on the state of media ownership at the point of manuscript submission (because ownership undoubtedly will have changed by the time you read this book).

Chapter 3 begins to define convergence both organizationally and systematically, using models developed during the course of the past several years. Chapter 3 offers some direction on differentiating among convergence levels.

Chapter 4 is generally a discussion of traditional management methods and the evolution of management theories. The chapter discusses these theories and their practical assumptions in a broad context, generally setting up the discussions on specific management tactics in following chapters.

Chapter 5 moves to management discussions at the organizational level. Paradigms developed in organizational communications, organizational psychology and other areas are examined and applied to convergence activities.

Chapter 6 attempts to reconcile the difficulties of change on the concept of creativity. All individuals possess and express creativity in different ways. Journalists are trained to channel creativity through writing and performance. Several models of convergence adoption are examined, and their impact on creativity is shown.

Chapter 7 begins a discussion on power, performance and risk in the newly mediated workplace. Formal and informal power structures are discussed, and the added complexities of convergence are added in the general political mix of news organizations.

Chapter 8 reviews the essentials of regulations over the past several decades in broadcasting and the influence that convergence brings to the regulatory mix. Issues of national policy and local application and enforcement are discussed. Several potential solutions to the concerns over local issues are examined.

Not everything about convergence is tied to journalism. In Chapter 9, some aspects of advertising and public relations are discussed in relationship to their applications in convergence and converging media outlets.

Chapter 10 brings a variety of factors together to talk about whether convergence is journalism's future or just another blip on the radar of journalistic conventions. This author believes that convergence is an intermediate solution to long-term media integration or what integration will ultimately take place. Despite regulatory concerns, media will be fully integrated in the not-too-distant future. Regulators and society need to prepare for this integration rather than fight it.

The future of journalism, whether it based on convergence, integration, collaboration or some name not yet in general use, is tied to these new technologies and delivery systems. Efforts to keep the media separate will be counterproductive in the long run. The notions of the past, based on embedded individual and organizational belief systems, will yield to the technological revolutions surrounding information dissemination.

Those leading the efforts to stop convergence should instead look for new ways to create an evolving set of regulatory and business models that both benefit and protect society while incorporating converging media into the milieu. Efforts in this direction will position the United States and other nations to improve the quality of journalism while increasing the sources of media to the public. I hope that the ideas presented here are a step in that direction, as well.

Kenneth Killebrew
February 2004

MANAGING MEDIA CONVERGENCE

Pathways to Journalistic
Cooperation

CHAPTER 1

Change in the Global Media Environment

"And there were giants in the earth, and time was theirs."[1] The time of giants has come again. These new behemoths have fallen on the media and have generally cleared the media landscape of family-owned lumber, nearly completing a task undertaken three decades ago. For more than 20 of those years, a battle cry has been raised by those who fear these giants will overtake the world and create a new hierarchy of information designed by elites.

Ben Bagdikian raised the alarm in 1983 with the publication of his book *The Media Monopoly*.[2] Bagdikian lamented the passing of family-owned newspapers, the destruction of the magazine industry and the insipid advancement of corporate causes over individual journalistic endeavor. Despite those warnings and more than 20 years—and six revised editions later—the power among media owners has continued to become more centralized and has reached beyond Bagdikian's earlier concerns of media concentration in the United States to one of significant global reach.

Robert McChesney also has been an active critic of increased media concentration.[3] He, with a number of other scholars globally, has entered into a great debate on the issue of media concentration. In the online debate vehicle "Open Democracy," McChesney and others have called for governments to stop the process that is eating away at competition and turning the media landscape into a strong-armed oligopoly.

> Twenty years ago, one thought of media systems as national phenomena first, with imports a secondary consideration. Today this is reversed. We must see the global system first, and then make allowances for differences

between nations and regions. This global media system is an indispensable part of the rise of global neoliberal capitalism. Indeed, it would be difficult to imagine 'globalisation' without the emergence of the international commercial media system.[4]

Standing at the top of these media chains are the likes of AOL Time Warner, Bertelsmann, Viacom, Sony, News Corp and Walt Disney. From the shores of Japan and Australia to the glass towers of Berlin and New York City, media giants are roaming the landscape.[5]

General Electric, owner of NBC and a variety of media operations, has made a move to join the largest of these companies by recently acquiring the bulk of the media properties from the French media company Vivendi Universal. Now NBC Universal is expected to be among the largest of the top companies in the world.[6]

Not to be outdone, News Corp. recently completed plans to purchase Hughes Electronics, primary owner of DirecTV, adding to its already impressive lead in satellite television holdings.[7] Then in February 2004, Comcast launched a hostile takeover bid for Disney. If that $54.1 billion merger takes place, Comcast will become the leading media company in the world. In 2001, Comcast was only an average sized cable company. It is now well equipped to play with the major companies.[8]

Darkness or Light?

Although Bagdikian, McChesney and others continue the written and verbal assault against media concentration, others aren't quite sure that there is a media doomsday on the horizon. Some dispute the claim that media ownership concentration has led to a loss of diverse voices; others don't believe that concentration itself is a culprit and want to know just how "ownership" should be defined. To them, those who point backward to corporations with centralized power of a century ago need to understand that today's corporations look vastly different.

Compared to ownership two decades ago, corporate media ownership today is concentrated among a small number of companies, but the control of those companies is now as diverse as the voices that Bagdikian and McChesney say are being muffled. Investment groups, retirement and pension programs, minority college fund developers and others are capable of compelling today's corporations to moderate from a single position that is corporately developed to a position where these multiple ownership voices are satisfied.[9]

While there continue to be personalities as strong as Rockefeller and Carnegie—News Corp's Murdoch and Disney's Eisner come to mind—their power has been transformed. At the global level, signs of competition exist in at least the way messages are delivered to viewers. These new messages tend to show up in the way programming is determined, but it also shows up in news organization activity. Media writers now term cable television's CNN as a liberally biased news operation, while FOX News is the conservative answer to that call. Less than a decade ago, there was no cable-based news from FOX, let alone the ability to label FOX as a conservative alternative.

Demers (2002) provides a strong antidote to those worried about media ownership concentration.[10] Demers points to the explosion of research in mass media influences as a reflection of the general interest and ability to study the nature of the media itself. He argues that a concentrated media bent on serving a single-minded approach to society would have found ways to suspend the myriad voices now working on media issues.

Demers also argues that critics have failed, among other things, to back up their claims of diminished voices and ideas with good empirical research; nor, as he points out, can those critics explain social changes that have benefited groups that challenge so-called traditional values or capitalism (women and civil rights organizations, for example). From this perspective, how would *Queer Eye for the Straight Guy* fit any definition of traditionally entrenched values?

It might also be argued that although media concentration is certainly underway, media monoliths frequently work to confound themselves. For instance, there has been some obvious remorse in the mergers arena following the feeding frenzy of just a few years ago. AOL Time Warner in early 2003 announced that bringing the broadband Internet company on board with the television and publishing giant had been a mistake. The companies had spent three years trying to work together but were discovering that a number of internal issues were difficult to resolve.[11]

AT&T, less than three years after acquiring one of the largest cable systems in the world, decided it didn't understand the cable industry. The telecommunications colossus sold off the cable unit to Comcast in 2002, creating a newly defined world leader in cable systems. In addition, the Vivendi-NBC deal took place only after Vivendi decided it didn't want to be a global media competitor and would be happy with its holdings in France. It was all about risk—which companies were willing to take the risks and which companies were worried about profitability.[12]

Benjamin Compaine, in his book *Who Owns the Media? Competition and Concentration in the Mass Media*, also portrays the media ownership landscape somewhat differently. According to Compaine, 50 companies owned the vast majority of media holdings in 1986, and by 2001, the number of owners remained about the same. Compaine believes that while media concentration appears to have grown, growth figures are misleading in real dollar terms. Compaine dismisses the growing concentration in the newspaper industry as a function of increased competition and tumbling circulation figures. After all, he says, "One can't expect a dying industry to do anything but consolidate."[13]

Although Compaine is correct that the number of owners in the mass media is relatively unchanged, the overall concentration of facilities and units among the largest owners has increased significantly in the past decade. In other words, while some companies have grown smaller, others have grown larger, including Viacom and General Electric/NBC. Comcast's bid in February 2004 to take over Disney for $54.1 billion is the latest example of the increased pressures from concentration.

Demers' view of media concentration critics is similarly skeptical. Although dubious of concentration where societal risks and loss of voices are concerned, he also remains convinced that government should keep a vigilant eye on the media to ensure that public interests continue to be served. This author's opinion is that the only way to ensure the protection of the public interest while allowing free market activities to continue is through some form of re-regulation. Ideas in that realm appear in Chapter 8.

Regardless of the view, changes in these media environments are likely to continue. Still, the emphasis on each of these changes appears to be based on two things: organizational compatibility and profitability. Individuals are not part of the ultimate concentration equation, and the public is recognized only as a market, despite Compaine's view that shareholders also are the public. Stakeholders often aggregate the "needs" of their shareholders and, as noted earlier, are the keys to the visions driving media operations. Governments, one time formidable players in these games, have seemingly been left at the curbside as the media companies move along their way.

From one industry segment to another, improving the organization's profitability has motivated the actions of these companies. Concerns over profits slashed the number of general interest news magazines world-wide in the early 1970s, yet the total number of magazines today is higher than it was in the mid 1970s. This is generally the result of niche marketing.

Likewise, the cable television industry has found profitability in niche marketing where competing head-on with the big networks failed. Fewer daily newspapers exist in the United States than 30 years ago, but other nations have suffered higher closure rates.[14]

Today, there are increasing efforts to link newspapers, television, radio and the Internet into converged media operations. This change is coming, not to increase the information power of these media outlets, but to increase their earning power as community-based oligopolies. Bringing the concept of oligopoly from the national to local level will be discussed more fully in Chapter 2.

Technology is driving these changes at one end, while increased profit motivates the changes from the other. We will deal with each on a global scale before integrating them into a discussion on management.

Techno-World

Although a great deal of effort has been put into discussions regarding the evolution of communication technologies, and particularly the Internet, it is not the development of the Internet itself that has led to the explosion in world communications; the Internet has been with us for decades. Two other things have made the Internet's current abilities more viable: digital capacity (the Net's carrying power through the "pipe") and more-sophisticated networking technology. The absence of powerful computing tools hampered the early ability of the Internet to take advantage of digital communications opportunities and linkages with the more traditional media of newspapers and television. "Streaming" video was likely to lock up computers, clog the information delivery system and even shut down some Internet service providers.

The gigahertz revolution in personal computing power began the process of solving those problems and opened the frontier to the general public. Video streaming, still slow by broadcast standards, is improving exponentially each year. This increased access has pushed the technology envelope until personal computing and Web surfing today are a way of life for many. As improvements continue, the revolutionary influences of technology on media will render further profound effects.

If, for instance, telecommunications companies, Internet service providers and cable systems continue to develop higher capacity links to individual homes, the expectation will be that traditional broadcasting outlets would be required to use multiple delivery systems or face substantially diminished markets in the next 10–15 years. Some researchers believe this won't happen, that traditional broadcasting will reach a smaller but stable audience level and remain there. This seems an unlikely scenario since we are dealing with media that is easily transformed from one technological base to another via the digital realm, i.e., broadcast to Internet. The evolution of some broadcasters away from broadcast licensing to accept only cable carriage is already a fact of technological media life. One expectation is that the next evolution would substantially complete that move away from traditional licensing (and its added governmental encumbrances).[15]

Although further discussion on licensing, particularly in the United States, will be discussed in Chapter 8, this book is not situated to deal in depth with the societal outfall of such a move. Moreover, those who have worried before, whether they are correct or not, will worry even more in a nonregulated freefall digital community. What we are interested in here is developing an understanding of how organizations and the individuals who gather and disseminate information for them are going to be affected by these technological changes, and how to manage those changes in the coming years. A more thorough discussion of the prospects of regulation and its influences on information gathering will wait.

Global Muscle-Flexing

In the early '90s, Rupert Murdoch, already flexing the growing muscle of News Corp, launched his Star-TV satellite over Southeast Asia to extend his corporate hold over the Asian media audience. It wasn't long before the mainland Chinese government threatened to find a way to shoot it down. Thus the Chinese were faced with dealing with a corporate entity in the midst of their continuing efforts to isolate themselves from the Western world's commercial influences. Conversely, Murdoch was faced with the first serious threat to his media empire—a threat that came in a way he had not originally predicted.[16]

Well before the incident with China, Murdoch had bought his way into a dozen nations, including Great Britain and the United States. In the U.S., some marveled at the speed with which the chief of News Corps received his citizenship, a condition of media ownership. It was clear that in America, money talks. Murdoch's arrogance is considered typical and symptomatic among global media owners. These owners, representing large shareholder groups, generally tend to ignore the cultures of the nations upon which they are trying to impose their media willpower. The media ownership culture is steeped in the halls of profit, the language is money; it is no wonder that many critics portray modern media owners as the "robber barons" of today.

However, there is little evidence to back up claims of Western media cultural imperialism, the term used to denote the local impact of global media insertion into other nations. The influence of Western media on disparate nations is generally considered weak. In fact, more than a dozen studies have found that the cultural influences rarely have a dramatic impact at all on the non-mediated nation . Cultural values are generally more embedded in these societies than those issuing warnings expect.[17]

In many ways, media moguls have had an excellent run. Their properties are among the most profitable enterprises on the face of the earth, with revenues running four to five times higher than that of traditional industry. The resultant earnings are far beyond the typical corporate earning levels of 7–12 percent, yet media owners seem perplexed when others chide them for high profit margins and quick fixes on the global landscape.[18]

In the United States, the checkbook is doing the talking in Congress, in the White House and through the administration's grip on the Federal Communications Commission (FCC). Deregulation is the mantra in Washington. Elected officials and financial gurus all believe that the free marketplace will solve the problems; however, some members of Congress under pressure from consumer groups have gotten another message…enough with the mergers and slackening rules, it is time to take back control of American media.[18]

Principal among those now worried about too much centralized ownership is Senator John McCain, war hero and former presidential candidate. McCain, along with others, was successful in mid-2003 in calling a halt to the FCC's planned removal of the thirty-year-old prohibition against newspapers and television stations within the same market being owned by one media company. Congress was reviewing the rule as this book went to press.[19]

In Great Britain, similar forces had gathered in the 1990s to unbundle the stranglehold the government-backed BBC had on the airwaves. Broadcasting in Britain and much of Europe had evolved through a series of laws designed to "protect" society by controlling the airwaves in government owned and/or operated stations. Nevertheless, by the early '90s, commercial companies wanted a piece of the lucrative audience in Great Britain. The pressure forced the government to remake its regulatory environment. The commercial ITN stations, allocated to add more channel selections to British television in the '80s had been hampered in its efforts to expand by the high-powered and publicly financed BBC. The pressure for profits helped Parliament move away from the two company system by reallocating the ITN broadcasting licenses and reducing over time the public monetary support for the BBC. The idea was to position all of the broadcasting companies in a somewhat equal competitive environment. The number of media companies operating on the British airwaves peaked at seven, but rapidly dropped to four by 2002.[20]

Equally daunting to the European media landscape was the development of pirate stations operating off the coasts of several countries and finally forcing government to capitulate and issue licenses to those who were operating offshore and outside of the geographic borders of the controlling nations. Issues of control have led some to suggest that some form of global regulatory action may soon be necessary.

World Trade, Alternate Culture Pressure

Questions exist about how global media should be operated in the future—how they should be organized and what should be the role of nations in organizing and enforcing those regulations. Quietly over the past decade, forces have been at work to relax the overall operating rules of media and bring them into a system managed generally by those who run the media now. The implications are enormous but point to how convergence, whether stalled in the United States or not, will likely have a place in a global media environment.[21]

The World Trade Organization (WTO) was established in 1995 to supplant the GATT (General Agreement on Tariffs and Trade) and first became known in the United States when world economic leaders met in Seattle, Washington, to formulate global economic policies. The WTO members were met with violence from those who believed that the corporate world was attempting to take over functions of government and destroy national identities.[22]

Critics once scoffed at the "idea" that the corporate world could undermine established governments, but the anti-WTO forces may be justly worried. WTO has, since its founding, worked untiringly to force the "liberalization" of nationalistic rules that limit trans-border trade.

This liberalization of laws and rules governing trade has a direct impact on the media industry. By subjecting rules to a global standard, the expectation is that fewer, not more, rules will be pushed into place because allowances for local cultures and mores must be made. With a liberal (read relaxed) system of rules, media organizations, currently tethered by nationalism, will be free to move from organization to organization, as well as from nation to nation to put in place their organizational goals.

A second agent of global change is the United Nations Educational, Scientific and Cultural Organization (UNESCO). UNESCO has battled with Western-controlled media and governments over the years as the discussion of the control of media messages has heated up. The organization, also an independent branch of the United Nations, has attempted to persuade Western media to invest in less-developed nations without adding their own input into operations and content.[23]

The issues of media regulation at a global level will be discussed more fully in Chapter 8, but the influence of media owners on both large and small nations cannot be underestimated in the long range.

While leaders in the United States and other nations work to find ways to control growth and ownership in media groups, they may have already handcuffed themselves by voting to favor global agreements like that with the WTO. The prophets of media change then are likely to have a better grasp of the overall situation than those individuals who work in their own media industries, but see the overall state of their industry from the narrow, rather than the global, view. This leads us to a discussion of just how dramatic the changes are likely to be as media ownership slides into multiple-platform arrangements.

Kawari Wars

The Japanese word for change is *Kawari*. Faith Popcorn, co-author and editor of the *Dictionary of the Future,* believes Kawari will soon become a universal word defining periods of sudden, almost violent, change. From a media management standpoint, it is likely that we are indeed in the midst of Kawari and may well be near the brink of revolution—a revolution that many in the deregulated high-tech media environment of today believe is already here.[24]

From a global perspective, media managers are faced with not only marketplace chaos resulting from concentrating ownership and value shifting by those owners but also revolutionary processes for providing content and how to best communicate with those often distant and distracted owners. It is part war, part race to see who, in the changing world of information delivery, will win. This war-race is being waged on two fronts: the technological front, which has received a great deal of attention (as we have noted), and the provider front where managers and journalists face significant changes in how they must do their work to survive.

Each front is challenged by a series of advances that are creating changes in how information is processed and distributed. At the human level, media managers must confront existing cultures, traditions and conventions while overcoming a frantic climate of uncertainty. Simultaneously, these managers must sound a call to action to engage competitively in the historic technological battle of change, all the while fostering the creativity required for product excellence.

The specifics of the global environment are as revolutionary and perplexing as the management issues that will ultimately be dealt with in later chapters of this book. Companies are swapping properties, joining in collaborative efforts, and out-and-out destroying competition where owners see a corporate "fit" or think they can stifle competition. The global nature of media continues to change.

As the Western model expands past its national borders, it will encounter stronger and stronger resistance from nations more comfortable in other systems of management and politics. This will further the Kawari concept and likely lead to conflicts. The News Corp-China example may have been just the beginning.

Beyond Nation States

In the past, nations sought to expand and impose their wills on other nations through the capture and control of the peoples of those nations. The will of the conquering nation often was imposed on these peoples with differing levels of effectiveness and success.

By the late twentieth century, non-government organizations (NGOs) and transnational corporations began a different form of expansion, one based on ideas. Those ideas centered on the concepts incorporated in capitalism. The World Trade Organization, formed with the United Nations following World War II, and its closely linked groups, the World Bank and the International Monetary Fund (IMF), worked to turn governments and populations toward a more capitalistic model of operating.[25]

Economic upheaval in a variety of second- and third-tier nations was often delayed or deferred by loans and grants from the bank and others. However, when these loans were called in by the World Bank or IMF, the result was often even more chaotic with rioting and wholesale revolutions.

By 1999, concerns over how the banks were controlling the political lives of other nations led to the protests that took place on the streets of the cities where global monetary leaders gathered. From Seattle to Paris, Washington D.C. and New York, those opposed to globalization efforts have taken to the streets. If and how these protests will eventually manifest themselves in change is still a matter or debate.

Money Changers

Media organizations are also deeply involved in this battle. At the heart of this warring media frontier is a desire to increase or maintain profit levels by media organizations. Global audiences provide more potential for profits without increasing media organizational needs to produce more products. The current buzzword for making the most of this need is "re-purposing."

Repurposing is an interesting concept. It stems from an old premise in business of using the Parsimony Principle. Under the Parsimony Principle, organizations find ways to use the outputs of production in as many ways as possible. Much as pharmaceutical companies have created drugs for one disease and then research ways to use the drug to assist in treating other medical conditions, the media has taken its products and looked for ways to extend those products to new audiences.

This repurposing has been utilized on a global level for some time. Most marketers of motion pictures made in the United States today concern themselves with international "aftermarket" runs of the film as well as sales of videos to markets around the world. This is because revenues generated from international sales are often three to five times higher than the monies generated from the initial release of the film in the United States.

Although many nations fear the influence of media from the United States, others are interested in how media products from their nations will influence the thinking of U.S. citizens. One can not have expansion in one direction without ultimately expecting expansion of the media products of others back into their own nation. In the U.S., discussions of cultural differences are often limited to a few minority groups; there is little discussion about how other peoples will react. The U.S. has become a nation that absorbs the cultural outflow of others, incorporating what it wants and discarding unwanted cultural intrusions.

Other nations, most notably France in Europe, China in Asia and a variety of fundamentally Muslim nations of the Middle East and much of

Africa, criticize Western "cultural imperialism." These nations seek to protect their traditional cultural values and see Western media products as ultimate examples of the evils of global capitalism. The fact that these same nations readily export goods to the U.S. seems lost in their arguments when defending their own cultures. This may be a fair assessment since the sheer volume of U.S. products often overwhelms the marketplace of other nations.

Although repurposing has not been well received by a number of other nations, many journalists and writers agree with concerns over globalization, but for different reasons. Individuals often feel that organizations are reaping undue profits from their work. Freelance writers and photographers often feel the pain of reuse the most. Recently, a freelance journalist reported that a health story she had written appeared in nine publications in seven languages during the course of two years. She was paid once.[26]

Conditions like these are at the heart of repurposing from a corporate level but are of great concern to not only writers and photographers, but to other nations as well. They argue that reports written in one language and prepared for one media organization appear internationally without respect to the nation where the material is targeted. In these "repurposed" materials, little concern for cultural or geographical differences exists. Again, the motive is profit.

Similarly, convergence suffers globally from these same workforce and government concerns. The cultural and economic implications have led some to worry that convergence will simply be used to eliminate jobs and decrease the number of sources of information available to publics on a global scale. Voices will simply dry up and fewer forms of expression will be available to the public.

Around the World

Earlier in this chapter we pointed out that China and Rupert Murdoch have not seen eye-to-eye on the Star TV satellite delivery system. Today, more than a decade after the open threats from the Chinese, there has been a shift in that country's philosophy.

China discovered that it could improve its markets by opening trade doors; interestingly, that has led to a relaxation in the types of television Chinese viewers are allowed to watch. Star TV affords Chinese throughout the southern half of the country with affordable satellite television and has brought many of their citizens an interesting and improved view of the rest of the world. China still holds the reigns, but the leash is a great deal longer where media is concerned.

Rupert Murdoch recently told the Chinese government that the nation has the potential to become a global media giant. Since his earlier encounters with the Chinese, Murdoch's News Corporation now controls and operates a major cable network, has expanded Star TV and is helping the nation improve its cable delivery system. Based in Hong Kong, News Corporation is working to reinforce its regional hold on the Asian basin.

Meanwhile, in Australia, News Corporation's home base, the government recently rejected a bid to liberalize its existing cross-ownership rules. Currently, owners may control no more than 75 percent of the national broadcast market. Cross-ownership of television, radio and newspapers in a specific market is forbidden. Because of its newspaper concentration, the rules have hindered News Ltd., the company's Australian subsidiary, in its attempts to move forward with media convergence and cross-ownership.

At the time this was written, News Ltd. controlled 68 percent of the national newspaper market, 67 percent of the local newspaper market and owned the major satellite television provider, Star TV. It also held a 25 percent stake in Foxtel, Australia's major wire service. However, its stake in the print and satellite media essentially was locking the company out of the television business in its home nation.[27]

Because of News Ltd.'s size relative to other media in that nation, there is a great deal of concern over changing the rules. Three other companies dominate the Australian media landscape with News Ltd., but none with the control of stake owner Murdoch and his people.

In the end, members of Australia's Parliament, citing both free speech issues and the centralized control arguments voiced by global media critics Noam Chomsky and Edward Herman, agreed that the media was unable to meet democratic needs because media's profit-making motives must be served first. In doing so, Parliament left existing controls in place.

Australian Screen Education magazine reported that one senator said, "Those who own or run media organizations are in a position of privilege and influence. They are members of an unelected elite who are not effectively accountable to the Australian people." Much the same could be said of major media in every democratic nation.

In Europe, the battle over media concentration and cross-ownership also is being fought in Parliaments and Legislatures. In London in late summer 2003, the House of Lords called for a series of hearings on media takeovers in Great Britain. Members of the House wanted to approve legislation that would guarantee a "plurality" of owners "committed to a balanced and impartial presentation of news and comment."

The Lords voiced serious concerns over attempts by U.S. media to buy into the independent ITV television network. At the same time, they worried that newspaper conglomerates in Britain would work to purchase Channel 5, one of several networks in the nation.[28]

In Latin America, the growth of media conglomerates (*Grandes Gigantes*) is influencing the south in ways that are apparently bringing a diversity of voices to the arena of public opinion, but only because media are becoming privatized. A mega-media free press apparently is still better than a press controlled by a despotic government.[29]

Throughout Latin America a variety of large companies hold most media...in Mexico it is Televisa, in Brazil, Globo. These giants have been around for years. In other nations, no more than two companies seem to dominate the media arena. For instance, in Argentina, major media holdings belong to Grupo Clarin and Telefonica. Telefonica is owned by its parent company of the same name in Spain. In Argentina there also is a great deal of cross-ownership in most media holdings. Columbia and Venezuela have similar two-group sets of owners controlling most media content.

Entire volumes have been written on media ownership, concentration and global issues. This was simply a sampling of international trends in media ownership. The concerns over media ownership concentration and its implications for convergence are obvious in every corner of the globe.

Conclusions

Keeping score in the latest series of media behemoth mergers is getting tough. Between late 2003 and early 2004, four major deals valued at hundreds of billions of dollars had been undertaken or completed. Global media companies continue their march toward ownership concentration, and the United States is at the center of these oligopolistic efforts.

Some experts believe that creating a systematic set of regulations from a global perspective will help offset the power wielded by these emerging media behemoths. Most believe, however, that nations still aren't ready to work closely enough with one another to create a unified global set of rules regarding media activity. The complexity of such an undertaking would be enormous and would likely set media progress back rather than drive it forward.

Creating a balance between market segments, governments and the various publics is of extraordinary concern. Convergence is adding to this concern as it eats away at traditional regulatory activities. From a management standpoint, attempts to reconcile global issues with local issues will continue to frustrate the hardiest of the proponents of convergence. Finding agreement among parties with significantly different motivations and priorities is not impossible but will be extremely difficult.

From a structural standpoint, American media may be least prepared to meet the management challenges being thrust upon it. In the United States, media management traditions evolved from the manufacturing industries and studies based on the work in those industries by experts in the fields of sociology and behavioral psychology. Management contexts have been examined in ways other than those considered traditional in the American marketplace for only a short time. American research is based solidly on quantitative outputs, but not all research lends itself easily to the arena. This structural bias often causes difficulties in organizations dominated by creative media personalities. Much of the rest of the world looks at media management in other ways.

In most nations, world media began with a focus directed by the government. Rules regarding journalistic activities in both Europe and South America are commonplace, even where generally "open" media systems exist. Great Britain has a complaint board that is able to fine journalists and their news outlets when their behavior is deemed unfair, biased or false. More restrictive societies regularly arrest journalists for reporting news that is unfavorable to the government or their elected officials.

However, in the past one and a half decades, these rules generally have been becoming more relaxed. As companies bought up media in other nations, they sought additional control in the marketplace. Governments have been reluctant to grant those wishes, generally based on past performance by media and other corporations where profit motives always find ways to drown out the need for diversity in news and programming. Still, most governments today have been adapting and following U.S.-directed "marketplace" models of regulation.

A. Michael Noll, a professor and former dean at Annenberg School for Communication at the University of Southern California believes that the latest rendition of convergence is nothing more than a myth. It is another false start in a media intent on consolidation.[30]

According to Noll, "The future will be determined not by the greedy wishes of a few, but by the confluence of a number of factors, such as technology, consumer needs, business culture, regulatory policy and finance."

This is a good position from which to begin any journey regarding convergence but is also a good place to use as a point of reflection. Noll sees the history of the term convergence and believes it is a disingenuous attempt to steal more power and consequently increase the value of media organizations. I disagree, based on Noll's observations that describe the need for a confluence of necessary factors to take shape before convergence will work. It seems to me that that confluence is here. Noll's advice to use caution is also well founded, lest the changes do allow all of us to fall victim to media-induced frenzies of folly.

Exercises:

1. Anticipating change has become a requirement for the information age. Do you believe that change is inevitable in the preparation and delivery of news? Why? Your explanation may cover both material in the book and your personal observations.
2. Is media as important to our daily lives as some authors report? Are the fears of those opposed to media concentration appropriate? Justify your answer.

CHAPTER 2

Corporate America and the Media

On a late morning in February 2002, officials from a top 25 broadcasting company met with several telecommunications and journalism professors at a university in the southeast. Their purpose was clear: help us with convergence (and hence its regulatory aspects) or risk seeing television newsrooms around the country "go dark." The gathering listened patiently but was unconvinced of the company's motives and less sympathetic than company representatives had hoped. There were simply too many questions and too much emphasis on bottom line pressures to warrant more than a tepid response to anyone's corporate mantra.[1]

Four months later, top journalists (from both print and broadcast), educators, publishers and news executives met in New York to grapple with the state of journalism in the United States. The forum, sponsored by the Carnegie Corporation, was lively and revealing and focused on the issues facing twenty-first century journalists. The rapport was engaging, but the outcome was limited. More study was needed, educators should be welcomed with new ideas, but the collective "we" was somewhat undecided in how to proceed.[2]

American journalism is in a period of turmoil greater than it has seen in nearly a century. Journalists and the owners of the media outlets that purvey the news have always been embattled with one group or another, but today the battle is being fought on more fronts than once thought possible. Public interest and trust in news and information is at a near all-time low. Media owners are faced with growing obligations to corporate giants and their shareholders, all while facing budget cuts and receiving fewer resources.

Table 2.1. Top 25 Media Companies in the United States ranked by earnings, 2001

Rank	Company	Revenue ($ Mil.)
1	AOL Time Warner	$40,258.0
2	Viacom	18,814.2
3	Walt Disney Company	15,675.0
4	Sony	9,298.6
5	Bertelsmann A.G.	7,765.8
6	Thomson	7,027.0
7	Omnicom Group	6,889.4
8	Interpublic Group of Companies	6,726.8
9	Reed Elsevier	6,618.8
10	Gannett	6,344.7
11	Hughes Electronics	6,304.4
12	WPP Group	5,791.7
13	General Electric	5,769.0
14	Reuters	5,639.1
15	Clear Channel Communications	5,627.2
16	Fox Entertainment Group	5,408.0
17	Tribune Company	5,193.9
18	Comcast	5,002.8
19	Pearson	4,969.9
20	McGraw-Hill	4,645.5
21	SBC Communications	4,468.0
22	Cox Radio	4,462.3
23	CSC Holdings	4,404.5
24	Verizon Communications	4,313.0
25	EchoStar Communications Corporation	4,001.1

Sources: Veronis Suhler Stevenson; Publishing & Media Group.

On the broadcasting side, the audience share is dwindling, and viewership among the hottest advertising group—those 18–24 years old—is down more than 7 percent from 2001 to 2002.[3] Pressure on television programming influences the pressure on television news. If no one is watching programming, who will the news departments draw onto the viewing plane? The overall viewing age among those who watch the top four broadcast networks is nearing 50, far beyond the arena favored by advertisers. Major advertisers are complaining that television costs are rising even as audiences dwindle. They want marketers and advertising executives to find new ways to meet the challenges of bringing their product messages to the marketplace.

Much of the continuing troubles with American media viewership and readership can be placed on the footstool of technology. The technology is evolving rapidly, even exponentially, according to some experts. Younger audiences quickly adapt and adopt new media strategies. As a result, they are now flocking to electronic venues that produce entertainment other than traditional broadcast programming. Computerized gaming, chat rooms, the Internet and its plethora of Web sites, even cell phones and the evolving technology of personal phone imaging, are all moving the younger audience away from traditional media.

A little more than two decades ago, cable television began a communications explosion of services offering viewers additional media choices. Still, by today's standards those offerings were paltry and woefully insufficient to meet the media demands of today.

Older audiences, generally more satisfied with their viewing and readership habits, are remaining faithful to traditional "appointment" media. This raises issues far beyond the pale of simply reaching an audience; it also sets in motion the likelihood that audiences have become more divergent, and traditional mass-mediated advertising can't respond easily to that divergence.[4]

Newspapers and magazines have already seen this fragmentation in action. Magazines in the 1970s collapsed under the pressures of the marketplace as readers moved away from general circulation magazines to niche magazines. Some general news magazines survived, but mainstream giants such as *Look* and *Life*, mainstays of the publishing industry, disappeared; although they occasionally reappear in special issues, they are but shadows of their earlier incarnations. Yet today, following the turmoil of the '70s, more magazines than ever before exist in the United States, although most reach targeted audiences. While this is good for niche marketing, general advertisers from Ford Motor Company to Proctor and Gamble have had to refocus their advertising dollars to meet the market where it lives.[5]

Newspapers faced a similar fate when consumers shifted work and family habits in a way that essentially drove evening newspapers across the United States out of business. At the same time, pressures from broadcasting reduced overall readership, and newspapers were forced to reinvent themselves in both their look and approach to the news. The advent of *USA Today* marked the beginning of the trend in "Mcnews," and the simplified strategy for many stories remains the main operational approach.[6]

Interestingly, although total newspaper readership is down somewhat from the heyday of the late 1970s and early 1980s, it remains substantially higher than post–World War II figures. Much of that readership was then attributable to the overall population growth. The real concern today is that although the population is growing, readership is not, so the overall percentage of individuals reached by newspapers is in decline. Newspaper circulation in general is static, not declining. Still, the economic pressure to produce more income has increased as large corporations have gobbled up smaller newspapers.[7]

Total time spent on media usage in the United States also is growing, albeit slowly, while audiences are shifting allegiances, bringing the need for new ideas once again to the forefront. Convergence is one of the latest additions to that idea front and will be discussed at length from a journalistic perspective in the next chapter.

Regardless, the media industry and specifically its presentation formats are in flux. The result has been a great deal of financial pressure. New

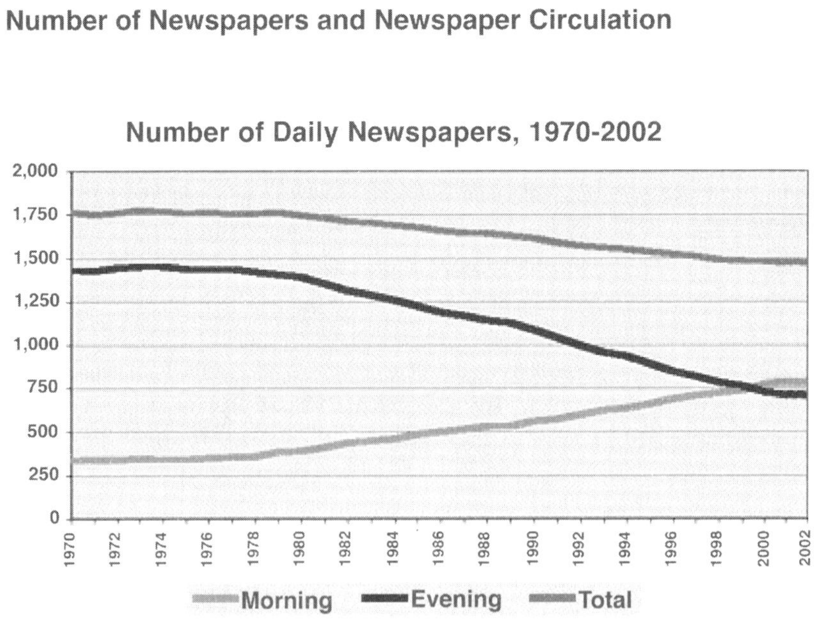

Number of Newspapers and Newspaper Circulation

Figure 2.1. The decline of total number of daily newspapers has been dramatic in the past 30 years.

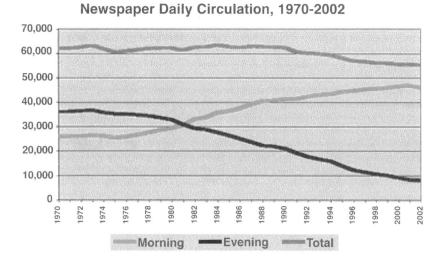

Figure 2.2. Although the number of newspapers is in decline, the overall circulation of newspapers has dropped only slightly in the past 30 years.

ideas for solving economic problems are rare, probably one reason why many publishers and broadcast media companies are looking to convergence as one solution to the uncertainty in the marketplace. Until now, the philosophy has been one of cutting costs while minimizing service changes. The losses have come in newsrooms, where replacement hiring has been on hold or in decline for more than five years.

Deborah Potter, executive director of NewsLab, reported in a recent *American Journalism Review* article that television stations across the country are losing reporters at an alarming rate. In Peoria, Illinois, WEEK-TV has lost 20 percent of its reporting staff since 1997. In San Francisco, KRON lost its NBC affiliation, and owners ordered an increase in on-air news presence of 40 percent. The station was allowed to hire new staff to cover only 15 percent of the expanded news hole.[8]

According to Potter's article, the approach is symptomatic of what is happening to stations around the country, as a large number of stations have had similar losses. Positions are being cut and openings remain unfilled to meet economic and profit concerns.

In journalism, cutting staff is like reducing the purity of silver in jewelry. It may still "look" the same, but the quality suffers. The final product is substandard, and the results are reflected in fewer people being interested in the product.

A recent study by the Project for Excellence points out that increased staffing results in increased audience. That is not a generalized finding but one that makes sense. Journalists, given the time to do their jobs well, will perform well, and the quality of news will improve. The public does notice good journalism.[9]

Some of those embarking on convergence activities see it only from the viewpoint that they will be able to siphon off resources from the newspapers to meet the growing demands of television news. Other research indicates that this too is a flawed approach to embracing convergence. These concerns are based on the fact that print journalists also are hard pressed to meet the growing demands of their business. Although the news "hole" in most newspapers has shrunk dramatically in the past several decades, the number of reporters also has fallen. This presents an interesting but un-

Television: Leading Source of News.

Primary Media Sources of News

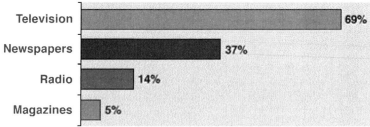

News Report Most Credible

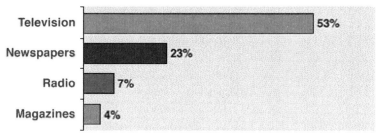

Source: Roper-Starch Worldwide, Inc., 1997   Adults 18+

Figure 2.3. Confidence in television as a news source among U.S. citizens continues.

acceptable proposition—that newspaper reporters, already fewer in number than in earlier years, now take up a new field altogether. This is a major complaint against convergence and one that is well taken. Media owners and management need to increase the number of reporters in both television and print staffs as a cost of doing converged business. We'll come back to this point in a bit.

Interestingly, convergence is likely to wind up as an interim category. As the speed of Internet delivery increases, the ability to send broadcast-sized pieces of data down the Internet "pipe" will increase as well. This will allow the true integration of televised programming and information over the Internet. Convergence will mean "fully converged," and journalistic training will come naturally across platforms. This evolution will not, however, take place quickly or easily.

John Pavlik, author of *Journalism and New Media*, prefers the term "contextualized journalism." He believes contextualizing information better explains the process of merging the information platforms of television, newspapers and the Internet because it requires writers and reporters to create information in ways that place the information in a context of understanding via its delivery platform.[10]

Pavlik's ideas are good, but his optimistic approach is currently somewhat tempered by the 2001 breakdown in the dot.com revolution. The torrent of money flowing into Internet companies suddenly dried up. This stopped or slowed both the expansion and adoption of converging activities. Several years later, the Internet industry is only now beginning to recover, and investments in dot.com endeavors are made in a much more cautious atmosphere. This translates into a slowdown in the adoption of convergence process.[11]

Because only a few Internet companies are making money, investments and expansion have slowed, thereby giving media industry critics time to bring other problems to light. These include the complexities of the marketplace, the interpretation of differing value systems between media operations, and the understanding and nature of timeliness in determining how news and programming is delivered.

Eventually, the advent of Internet-delivered programming will effectively end "appointment television." It will be offered on demand, and that will mean the face of journalism will change, as well as the face of programming. We will return to these issues later in the chapter. Investigating journalism in the United States and how the concentration of media ownership is influencing its structure needs to be discussed further now.

Beyond Concentration and Ownership

The look of media ownership in the United States is under dramatic change. Today, only five conglomerates dominate the bulk of the vast media holdings in the U.S. Another 15 or so companies, smaller but still significant operations, round out the major ownership and control of this nation's print, broadcast and entertainment media.[12] Some sources estimate that the four major television networks, all owned by major media conglomerates, account for most television viewership in the U.S.

Ongoing media consolidation has forever changed the ownership landscape; it is difficult to point to a time in the past three decades in which some consolidation wasn't underway. Before 1996, however, more barriers had forced consolidation to move at a slower pace. While some companies had wanted to break down those barriers, until technological convergence became a reality, few companies had a true interest in pursuing that option. Some would argue that media ownership is only part of an overall trend to put democracy on notice. Ted Nace, in *Gangs of America: The Rise of Corporate Power and the Disabling of America*, writes that corporate power via "rights" has been developing through a series of U.S. Supreme Court rulings over the past century and a half.[13] He lays the problems in both the courts and in legislation. Three phases have punctuated the increasing power of corporations: quasi-rights, corporate constitutional rights and corporate global rights.

Quasi-rights for corporations grew out of a variety of local and state statutory revisions protecting shareholders of corporations and allowing corporations perpetual existence. Constitutional rights were granted at some level when courts in the late nineteenth century first gave corporations similar rights to those of "persons." The third set of rights, underway today, deals with the breaking down of border controls by nation states. Through free trade agreements, corporations have been able to expand more easily outside of their national borders. Corporations are free to roam from nation to nation to create the best marketplace for their products.

Nace believes these are just a few of the factors leading to the concentration of ownership of various industries, including the media. He believes that these corporate "gangs" are out of control and that dramatic action needs to be taken to curtail their power and influence on the public sphere.

Still, one needs to put some of the worries about media concentration into context. In Chapter 1, we discussed the concerns about media concentration voiced by Bagdikian and McChesney. Concerns over big media itself are even older, particularly in regard to newspaper ownership.[14]

Stephen Bolles, grandfather of murdered journalist Don Bolles, spent nearly two decades as the editor of the *Janesville Daily Gazette* in Janesville, Wisconsin, during the early part of the twentieth century. As president of the American Society of Newspaper Editors (ASNE) during the mid- to late 1920s, Bolles wrote frequently of the growing threat to small newspapers from chain newspapers. It was his personal mission as a small newspaper editor to fight chain ownership.[15]

Bolles was convinced that chain ownership would destroy small-town newspapers and that newspapers in general should organize themselves to ensure that there would be a long-term commitment to the preservation and development of local newspapers. He challenged then-President Franklin D. Roosevelt and his cabinet to reach beyond the New York and Washington newspapers. He even chided the White House for focusing on big city newspaper coverage in setting the political agenda and pointed out that more than 900 of the nation's 1400 newspapers of the day were in small cities. Seventy-five years later, this all sounds familiar. Not much has changed in the intervening decades; however, chain newspapers generally have been replaced by conglomerates with interests in all media.

The major corporations that own media entertainment holdings also have holdings that include news operations. AOL Time Warner, Disney, General Electric, Viacom and News Corporation provide information and entertainment over the same airwaves and often through related production offices.

Time Warner owns and operates CNN, Walt Disney owns ABC, General Electric owns NBC, Viacom owns CBS and News Corporation owns Fox News. Each company also owns numerous broadcast stations that operate under the corporate banner as O&O (owned and operated) stations. With Comcast's attempts in early 2004 to purchase Disney, the slate may change even further, but what this will mean for managing news operations is still an issue for the crystal ball.[16]

Peter Jennings, principle anchor for Disney-owned ABC News, said in late 2003, "I have been pleasantly surprised that Disney, in general, has kept its hand out of our news department." He also indicated that the corporation had usually been helpful in providing the resources needed by the news operation.[17]

Various outsiders disagree with Jennings' observation and believe that Disney has painted ABC with its mouse-driven brush from one end of the broadcast news operations to the other. Regardless of one's viewpoint, the issues remain: How should the ownership of media in the United States look? Who should shape that ownership and what are the various impact factors on that ownership makeup?[18]

The evidence, as reported in Chapter 1, is not convincing that current ownership is wrongheaded. While little likelihood appears that the dooms-day machine is on some inevitable path to destroying minority voices in this country, that doesn't mean that regulators and citizens' groups should keep quiet. It may simply mean that the United States hasn't reached crit-ical mass on the ownership concentration issue. Now may simply be the best time to plan for a future that serves both the public and media own-ership. We will return to the issue of serving both groups in later chapters.

Expectations of the Field

Ownership and Journalism

So far, our discussion has taken a broad brush approach to issues influ-encing media in the United States. We have heard from owners, special in-terest groups and other experts in the field, but the real work of journalism takes place between journalists and their constituent communities. How is ownership creating an impact on the public at the local level? Is it creat-ing change? Is change simply a predictable aspect of time? Is cross-own-ership an inevitable aspect of convergence, and will the voices of change shout down the voices of reason? These questions are difficult to answer. As usual, one's perspective is as much a part of the answer as the issues themselves, but some research is now providing a clearer understanding of ownership influences on news reporting.

Miller, who sees media concentration as potentially falling victim to "The Frankenstein Syndrome," worries about the new information para-digm's lack of "modeling ethical behaviors." To Miller, there is a bit of the running "willy-nilly" among journalists assigned to producing news in media environments undergoing dramatic change.[19] He worries that the emphasis on transition and technology is undermining the ethical sense journalists should have embedded in their psyches; his concerns apply equally well to the expectations of convergence.

Miller notes that ethical behavior is the result of habits modeled and de-veloped through practice. He urges conglomerates to employ strong lead-ership models that will produce those ethical habits.

Williams studied the influence on news content that conglomerates exerted from the standpoint of added layers of ownership and a desire to protect their organizations. The researcher pointed out the inherent contradiction of newsgathering in both print and broadcast journalism— that despite the news media's need for profits, it seeks a non-business approach to gathering and reporting information. In other words, it seeks neutrality in a non-neutral environment.[20]

Drawing from Shoemaker and Reese, Williams points out that those charged with keeping to editorial values and goals always report to people who are interested first in satisfying economic goals. This is the continuing tension in journalism.[21]

Williams' study showed some promotional influences from the parent companies of media, but none were generalizable, and in all instances, self-promotion represented only a small number of the overall stories on a specific business.

Perspective, as noted earlier, is important. In Chapter 1 we saw that a great deal of difference exists between those who fear media concentration and those who believe it is simply an evolution of media activity. This section examines how managers and leaders of the media view the changes and challenges presented by increasing media concentration in the United States.

It is obviously important that we must hear from those who lead the journalistic efforts around the country. Leading editors, executives and educators met in New York at the Carnegie Foundation to discuss the "Business of Journalism."

Collaborations and Journalism

Tampa Tribune Publisher Gil Thelan likes to talk about convergence and bringing it into newsrooms across the media general set of properties; however, he rarely uses the term convergence anymore, preferring the terms collaboration and partnerships. Thelan is among a growing number of managers who have had to deal with the backlash from convergence, a backlash that is only partly deserved. Still, some want to throw out the innovation when the problems are actually with managing change. We will look at change and its impact on convergence later.[22]

Pavlik reports that convergence results is "an unprecedented opportunity for creating collaborative approaches to reporting." He adds that the rapid convergence of computing and telecommunications technologies is rapidly rewriting the traditional assumptions of newsroom organization and structure. Based on Pavlik's expectations, the newsroom model of the future may not yet exist; instead of centralized newsrooms, there would be disparately placed reporters filing stories electronically through wireless systems that integrated the information and contextualized that information into a format compatible with the expected upcoming newscast. In Pavlik's vision, even traditional broadcast studios could become a thing of the past as broadcast organizations present 24-hour coverage of on-scene events and investigative reports.[23]

Pavlik's vision is only one of many expectations about news, collaboration and the need to move to the next adaptation of information presentation. Most of those people who see the evolution of the technology tied to the potential for improved journalism understand that some form of convergence is likely—only the form remains uncertain.

Meanwhile, others in the journalism family oppose convergence and collaborative efforts from the standpoint that the diversity of voices will be lost. Much of this discourse is coming from the print journalism arena. Their arguments are generally based on the premise that it is likely that convergence cannot take place unless the broadcast and print media outlets are owned and operated by the same organization. This brings the notion of cross-ownership back into the picture.

Cross-ownership eliminates a layer of voice. The company that owns both the print and broadcast operations sets the voice for both organizations. The questions from this then are what is the impact on a community from the elimination of this voice? Does the community suffer? Have both the newspaper and the broadcast outlet cast a wide net in influencing the decisions of the public through their diverse voices? And is something important now eliminated? The answer is simple. We don't know.

In the broadcast industry, editorial comment was often and explicit through the early 1980s. This voice of concern for local issues cast a broad net, but following a decade of deregulation, those editorial voices had all but disappeared by the early 1990s. By the turn of the century, only a few television stations in the United States still carried any form of editorial opinion. Perhaps the critics are concerned not for the loss of an editorial voice but that the divergence of coverage of events through an expectation of relative sameness from the print and broadcast partners is lost. This argument also may be somewhat difficult to prove, but it should be investigated.

There is some evidence that much of broadcasting's ability to conduct meaningful enterprise reporting has been compromised in recent years through the reduction in appropriate reporting staffs discussed earlier. Whatever the arguments, cross-ownership has brought the FCC to a standstill in its efforts to deregulate the broadcasting industry further. At press time, commissioners were holding a series of public hearings on localism around the country.[24]

While social activists and journalists seem extremely concerned about cross-ownership, broadcasters seem more ambivalent on the issue. This may be that they are more accustomed to technological change. Then again, there may be fewer challenges to the traditions of broadcast news preparation and presentation because it has been dependent on technological innovation since its inception.

Management and Journalism

Jim Lehrer has spent more than 30 years in public broadcasting and had a distinguished newspaper career before that. Lehrer has said, "if you want to be entertained, go to the circus."[25]

What does this statement have to do with management and journalism? Everything. Journalism has bet its primary functions and foundation on the technology of today. Management has done a great job by allowing technology to rule the edicts of the newsroom. This focus is brought out in comments like: "if it doesn't sparkle, it isn't interesting. If it isn't interesting, it isn't news." Or from the television side: "if there's no video, there's no story."

Management is about making money. A 1999 report from the PEW Research Center indicated that news staff members feel caught in a "pressure cycle" from business pressures. The report indicated that those pressures undermine the quality of journalism while focusing on the bottom line. At the same time, news and corporate executives disagree, believing that business pressures create little impact on journalism.[26] Once again, this is a notion that is based upon perception. The following story should illustrate it well.

Once, at a management seminar that I attended, a speaker showed how these differences in perception influenced the output of employees. The speaker used a very large device, perhaps seven feet tall, filled with wheels and gears, all attached to one another. At the top of the machine was a very large gear, about 24 inches in diameter. At the bottom, after traveling through the maze of another dozen or so gears, was a small gear, about four inches in diameter.

The speaker, in order to show how perceptions changed, turned the large gear at the top just one "click," or about two gear cogs (out of 40 or so). The machine instantly sprang to life. Each gear began moving simultaneously, and at each level down, the smaller gears moved faster and faster until finally, the bottom gear spun wildly and nearly out of control. It wobbled on its hub and kept spinning long after the other gears had stopped.

This is the influence of perception; this is how management decisions influence journalism coverage. What management believes is a small move is perceived by those lower in the organization as a frantic effort to fulfill one need or another. When management doesn't understand that its actions will result in full scale activity, it incorrectly reads the impact of its actions.

In journalism, bottom-line pressures have been controlling the field since its inception. However, most managers recognized that it was important to insulate working journalists from the turmoil of the business side of news. In the past several decades, those insulating walls have been breaking down as larger and larger corporations have dictated how information is handled. These dictates are not directly targeted at content, but the result is the same as censorship. If the information won't sell papers or increase ratings points, then what is its advantage? Critical stories—those that require time and patience to develop—are left behind. The "easy" news gets the reporter's byline in the newspaper every day, their face on the newscast every night. Difficult stories, deep stories, take time. Those stories won't get covered when someone is counting. Unfortunately, financial management is all about counting.

The easy stories take us back to Lehrer's circus. Often they take journalists to the circus every day. Once, as a reporter, I refused to cover a funeral because the family of a murdered teen needed a break from media attention. Today, I would be fired—no questions, just fired.

A recent abduction and murder of a child in Sarasota, Florida, resulted in a circus that reached national proportions all because the abduction was caught on videotape by a camera at a car wash. The 12 seconds of video were not very revealing, but they were 12 seconds of video. Two weeks after the girl's body was recovered and the suspect arrested, local television stations were still spending 10–15 minutes of newscasts to cover "live" memorial services. It didn't matter that the official services had been over days earlier or that the groups holding the ceremonies held little import to the girl's life; it was part of the circus…and the show must go on.[27]

Maudlin is a word that doesn't begin to describe the coverage. Television news outlets should have been embarrassed, but instead, they were ecstatic. It all happened during February sweeps and would likely prove profitable in the near-term ratings race.

Bottom line pressures from management are to produce higher ratings, at nearly any cost (journalistic cost, that is). The news departments in these television stations merely responded to the moving cogs of the big machine of corporate decision-making. It is doubtful that most corporate managers would relate the coverage to profit dictates, but those who actually run the newsrooms know this is exactly why they responded with little restraint and a great deal of cheaply produced titillating "news."

Convergence is facing some of the same potential for misuse. Now the opportunities for profit are higher, and the resources that may be needed to produce those profits could be lower. Managers in converging operations need to understand that they must rebuild the deteriorating walls between business pressures and reporting pressures if they want to capture the full potential of journalism's newest venture.

Four years ago, I was asked my opinion on convergence. The response was and still is that if convergence is done for journalism's sake and to increase the effective coverage of meaningful stories, it is a welcome and useful extension of our field. If, however, convergence is embraced by management as a way to create economies of scale, produce information more efficiently across platforms and increase profits without improving journalism—it *will* fail. That jury is still out, and that sentiment is the core focus of interest in writing this book.

Voices in America

The nature of voices, discussed briefly in an earlier section, needs clarification. Throughout the world, apprehension from media experts has focused on ensuring that all who wish to speak have an opportunity to do so and that they have outlets for that speech. This is a democratic and open approach. As the world has grown, the number of voices, according to some experts, also has grown. However, many of those who look at media ownership concentration with apprehension believe the number of outlets for those voices has diminished as owners set narrower and narrower agendas for getting messages into their pages, over the airwaves and onto the Internet.

In the United States, these fears have led to the belief that convergence, as a partner in media concentration, should be discouraged. To discuss this issue thoroughly, we must talk about the nature of agenda setting and who is setting the public's agenda and for what purpose.

Agenda setting, as a theoretical concept, was introduced in the early 1970s by Shaw and McCombs in what is now considered a landmark study on how public opinion is shaped. Agenda setting formalizes a statement made 10 years earlier by scholar Bernard Cohen in that "It [the press] may not be successful much of the time in telling people what to think, but it is stunningly successful in telling its readers what to think about."[28]

Here, the idea is that people have a limited amount of interest and time to spend on learning about issues. The media, through its decision-making processes, creates a "set" of stories on a variety of issues, thereby framing the specific issues that appear in its pages or on its airwaves. Some researchers have even discovered that most people can focus on no more than seven issues at a time. We are either too busy or too uncaring to add more items to our personal issue agendas. Although this is a generalization, it sets the tone for what the public hears, sees and reads.

Maxwell McCombs, in the past decade, has come to believe that perhaps the media does tell the public what to think—a major step forward from the earlier agenda-setting positions. This makes big media even more of a concern to media watchdogs, for under this scenario, the media not only sets the agenda but also controls all of the activities related to the issue agenda.[29] From this standpoint, the number of voices is automatically determined by the media, and as media concentration narrows the editorial control to a few, the fear is that more voices are snuffed out.

Although some danger exists in using sports metaphors at this point, bear with me as we briefly examine the agenda-setting process by using college football in America today. I believe that although many agenda-setting concerns are valid, the issue of voices is somewhat different than many think. College football, through a variety of polls and computer measurements, each year creates a list of the top 25 or so teams. Teams rise or fall in the ratings based on their results on the field. If they win, they tend to rise in the polls; losing will surely find them falling in the polls.

The top 10 teams often find themselves with lucrative contracts to play before national television audiences. In these instances, the top teams generally show up on the major networks, depending on who has the contracts to broadcast NCAA games in any given year. ABC, NBC, CBS, and FOX will march out their first-team broadcasting crews to give coverage of these games.

Additionally, lower ranked teams will show up on games in other television venues, primarily cable. The number of outlets here narrows to ESPN and its other cable nets, FOX sports and several independents that carry games and broadcast them back to locales for local audiences (Jefferson Pilot, Sunshine, etc).

Who gets airtime is again controlled by the networks, the polls and the NCAA. The big-time football programs get more airtime because they are division I teams and have a history of winning; however, this metaphor doesn't show the networks or the NCAA truly conspiring to constrain the number of games that are aired. Indeed, compared to 30 years ago when audiences could view no more than three or four games per weekend, the public now may watch as many as 12 or 13 games without any special additional equipment. With other equipment, i.e., pay-per-view, that number explodes.

When we take this back to agenda setting, the ability to get a football team on air is not a one-dimensional media problem. Rather, agendas are multi-faceted sets of priorities dependent on numerous variables, one of which is the media.

Critics will argue that this is not the issue, that news is the issue. Today, more news outlets exist on television than ever before. The availability of information has exploded in the past two decades. Even the source of that information has diversified, with FOX and NBC entering the cable news market with CNN. Still, these outlets are owned by the few, and the few are what concern media critics.

The issue then truly isn't about quantity, but about quality. Here is where the critics should be making their point. Rather than focusing on controlling who owns current media, critics should be fostering ways to add media content to the mix. Some of this is taking place, but critics have failed to take serious notice. For instance, nearly every major city has at least one "underground" newspaper. In many locations, these newspapers pump out stories on unconventional lifestyles, take on local politicians and propose alternative positions on local issues.

Still, some worry that as these underground newspapers have become popular and profitable, they have been gobbled up by media conglomerates and "mainstreamed." The result, they say, is a tepid version of the controversial missives of earlier issues.

Still, there is support for creating more underground newspapers that are well written. Alternative voices have not been quashed, and in the

United States they never will be for long; history is on the side of those
who believe they are losing their voice. Groups rarely go quietly into the
night.

Less than a decade ago, a little-known Internet reporter, Matt Drudge,
began writing about issues in Washington, D.C. His underground Internet
site, "The Drudge Report," was filled with gossip. He was dismissed by
the mainstream press and most political mainstreamers. His reports on
President Bill Clinton regarding a torrid affair changed that perception.
Today the "Drudge Report" is well read and often cited by mainstream
journalists as a source of information. Drudge's reports still may be based
on gossip, but the Washington press has come to understand that the gossip is well placed.[30]

Most arguments regarding voice deal with the issues of minority groups
seeking an outlet for discourse about their ideas and issues; however, some
believe that broadcasting's voice will be subsumed to the voice of the print
press if convergence moves forward. This outlook obviously makes more
sense from a journalistic view than a societal view; however, in this case,
the argument should be made for good journalism based on good platforms. How journalists act across those platforms should change based on
the needs and characteristics of the platform and public, not on the broadcast industry itself. Good journalism is good journalism.

Conclusions

This chapter has examined the impact of media ownership and convergence on the United States. The jury is still out on how convergence will
ultimately be received in this country as in others. We have attempted to
point out some of the problems and issues with multi-platform journalism
and the intrusion of corporate management into the newsroom. Along the
way we have discussed how convergence should succeed and how it can
fail.

One other issue needs to be examined—the battle for localism in an era
of mega-media. Localism is based on the concept that the local community knows what is best for its citizenry and that those communities should
have control over how media is interpreted and used in their areas.

During the early development of broadcasting, a great deal of emphasis was placed on localism, but as the nature of the Federal Communications Commission shifted its emphasis from one of trusteeship of the
airwaves to arbiter of the marketplace, localism began to get lost. News-

papers, even those owned by huge conglomerates, know that the local audience is best served with local news. However, television stations now offer programming that "sells" only from a national level. How can broadcasting be brought back into the fold of creating services for the local community? A thorough discussion of potential actions to take to improve localism is addressed in Chapter 8, but it should be noted that convergence may be one of the best opportunities for localism to make a resurgence in the smaller cities and towns of America.

Convergence offers the ability to create understanding of local issues across a number of platforms. It also allows for the potential access to the media of more people because space and time considerations are less important in a converged environment. Still, solutions will depend on government creating a regulatory environment that encourages local activity, allows corporations to make a profit and balances the expectations of the community with the needs of the marketplace.

Exercises

1. In trying to understand the nature of news as a business, locate the financial annual report of a local media outlet. How profitable does that media outlet appear to be? Compare it with another local company. How do the companies differ? How are they similar?
2. Investigate a local issue…not a local event, but an issue. Is this issue being covered in the media? Try to determine why or why not. What approaches might be taken to improve the coverage of that issue?

CHAPTER 3

The Newly Mediated Workplace

Convergence and Mass Media

As pointed out in Chapter 2, media owners have continuously examined ways in which to maximize the returns on their investments. In the early years of broadcasting and newspapers, media businesses tended to be family-owned. Privately held entities allowed closely held businesses to reap the rewards offered from media holdings without making much information about that profitability available to the public. In the latter half of the twentieth century, the heirs to those families began to sell their media properties to larger and larger organizations. These conglomerates developed primarily into media holding companies. The potential for profit, no longer "hidden," soon drove a buying frenzy. By 1980, the number of family-owned newspapers had plummeted, and by 1990, the broadcasting industry had followed close behind.

The media buying frenzy didn't stop, however, and some sought quick profits in turning over the properties. This turnover led to higher and higher acquisition costs and ultimately cut the profitability of a great number of media properties. However, the expectation of a large payoff, stoked by merger fires, has kept media investors from relinquishing a belief that higher margins are a "requirement" in media stocks. This has led holding companies to devise profitability scenarios that would keep up the unrealistic rate of return levels, the latest of which is Convergence.

Defining Convergence

A great deal of discussion has taken place during the past 20 years regarding the ultimate form of our information media. Convergence is a movement in the field of mass communications undertaken in the late twentieth century and now moving quickly in the early twenty-first century, that weds previously competitive media delivery formats (platforms) to one another. We should note, however, that convergence is not one thing—it is at least two: the technological delivery (system of transfer) of information and the interpretation via partnering of information purveyors to utilize the new delivery system.

To understand convergence, one must first understand that there are three distinct platforms currently involved in information delivery: print media (newspapers and magazines), telecommunications media (broadcast television and radio, cable and satellite transmissions) and the Internet (all Web-based formats). From the technological side of the discussion, the general concept has been to bring the platforms together to provide information to the public through shared multiple technical resources or pipelines. These pipelines care little for what is transmitted or how it is transmitted, only that the technical capabilities are linked together.

On the information or content delivery side of convergence, the founding idea was to ensure relatively equal distribution of information through each platform, thus creating a partnering of equal information providers. In reality, however, that idea has been displaced to create super-competitors using economies of scale to combat or eliminate less-ready significant media. Today, the largest efforts in convergence occur between newspapers, the Internet and traditional broadcasting, generally television (both cable and broadcast).

The emphasis among owners and managers of converged media has been on either the delivery systems themselves or the subsequently changed marketplace. This is perhaps in response to the advent of the technology and the desire to implement the technology because it creates new economic markets through multi-platform delivery while remaining rather efficient. Another factor working in this marketplace process may be what Shoemaker and Reese term the "primacy of economic goals."[1] In such instances, presenting information in multiple platforms creates the ability to cross-pollinate audiences with the promotional (read additional advertising revenues) aspects of the additional reach. In many instances, these decisions have been made without determining the groundbreaking and disruptive influences in the news gathering process and those who are responsible for the content: reporters and editors.

If we view convergence from a graphic sense and based on the work of journalists, two models of full convergence currently compete on the world's news landscape. The first, a model currently in use in several U.S. media markets, would look something like Figure 3.1.

The existence of a stand-alone staff engaged in the newsgathering and dissemination process at each location is a key component in producing an environment where there is true transference of information and not an environment designed simply as a series of pass-throughs created by linking the various media at their Web site (URL) addresses. The series of solid lines is used to show that each news staff shares equally among the platforms to ensure that each platform receives appropriate information on stories to post in its form. This model focuses on maintaining the traditional media while information is shared.

A second model, now being used in several markets in Europe, particularly Spain and Germany, looks like Figure 3.2.[2] Whereas the emphasis in the first model is on the platform, the emphasis in the second model is

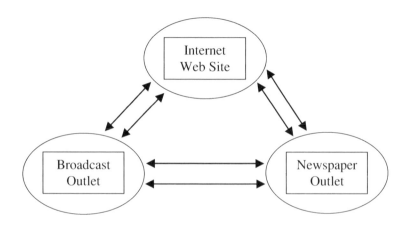

Convergence
(fully shared two-way flow among all components)

Figure 3.1. Full convergence is a fully shared two-way flow among all components; however, the emphasis remains on the platform, not the journalist. This creates an environment in which the journalist has less control over product.

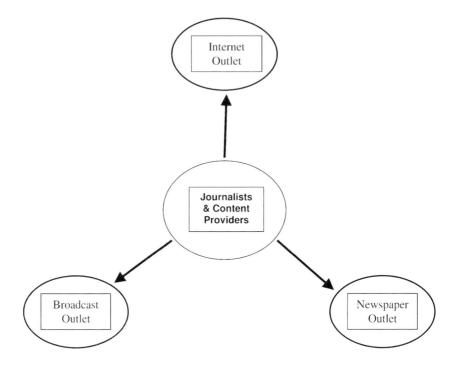

Journalistic Convergence
(Reporter / oranization based)

Figure 3.2.   Journalistic Convergence (reporter/organization based) is
"true" convergence, showing the journalist, not the platform, as central to
the news story process.

on the information "gatherer" or reporter. Contextually, the reporter is
placed in an environment where he or she can file stories in a multi-platform method, rewriting the stories to fit the particular stylistic needs of
each media. Generally, the photography and videography are developed
and presented by one individual in charge of the visual aspects of the
story.

Each of these models places the information gathering emphases in different regions. Each produces an information product based on differing
criteria in the newsroom managing process. Both need to be explored from
a management standpoint, but before undertaking that discussion, it is important that we examine the evolution of the process.

If these two versions of "full convergence" are viewed as the probable endpoints of convergence (albeit perhaps temporarily), then at least one primary question is raised: How has "convergence" evolved to this point? We need to look at other definitions and inter-platform relationships to see where the evolution has come from.

Defining Multimedia

The evolution of news platform flow to what we now call full convergence has occurred in a relatively systematic fashion. It has been following a path that began with multimedia and led slowly to various configurations of partially converged media and then to the more fully defined state we see now. Early discussions of convergence today would be looked on as simply a multimedia platform trade. These are models that are more simplistic than later, fully converged models, and some are indicative of how a variety of newsrooms still define their "converged" presence. Let's discuss each, beginning with multimedia.

The systematic transfer of information from one or two platforms (broadcast, newspapers or both) to a third platform, generally the Internet, is the key differentiating characteristic of a multimedia platform. This means information transfer only. It also means that for the most part, the contributing platform supplies its information to the Web via its traditional delivery system, i.e., newspapers supply print-style stories with accompanying still photos, but broadcasters supply uploaded scripts with video and video packages. No information sharing exists, and the stories, links, photos and issue discussions end there. Most newspapers and television and radio stations have a multimedia presence. Many go no further.

Multi-Media Function of Press
(non-converged)

Figure 3.3.   Multimedia function of the press (non-converged).

Figure 3.3 describes graphically the limitations of this process. Here we see, represented by solid lines, the transfer of platform-dependent information to a "host" Internet provider. Dashed lines indicate linkages back to the primary information provider but show that the information is channeled not from a user-source reportage balanced approach but from a single direction source, i.e., the newspaper, television or radio station. The information is simply a pass-through, and the Internet is used (or under used) to supply only content from another source.

The Internet is generally used by host platforms as an opportunity to reach a secondary audience that would not normally be reached through its traditional platform. As Gentry has suggested, sometimes media use the Internet for promotional rather than substantive purposes, but the information is always for posting; there is no backward sharing because there is rarely an active staff gathering information exclusively or primarily for the Web-based platform.

Partial Convergence

The evolution of the multimedia environment to a converged phase of information collection and dissemination is at the heart of the now overly used term that often adds more confusion to the process: "new media."

Although convergence generally means that all component platforms available for delivery to a Web-based operating system contribute to the overall information product, it also implies that at least some level of two-way information sharing and enhancement takes place along the way. As we have seen, in the best of all worlds, the three platforms share information equally and strive to improve the products of all three.

Many newspapers and television stations have used (and are using) a sharing model to ensure that information flows through the system. However, there have been limitations on how the systems have been allowed to work, and full convergence is generally difficult to maintain. True convergence requires extensive resources to ensure equality (or at least a general perception of equality) among the partners. It also requires that journalists from different cultures and competitive structures work together. This is not always advisable or possible and sometimes leads to an overall breakdown in the sharing process. The mechanisms that lead to these breakdowns are not part of this research but should be considered by educators attempting to help students work through the process of learning how to operate in a multi-platform environment.

Three system conditions are readily identified in discussing the potential shortcomings of full convergence. They are demonstrated in the accompanying figures. Each deals with emphasizing the information side of the sharing equation and identifies the failures where the information flow becomes one-directional on any platform pair.

Bias among "Partners"

Because of the relative newness of the converged environment, it seems logical that the media platform that is the most entrenched (as examples, strong broadcast ratings versus weak newspaper circulation, large metropolitan daily newspaper versus medium-sized television station or newly created Internet sites) may exercise a level of influence on the other partners in the convergence process. Three conditions are described in the following discussion, and each is explicated to further understand the limitations and levels of convergence in the modern media marketplace.

Figure 3.4 shows the interrelationship and content bias represented by a semi-converged set of media platforms in which the newspaper is dominant in the scenario.

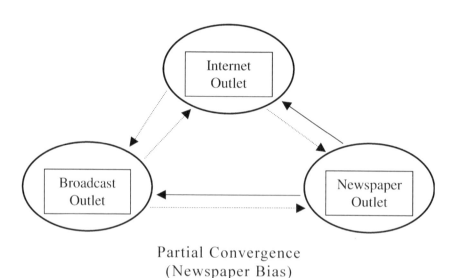

Partial Convergence
(Newspaper Bias)

Figure 3.4.   Partial convergence (newspaper bias).

In this scenario, the newspaper is clearly the primary source of information in the dissemination process. The newspaper, because of its partnership with the broadcast and Internet outlets, is supplying these platforms with significant primary information sourced through newspaper reporting and editing staff. The broadcast and Internet platforms provide space and time for the newspaper copy and provide linkages back to the newspaper regarding content available from their affiliated services, but the linkages do not include material created, initiated and reported by the other platforms. There are benefits to the platforms not involved in creating content because there are definite advantages to having more information available than the staff (or lack of staff) can provide in these outlets on their own.

The newspaper also benefits through the promotional process. In most converged environments, regardless of the degree of the convergence, there is a general acknowledgement between the platforms that they will quote or name the primary outlet in the story.

In Figures 3.5 and 3.6 we see a similar configuration with the emphasis on one of the other platforms.

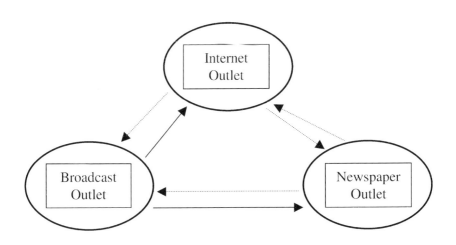

Partial Convergence
(Broadcast Bias)

Figure 3.5.   Partial convergence (broadcast bias).

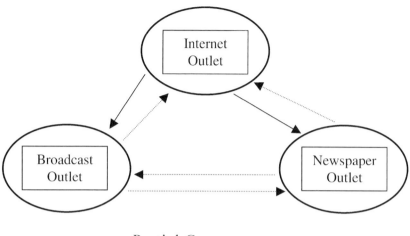

Partial Convergence
(Internet Bias)

Figure 3.6.   Partial convergence (Internet bias).

In each of these figures, the conditions that depict information source bias depend on the primary source of the information. It is noteworthy that these "biases" offer a variety of scenarios, depending on the convergence "partners" in a particular news and information configuration.

These scenarios provide a wealth of descriptive information useful in conveying the current status of convergence. Each is fraught with difficulty, and each is technically tied to an evolution (or some might say revolution) in the newsgathering and dissemination process.

Bob Gremillion, President and Publisher of the Sun Sentinel properties in Fort Lauderdale, Florida, believes that some bias is probable, and likely desirable, in all convergence activities.[3] Gremillion believes that each platform brings specific opportunities and resources to the table when a convergence activity takes place. He also expects that one of those platforms will bring more to the table than the others. It is important then to understand, according to Gremillion, that the platform making the largest commitment and generally taking the largest risk should be recognized for that commitment. He adds, however, that there must be no quid pro quo, or the organization will face internal battles over which platform is helping "more" than the others.

With the expectation that some form of convergence is here to stay, it is important to remember that change will continue, and as it does, it is also imperative that journalists prepare themselves for those changes. Other ways of examining convergence are also on the rise and now will be examined.

The Convergence Continuum

Daily, Demo and Spillman created what they call the "Convergence Continuum." In it, the authors discuss the evolution of convergence from its early stages into the full convergence process.[4] At the minimum, it shows information organizations gathering information on their own but cross-promoting other information products across platforms. At the fullest extent, news operations are fully integrated information machines.

The Convergence Continuum looks at how convergence operates from one group to another, creating methods for determining how close a company is to delivering a full convergence environment. At one end of the continuum is cross-promotion, at the other end lies full convergence. Between those end points are cloning, co-opetition, and content sharing.

Cross-promotion is a marketing effort that places the "brands" of each information-sharing partner in front of the public through its other information partners. For instance, stories originating in the newspaper also air on the television station. The station describes the newspaper as the source of the story, thereby marketing the brand through the second medium, television. The newspaper may carry weather information generated by the television station's meteorologists. The newspaper then identifies the source of the information as the television station, once again cross-promoting.

Two companies deeply involved in cross-promotions are Media General Company through its flagship operations in Tampa, Florida, and the Tribune Company through its *Sun-Sentinel* properties in Fort Lauderdale, Florida.[5]

The Tampa convergence partners include the *Tampa Tribune*, WFLA-TV and Internet site TBO.com. The three trade branding information and share cross-promotional activities on numerous stories daily. Because all three are located in the "NewsCenter," a facility completed in 2000 to house all three information outlets, knowledge is easily transferred from one partner to the other.

The *Sun-Sentinel* partnering situation is more complex. Located in Fort Lauderdale, Florida, the primary partners include the *South Florida Sun-Sentinel* newspaper and WBZL television directly. But Fort Lauderdale is split by two active television markets, Miami and West Palm Beach. Rather than ignoring the challenges of brand placement in two markets, the *Sun-Sentinel* management team created branding partnerships in both television designated market areas (DMAs). Those partners, both NBC affiliates, include WTVJ in Miami and WPTV in Palm Beach County. Unlike WBZL, WTVJ and WPTV are not owned by the Tribune Company. This creates management issues that will be discussed more completely in other chapters. To assist in the partnering arrangement, the newspaper's newsroom also houses a television set and television news reporters to provide Fort Lauderdale content to the other two newsrooms.[6]

The circulation zoning for the *Sun-Sentinel* is comprehensive. Where possible, each television brand appears in the appropriate zone every day in the newspaper. Conversely, the television stations brand the *Sun-Sentinel* partnership on all stories originating from Fort Lauderdale's partnership. It has worked well, and circulation has stood up well for the newspaper during the several-year period that the project has been underway.

Cloning is the unedited display of a partner's product. Because television and newspaper products don't transfer well from one medium to the other, this part of the Convergence Continuum generally shows up in repurposed material on Web sites. In this, the newspaper stories would be placed on the Web page in exactly the same format as they appeared in the newspaper. Television stories would be streamed onto the Web site to provide the same content as the original television news story, often with a written note leading the Web viewer to the streamed story.[7]

This is used effectively by Media General's TBO.com entity. Stories appearing in the *Tampa Tribune* and on air with WFLA are often redirected into content pieces on the Web. There is generally little editing. The end product produces coverage of stories that have often appeared from different perspectives on both of the primary mediums, thus building branding and cooperation among the media entities to place the news before the public.

Co-opetition is a concept that recognizes that competitors can sometimes cooperate to bring added value to both of their products. In the information business, in which television and newspapers have been heavy competitors for more than 30 years, the notion is becoming accepted because there are clear added values to the products.

The ability to place the name of your brand in front of an audience is one clear way that co-opetition takes place. In the scenarios for both the Media General and Sun-Sentinel properties, the co-opetition activity has been profound. At Media General's Newscenter, the close placement of the media competitors has resulted in access to the newspaper's archives for the television reporters. This is a luxury unheard of in most television newsrooms. Archives exist with television stations only as long as a television reporter or producer stays at the station. When they leave, their collective memory goes with them. Newspapers have always needed to keep a record of the stories they publish. That need has led to complex library resources, and this resource is an added value for the television side of the business.[8]

On the newspaper side of this added value equation, the *Tribune*, which is in a very competitive market with the St. Petersburg *Times* across Tampa Bay, gets branding on the daily newscasts of WFLA. Every story that appears on air but had original content in the newspaper receives a visual branding during the newscast. In the three years since launching the effort, the *Tampa Tribune* has actually gained circulation, an almost unheard of achievement in the modern newspaper world. Although not all of the gains can be placed on the shoulders of this cooperative arrangement, the arrangement has certainly helped.

Beyond co-opetition in the Convergence Continuum lies *content sharing*. In this scenario, the news partners meet regularly, exchange ideas and work together to bring stories to the public. Major projects, including elections and investigative pieces, are often a joint effort by the partners. The results are sometimes stunning.

Two recent efforts at Media General's properties resulted in major investigations by the state of Florida. A chemical plant in a nearby city was accused of dumping harmful pollutants into area creeks and groundwater. More than a dozen stories appeared on both WFLA-TV and in the *Tribune*. The lead reporter was with the newspaper, but several television reporters made significant contributions and both groups worked together to bring about the investigation. In the second set of stories investigated, a local charismatic minister was called to task regarding fundraising and the use of church monies for not-so-church-worthy activities.[9]

The final concept on the continuum is full *convergence*. Convergence in this context is a "level at which partners have shared the assignment/editor's desk and the story is developed by team members who use the strengths of each medium to tell the story." Full convergence has been elusive for most integrated media efforts in the United States. For full convergence to work properly, the partners and their reporters need to understand how each platform works best and then be satisfied that the selected placement is a sound decision.

Media General has struggled with the notion of full convergence. Early on, the Newscenter was expected to use a joint assignment desk on the second floor of the operation. That has not happened, and for the most part, that desk has been used by the broadcast and Internet partners to go over daily newsgathering activities. Meetings with the newspaper partner often occur in other locations and still tend to focus on special projects rather than daily news assignments.

The *Sun-Sentinel* is not co-located with its partners and has not reached that level of converged activity as yet, either. Only time will tell when or whether these operations will eventually evolve into full convergence operations. A great many structural problems and issues still need to be overcome before this can take place.

Stress Factors in Convergence

Although the structure of converging media is important, equally important is understanding that convergence is not going to happen simply because someone says "make it so." The relationship between media partners is extremely complex, tied up with cultural values and editorial issues. Even definitions of what constitutes a good news story are different from platform to platform. When these differing values are situated next to one another, the stress factors in play become enormous.

Gil Thelen, publisher and president of the *Tampa Tribune* and one of the earliest proponents of convergence, has come to dislike the term altogether. He now prefers to use the term "coverage partners." This is likely the result of years of controversy that took place inside the newsrooms of the Newscenter. Today, Thelan likens the term convergence to that of a "traffic accident."[10]

"Trying to get the lions and lambs to lie down together has been an extraordinary challenge. We have learned that trying to create omni-competent journalists is impossible. They may be very good in one platform, pretty good in another, but never (or rarely) excellent in both," Thelan notes. "We are moving from what was initially a shotgun approach to a rifle. We want to target resources and make them work exceptionally well."

Media General is working toward that end by identifying what information the public wants and where that information crosses the platforms and plays well in multiple areas. How that will work for general news other than major events is unclear, but the company is identifying areas of interest—including health, weather and public safety—that they believe transition easily.

The *Sun-Sentinel* has had fewer problems with cultural issues. Bob Gremillion is president and publisher of Fort Lauderdale's convergence opportunity at the *Sun-Sentinel*. Gremillion doesn't believe that convergence is ever a truly "shared" activity: "One partner or the other is going to contribute more to the effort than the other. It is essential that the organization, not just management, understand this fact, recognize the fact, and promote it to others within the organization."[11] Gremillion says that "It may not be fair, but it is what works. Generally, a newspaper will have the largest number of assets to make use of in a converged operation. It is also essential to understand that some compromise is necessary in attaining that cooperation between platform partners."

The real questions that arise about form and substance in these new formats, however, still must address how to best communicate with new and existing audiences and how to best present information in ways that will assist both those reporting the news and those receiving the news. The next section describes some of those issues.

Traditional Media in Change

In Chapter 2 we discussed the pressures on media in the United States and the changes that are being required of owners and investors, but other changes are likewise important, particularly in the news and information work place. It is therefore important to examine what is taking place in the traditional media workplace or how convergence and ownership are playing out in the newsrooms of the globe. The starting point for this is with the journalist. These individuals sit at the fulcrum of the advancing battle between people and technology, owners and investors, profitability and financial disaster.

Journalists are tasked with moving the information environment from their traditional platforms to a technologically converged environment. At the same time, journalists must deal with corporate owners who have grown more distant, are often international and have differing value systems than they.

Although this chapter has spent a great deal of time discussing journalists, we haven't defined what the term means. In our current context, including convergence, the term "journalist" may be generally defined as an individual who purveys information to mass audiences through print, broadcast and the Internet or World Wide Web. Many journalists today are at a crossroads; although the acquisition of information is a fundamental first step for journalists, how it is presented is the result of specific training. Each journalist may be gleaning the wheat from the chaff, a function that separates the profession from the public, but how that gleaning takes place differs greatly from platform to platform.

While web journalism is still relatively new, traditional journalism training has focused on providing specific, yet significantly different, skills to print and broadcast journalists. In fact, since the explosion of broadcast journalism programs in American universities during the early and mid-'70s, there has been a distinct divergence in training from print reporters. Much of that change is a reflection of the profession, where an emphasis on consultants, image and ratings has pushed broadcast news programs in new directions. The changes resulted in a shift by broadcast educators from an emphasis on training that provided audiences dense content to an emphasis on techniques that provide viewers simplified information with strong and often emotional performances from broadcast reporters. Now, nearly 30 years later, those training techniques are considered standard and have given us more than a generation of broadcasters who emphasize action rather than content.

Print media reporter training has remained largely unchanged. These reporters have been trained in the art and science of information gathering, the inverted pyramid (though sometimes denigrated today) and have placed emphasis on depth content while remaining literary where possible. Broadcasters have been trained to emphasize the visual aspects of their stories, to shorthand the details and bring the story's "essence" to the fore quickly.

The advent of the Internet has added an additional layer to the global aspects of the media. The Internet, coupled with current experiments in convergence journalism, is putting today's reporters and editors in a new and sometimes frightening environment. It is therefore important to discuss the conditions that are leading to a dissonant atmosphere in many convergence attempts.

Media Management

Most media management activity takes its cues from general business management structures. The thought is and has been that managing people rarely transitions from one business to another, but some would suggest that highly creative people are more receptive to change through proactive mechanisms.

The authors of *Media Management, a Casebook Approach* recognize that team building is an important activity in creating positive work strategies in media organizations. The authors discuss the three stages of group development, orientation, dissatisfaction and resolution.[12] They see four groups of factors involving job satisfaction among television news employees. Those factors included leadership, individual factors, market factors and organizational factors, and each influences how journalists perceive the success of their organizations and the goals that are embodied in successful workplaces.[13]

The most important factor discussed in *Media Management* seemed to be leadership behavior. In newsrooms where news directors took a human relations approach and developed positive relationships with employees, a higher sense of job satisfaction existed. The relationship between newsroom managers and reporters in both print and television newsrooms is extremely important. I have found that reporters held their managers and editors in higher esteem in instances when those managers worried about the satisfaction of their workers. The implication in that study was that the concern for employees showed through in the actions and activities of the manager.[14]

Others point out that "human nuances and individual perceptions of reality ebb and flow within the interactions of the social beings of which groups are composed. Media organizations are even more so because of the combination of mechanistic and professional aspects to the activity…as well as the inherent difficulty of managing creative people."[15]

Zavonia and Reichert (2000) examined the issues of workflow and its impact on the evolving environment of visual journalists in the converged workplace. They examined the Web site created by a joint venture between the *The Dallas Morning News* and *The Fort Worth Star Telegram*. The authors noted that although research has examined the technological and educational factors in converged platforms, little has been done about workflow or decision making.[16] They found that the majority of activity in online publications is done without clear communications from hardcopy counterparts. In the instances when communication and decisions were shared, the authors termed those activities as anomalies. If we are to believe that a merged/converged environment is inevitable, then the study points to the likelihood of serious problems in the converged workplace in the future.

Gremillion echoes those findings from a working standpoint at the *Sun-Sentinel*. He agrees that management leadership is among several factors required for understanding and compliance from a news staff. Gremillion also reports that those leaders must have media knowledge (they know and understand the media business), have a clear vision that is easily transferred to employees and are clear about the expectations and the way those expectations are set and transferred among employees.[17]

Influences in a Changing Workplace

Change, by its nature, puts the expectations of safety and awareness at a disadvantage. The degree to which an organization embraces openness to change is likely an outcome of the interrelationship between values, structure and climate. When organizations have been open in the past and organizational members feel there is a continuation of accurate and reliable information and actions, a greater degree of acceptance to change will likely exist.

Understanding how these concepts fit into the changing journalistic workplace is extremely important. Reporters, editors and the supervisors charged with making convergence or "new media" journalism a reality are finding a great deal of dissonance in the workplace today. Organizations and people unwilling, uncertain or just plain fearful of change may soon be left behind. Regardless of one's long-term view of these changes, it is likely that convergence journalism will be disruptive to the process of collecting and presenting news and information in the short run.

Still, the changes are coming. Journalists must be prepared to either cross-train themselves or seek training from other sources while management must be prepared to give them the opportunities and time to do so. How does this jibe with the news requirements of immediacy and media-specific content? How would a newspaper reporter handle turning over an exclusive story to the newspaper's Internet cousin, where it would likely be published in time for the newspaper reporter's print competitors to respond? Many reporters would rather face a firing squad than lose an exclusive story. Meanwhile, reporters and editors are tasked with providing new products while their cross training is ongoing. Stress and disenchantment with the news organization will likely follow.

Couple these questions with the organizational disdain that exists between print and broadcast reporters and factors create a mixture crying to explode. Print reporters often refer to broadcasters as the "hair and smile" people; of significance is the number of newspaper cartoons that often portray broadcast journalism schools as "Hairstyling 101" or "Smirk

School." In contrast, broadcast reporters think of print journalists as ponderous and too rigid to get the story done in a way that the public will either read or care about. Melding these cultures would be a seemingly endless clash of individuals and values, yet that is what convergence calls for if it is to be done correctly. Add to this the continuing centralized power of media conglomerates emphasizing profitability, and the potential for confrontation increases exponentially.

At this point the principal issues seem to be management readiness, employee readiness, value structure differences between the merging groups (even when the groups remain physically separate), organizational attitudes (both in culture and climate) and issues of structural/relational differences. We will deal with the specifics of these issues in later chapters, but some conclusions may be drawn at this stage.

Readiness and Preparation

The tension resulting from these unanswered questions raises issues about the complexity of group/organizational integration. Each of these is a major threat to successfully meeting the challenges of change. Management readiness and employee readiness are two sides of the same coin. Managers who are ill-prepared to cope with the stress of change in the move to a converged news environment will increase the level of stress among employees who are being asked to work in a new cross-platform environment. While eliminating stress is likely impossible, improving management readiness will reduce the power of stress in the transition phase. Readiness is an issue of training, but not training in the traditional sense; although managers and employees must be trained and made comfortable in their new platforms, they must also be trained in working under new conditions.

This means that training shouldn't be limited to advancing the skills of the managers and the practitioners but should include a process for identifying the individuals who will most easily adapt to the new strategies and placing them in the forefront of the changing activity. In the near term this may be disruptive to the traditional hierarchy of the newsroom, but it will be essential for long-range success in the convergence process. These frontline managers who understand, adapt and adopt the converged process will provide a more confident source of new structure for employees.

Most news organizations proceeding with technological convergence have examined the issue of management and employee readiness at superficial levels. The selection criteria used to identify cross-platform managers and workers have frequently focused on singling out people who are talented in one area and pressing them into service in the cross-platform environment. The thinking has been that creative people who write well should be capable of adapting their talents to multiple platforms. Although this is partially true, proceeding with convergence and using talent as the primary criterion may actually undermine the process. The training process therefore should identify managers and employees who are not only flexible and competent in cross-platform reporting/writing/presentation but also interested as well.

Several points should be understood by those undertaking converged news environments: 1) identify and train good reporters, 2) hire slowly and thoughtfully for the new organization, 3) take the time and investment to create an excellent product, 4) have patience, 5) evaluate constantly and consistently, and 6) when problems arise, avoid quick fixes. These issues will be discussed more thoroughly in later chapters.

Conclusions

The availability of a diverse technological delivery system for information is creating an environment of change. Many media organizations are already well on their way to either implementing or studying convergence and already have a multimedia presence. The technology offers owners and stakeholders further opportunities to expand and diversify their print, broadcast or Internet holdings. Convergence is financially viable and could provide enormous economic benefits to both owners and their audiences.

That means convergence is here to stay. Anyone who believes that "old school" journalism thinking will suffice for the twenty-first century is sadly mistaken. What needs to be understood is that convergence is neither an end-all or be-all, it is simply the next step. Managers who plan on using convergence only for more efficient operations likely misunderstand the nature and power of this emerging tool of information. The New Media workplace will indeed be new, but managers and media owners should understand that the technology is not the most significant addition to the journalistic toolbox; it is rather the ability to conceive and deliver an effective reach for effective journalism and effective public understanding.

Issues of a changing workplace, and organizational change in general, particularly where owners mandate convergence while continuing to emphasize cost cutting and work force downsizing, will be discussed in Chapter 6.

Exercises

1. Describe an instance in which you believe news coverage of a local event would have been enhanced if the local newspaper and a television station had acted together to provide the most comprehensive yet immediate coverage possible. Where do you see the benefits of this action? What might have been the pitfalls?
2. Interview a local reporter. If they have heard of convergence, ask them what they think about the process. Regardless of their positive or negative feelings, keep the assignment for discussion in later chapters as well.
3. Call a news manager; this could be a publisher or a news director. Ask them what their opinion is of convergence and if they believe that sharing information or working together has benefits, both financial and for the news operation itself.

Case Study

The *News Journal* (fictitious) has just been allowed by the Federal Communications Commission to purchase the local CBS television affiliate. The *News Journal* publishes a daily morning edition. The television station has five newscasts daily and a morning show that also features a great deal of news and is anchored by newsroom personnel. The television station is located across the street from the newspaper's editorial offices. The newspaper has a daily circulation of 98,000. The television station is ranked #2 in a three-station market. The owners of the newspaper want to integrate the newsrooms quickly to take advantage of some tax issues and stave off the potential for the FCC backing out of the approval because of some concern by media activists. Should the management move quickly to integrate these properties? Based on the reading so far, is this a good move or a bad move? If you decide yes, explain your position. If you decide no, examine other options available for the owners and explain why you think those options might work better.

CHAPTER 4

Evolution of the Modern Media Workplace

Take a walk through the aisles of any contemporary American bookstore and you will find the stacks filled with offerings of ways to manage companies. We have become organizational animals, and the ability to determine how to manage our organizations well has led to a plethora of special interest books on the subject.

From *Six Sigma* and its emphasis on creating ways to reinvigorate companies around a structural model to the symbolic approach advocated in *From Worst to First*, significant opportunities exist to apply these management techniques to journalism. Before delving into the significance of approaches to management in journalism, it is important that we have an overview of how we got to this place in management. It will also be helpful to begin the discussion as to whether any of these growing traditions is helpful in controlling the tumultuous changes accompanying convergence.

For the most part, management theories and techniques are an outgrowth of the industrial age, and most of the theoretical development about how management works has taken place in less than 60 years. This means that from both a philosophical and strategic view, management theory is a relatively new undertaking.

Many of the fundamental notions of management today are based on the expectations that people will work if they are paid (termed a money economy) and that employers can expect a reasonable level of work for the pay their employees earn. This concept is an outgrowth of Adam Smith's classic book, *An Inquiry into the Nature and Causes of the Wealth of Nations*, generally referred to simply as *Wealth of Nations*. Until

Smith's treatise was published in 1776, the world of business (and early economics) had been positioned on a two-tiered system of mercantilism and peasantry.[1]

Mercantilism was based on the rise of a trading merchant class and the expectations of nations of shopkeepers who would provide for one another through barter and the exchange of goods and services. Peasantry was directly related to the earlier feudal times when servants worked for those who ruled. These definitions are both overly simplistic but give you the idea of how business operated in the late eighteenth century.

Smith had what he thought was a better idea, based on the creation of goods and the value of the production process through labor. Smith argued that if you could increase the productive capacity of a nation, you would be able to create wealthier nations. How could that productivity be increased? Smith showed that the way to increase productivity was through the division of labor. This was borne out by creating tasks that were efficient. Smith articulated three premises to increased productivity: 1) specialization of labor to increase agility, 2) time savings based on increased efficiency of the workers and 3) the development of machines to further increase production because the process had been simplified and specialized by creating individual production steps. By taking these premises together, Smith estimated that increases in production would skyrocket.

In Smith's time, workers tended to make products from beginning to end. Each was charged with completing finished products from raw materials. Smith thought this inefficient because he believed that it was important to place people in jobs where they could do a few tasks very well. Together, workers could create more products by individually creating the parts of these products more efficiently and generally with fewer mistakes.

Smith's ideas were not universally accepted, but everyone understood the assumption that increased wealth meant increased power. They also understood the likelihood that people wouldn't mind getting paid for their work and that the more they worked, the more they might be able to earn.

Smith also coined the term "the invisible hand" of the marketplace. This concept held that the forces of the marketplace would lead to greater competition and that market forces, unseen, would control the threats of aggregation or monopolies. He believed that economic power could become centralized, but only for a short time before those market forces reintroduced competition.

Smith also was suspicious of corporations, or what were then termed joint-stock companies. He preferred to emphasize production development in the hands of sole proprietors and partnerships.

Smith's writing appeared before the industrial revolution of the early-to mid-nineteenth century and onward, but the timing of it was such that company owners seized on his methods of creating efficiency and wealth and never looked back. The United States' business climate was shaped and likely will forever be linked to perspectives in Smith's work.

Managing and Management

According to Alan Albarran, "Management is defined as the process through which individuals work with and through other people to accomplish organizational objectives." Process can be defined as "a series of actions or events marked by change."[2]

Management therefore is appropriately defined as a process because the activities involved in managing are ongoing, evolving and constantly changing. Television and radio stations, cable systems, and newspapers operate continuously, and their products are based on change. News and information are therefore very much subject to process.

Management has been evolving, and the development of management theory has borne out that evolution over the past century. To examine the historically-based evolution of management, we need to start at the beginning. Although some dialogue on convergence will be added during the review, most of our discussion will be saved for the end of this chapter.

Classical Management School

What has come to be known as the classical school of management is an outgrowth of the origins of the industrial revolution. Today, it is also referred to as structural in nature since the elements leading to creating products efficiently are foremost in these designs. Until the mid- to late nineteenth century, work was generally performed in small groups and was extremely labor intensive, placing an emphasis on an individualistic perspective of the workplace. With the advent of machines, first with steam engines and water-driven machines, doing work changed the emphasis from the worker to the product. As the twentieth century dawned, various perspectives evolved from these early industrial settings based on generating increased production, but it wasn't until after World War II that specific theoretical components were set down.

Scientific Management

Among the first management theories developed was scientific management theory. This theory, more properly a set of preferences, held that principles of work should be based on the effective arrangement of tasks and the careful acquisition and selection of employees for different positions. In other words, it was one of the first efforts to "fit" people to their specific tasks.

Frederick Taylor (1947), a mechanical engineer, created scientific management and arranged tasks based on production values, not on how a particular individual thought or wanted to work. Rather, the work was based on the individuals' physical attributes and "fit" to do the work.[3] For instance, women were selected to perform skills that required small hands and a great deal of dexterity. Men were often selected to do work in which physical strength and endurance were valued. Taylor measured the size of shovels used by workers and assigned the shovels based on the size and ability of the worker to do the work. Workers who did more work than their assigned share would receive a few dollars extra as an incentive.

Scientific management also called for training and development of the workforce and the inclusion of economic incentives to motivate employees. Each part of the production process received careful scrutiny to increase production output to its fullest. Scientific management also proposed that workers would be more productive if they received higher wages for their labor. Although later studies would show that workers needed more than higher wages to increase productivity, this was a radical proposition at the time.[4]

Many components of Taylor's work are still found today, including detailed job descriptions, careful employee selection processes, and training and development.

Administrative Management

About the same time as Taylor's creation of scientific management, Henri Fayol (1949), a French mining executive, created the basis for administrative management theory. Fayol developed a Principles of Management philosophy containing 14 specific values based on the assumption that organizations operate best in a hierarchical environment (Table 4.1).[5]

Table 4.1. Administrative management: Fayol's Principles of Management

1) Division of Work—Work should be divided according to specialization.
2) Authority and Responsibility—The manager has the authority to give directions and *demand* compliance along with appropriate responsibility.
3) Discipline—Respect and obedience are required of employees and the firm.
4) Unity of Command—Orders are received from a single supervisor.
5) Unity of Direction—Similar activities should be under the similar direction of a single supervisor.
6) Subordination of Individual Interest to General Interest—Organizational interests outweigh those of the individual workers.
7) Remuneration of Personnel—Wages should be fair and equitable.
8) Centralization—Organizations must discover the necessary level of centralization of authority to maximize employee productivity.
9) Scalar Chain—Organizations create a specific line of authority from top to bottom
10) Order—All necessary materials must be organized in their appropriate places to maximize efficiency.
11) Equity—Fair and equitable treatment is given to all employees.
12) Stability of Tenure of Employees—Organizations allow employees adequate time to develop and adjust to their new work skill demands.
13) Initiative—Ability to implement and develop a plan is crucial.
14) Esprit de Corps—Organizations promote spirit of harmony among employees.

Fayol's work is important because it was among the first to look toward how an organization should operate based on a set of values created to make work more efficient. This set the stage for further designs in the workplace that would be based on increased production in an efficient manner.

Bureaucratic Management

Max Weber (1947), a well known philosopher and sociologist in Germany, developed the bureaucratic management model. Weber theorized that the use of an organizational hierarchy or bureaucracy would enable an organization to produce at its highest level. This model formalized themes calling for a clear division of labor and management, strong central authority, a system of seniority, strict discipline and control, clear policies and procedures, and careful selection of workers based on technical qualifications.[6]

The classical school was noted for its emphasis on production and efficiency, and its models reflected strict regimentation and hierarchy. Early production-based organizations had few models to guide them in working with large numbers of skilled and semi-skilled laborers, so the early models were based on the only other large organizations in which many people worked together—the military. Many of the companies that first came to prominence found a military rule of order particularly appealing; the close organization and monitoring allowed owners to control every aspect of the production of their companies. Globally and nationally, these company owners positioned themselves to be the heart and soul of their companies. Individuals who worked for these often rigid business operators knew and understood that there was little leeway in management functions. Orders were given, and orders were followed.

As the classical theories were beginning to be formalized, others began to question the models that had developed in the workplace. It became apparent to some efficiency experts that the models worked well for a time but that in certain types of jobs, particularly jobs in which more skills were required, some aspects of the classical models began to break down.

Skilled labor had become more important as the sophistication of manufacturing had consistently evolved. Skilled laborers had something that early models didn't account for—interest in their work, or sometimes even a lack of interest in that work. Experts began to realize that economic factors were not going to be the only motivation for workers to increase production and continue on an efficient path.

This interest in workers rather than strict management led to the development of a series of new management theories that were ultimately called the Human Relations School of Management or human resources approaches. Some have called it the behavioral school, but for our purposes, we want to emphasize the human aspects of management in these approaches rather than placing the emphasis on making people behave in a certain manner.[7]

Human Relations School

Some of the earliest studies looking at workers and their working conditions were conducted by Western Electric Company at its plant in Hawthorne, Illinois, a Chicago suburb. Western Electric was a subsidiary of AT&T and was involved in the development and production of telephone equipment. Elton Mayo, a business professor from Harvard, was called in to study working conditions and their relationship to productivity. Mayo believed that improving working conditions would improve productivity.[8] Mayo developed several experiments, including studying the influences from differences in lighting, noise and heating, and pay incentives. The study first found that when workers were placed under improved illumination, their productivity increased. Mayo then reduced the level of illumination, but the results were confusing because worker productivity still improved. Using similar tools, Mayo's research team looked at the other variables, only to find results similar to those in the illumination studies.

Mayo concluded that the illumination had little to do with productivity but that workers were highly aware that they were being observed, and knowing that management was paying attention to them led to increased productivity. In other words, greater interaction with management meant higher levels of production from workers. This effect became known as the Hawthorne Effect. It also showed that incentives beyond pay and working conditions influenced productivity.

From a management point of view, Mayo's studies launched the human relations school, and additional studies began to focus on how management's treatment of employees would influence productivity.

Maslow's Hierarchy of Needs

Abraham Maslow created a theory based on his observations of people. The Hierarchy of Needs is generally shown as a pyramid or ascending diagram. Maslow was a psychologist and was among several researchers who looked at people, their surroundings and their motivations. Maslow believed that people were first motivated to fulfill their *physiological* needs—needs defined as simply living, the need for food, water and shelter. In this instance, a job is important at a physiological level. Many workers through the late nineteenth and early twentieth centuries were primarily interested in meeting employees' physiological levels of need.[9]

Moving upward on Maslow's scale, the second level is safety. Once individuals meet their physiological needs, it becomes of interest to keep meeting those needs. This means that the individuals must be physically able to keep doing the planned work; if they are harmed, so is their ability to do work, which leads to concerns for safety, both physically on the job and financially away from the job.

The third level of Maslow's hierarchy is social. Maslow recognized that all individuals need to interact with other people; as some have said, people are the products of their environments, which are created both by home and work.

Once social needs are met, people seek to move to the next level. Individuals want both self-esteem and recognition from others. These needs show the way to individuals feeling good about themselves. People look for "affirmations," positive influences in their lives that will motivate them further.

Finally, at the top of Maslow's scale is self-actualization. People who have achieved well at the other levels now seek the ultimate challenge—becoming all that they are capable of being. This is the idea of maximizing one's potential. People will become what they must.

Maslow's Hierarchy of Needs has a great deal of utility in explaining the human condition—what motivates people when. Maslow theorized that people will respond differently to this scale at different periods in their lives and will emphasize different aspects of this pyramid in different periods of their life cycles. Because of this, Maslow's enduring contribution to the human relations school may be the recognition that people are not static or linear and that they move upward and downward through the hierarchy depending on where they are in life.

Herzberg's Hygiene and Motivation Factors

Frederick Herzberg, another psychologist, studied employee attitudes and developed factors that were designed to be more structurally understanding of human motivations.[10] Herzberg divided these factors into two groups. The first group is composed of the hygiene factors. Hygiene factors are defined as elements that represent an individual's working environment. These factors include working conditions, both technical and physical; company policies and procedures; supervision; the work itself; wages; and benefits. Herzberg's second group was labeled motivator factors. These factors included aspects of the job itself, including recognition, achievement, responsibility, and individual growth and development. Motivator factors are so named because they imply that the factors would have a positive impact on employees' satisfaction with their jobs.

Theories X and Y

Other people also were examining the human condition as it applied to the workplace. Most notable among these was Douglas McGregor, who in

1960 formalized these concepts into management theories. He expressed the classical school mantra as Theory X. Theory X emphasized such management practices as control and coercion in motivating employees.[11]

Employing the concepts brought forward in the human relations school, McGregor posited his Theory Y of management practices. Theory Y assumes that workers want to achieve. When workers want to achieve, they are generally motivated toward self-improvement and are capable of exercising self-control in the workplace. Under this theory, workers do their jobs based not on direct supervision and control but on a set of motivating factors. This changes the focus of the manager's role in the workplace; the manager is now charged with discovering the worker's proper role in the organization, placing him in that position and working to create a reward system that assists the employee in his individual advancement.

Theory Y then focuses on supplying workers with an appropriate system of rewards, which are expected to lead to interest in the further personal development of the worker. It is a fundamental theory in the human relations school. Interestingly, traits from both Theory X and Theory Y are found in most modern management situations or contemporary organizations.

Theory Z

While Theories X and Y were based on existing trends in management, Theory Z was written as an outcome of the examination of working conditions in organizations in Japan. William Ouchi, a management consultant, had attempted to take his ideas to American industry, but some of his methods and expectations worried traditional management leaders in the United States. At the time, however, Japan was emerging from the devastation of World War II and was willing to look at Ouchi's unusual approach to work. In fact, because of the cultural nature of the Japanese people, Ouchi's theoretical ideas were an excellent fit.[12]

Theory Z, like Theory Y, emphasizes employee participation in management. The development of individual traits is crucial to the overall health of the organization; however, Theory Z also draws from Theory X, calling for strong central authority and requiring management to make key decisions. Much of Theory Z emphasizes teamwork while focusing on individual concepts and the interrelationship between managers and "managees." Theory Z's focus on creating an atmosphere in which group participation was central is a key factor in what makes it work. Japan's cultural heritage of working as a "family" and honoring leaders was well positioned for the move into creating organizational structures based on Theory Z.

Theory Z was heavily criticized by some more traditional managers in the United States, particularly those concerned about cultural differences in the workforce. In the United States, an emphasis on individuality has always existed. Although that is often true of workers in the U.S., a number of work situations have found that Americans, properly trained and motivated, do well in Theory Z-style team environments, but only when everyone is carrying his or her own share of responsibility.

Theory Z tends to bridge the traditional management schools and bring together the primary goals of both the classical and the human relations schools, but more theoretical advancement has taken place since the development of Theory Z. Most of these advancements fall into a less-than-theoretical range but provide excellent material for examining where organizations are looking for management practices today.

The Modern School of Management

The modern school of management is punctuated by four primary areas of study: management effectiveness, leadership, systems approaches to management, and quality management approaches. More recently, scholars have added to this milieu by creating a series of incremental management processes. We will discuss these following an overview of current trends in management.

Management effectiveness is an outgrowth of considerations generally unaccounted for by Theories X and Y. Theory X focused on managerial efficiency and control while Theory Y emphasized employee needs and wants. Neither model focused on the effectiveness of the management process or asked questions about how tasks were accomplished that benefited the organization other than through production. Management effectiveness asks whether the goals of the project were met and how those goals influenced the workers involved in the project.

Everyone is familiar with the saying that it's difficult to remember that the original job was to drain the swamp when everybody is up to their eyeballs in alligators. That may be a bit of a more politically correct version of the statement than its original incarnation, but readers should understand the idea behind it. Researchers in these instances were trying to understand not only the outcomes of management but also the processes of management that led to the development of new approaches in managing the workplace.

Management by Objective

Management by objective (MBO) presented an early model that tried to formulate a way to answer those questions. Here, the focus switched from emphasizing organizational output to emphasizing the roles of managers and workers in creating that output. In other words, leaders asked "What roles do managers and employees play in creating the desired outcome of a project and what is that relationship to the organization's goals?"[13]

In the MBO system, upper- and mid-level managers identify goals for each area of responsibility. Tasks are then designed in a manner that will, or should to some extent, meet those goals. In the earliest development phases of MBO, employees were assigned projects with specific results. It was not the role of the manager to decide how the employee reached that goal, but managers were to facilitate the employee's effort.

In this way, the employee had a great deal of self-direction. The difficulty in this system came in understanding how goals should be set. Since MBO's inception, many MBO-driven organizations have included employees in assignment creation, thereby overcoming some of those obstacles. Employees generally know best the number of projects and deadlines under which they operate best. They also generally know where the loggerheads to completing the assigned task will be. Working together, managers and employees are more systematically able to identify timelines and goals for all projects. This approach avoids strict goal-setting and timelines and helps prevent management-by-objective approaches from breaking down.

Leadership

Much of the organizational literature today deals with the concept of leadership. Leadership is a concept that has created a number of concepts and is generally defined as the process of influencing the activities of an individual or group in efforts toward goal achievement in a given situation. In general, we should add "without coercion" to that statement.

Leadership has been variously dealt with in business schools, organizational psychology and organizational communication. Those examinations

have ranged from defining notions of charisma to locating factors that influence the development of leadership skills. We will be examining leadership and its relationship to power in Chapter 7. For now, we need to
understand leadership as a management component and how it operates in
the workplace.[14]

The Situational Leadership Model

One of the principle leadership models is the Situational Leadership
Model, which is based on three variables: 1) task behavior, the amount of
guidance and direction provided by or needed from the leader; 2) relationship behavior, the amount of support (socio-emotional) provided by
the leader and 3) the level of readiness that followers exhibit toward a task
or objective.[15]

This is a contingency-based approach to leadership. In other words, the
leader decides which style of leadership to adopt depending on the project
or goals and the readiness of employees or followers to perform the task.
In this model, the method and style change as the project changes. Some
believe this is an excellent way to manage in the electronic media because
of the wide variety of tasks and skills used in an electronic medium. It may
also look schizophrenic to some who believe that managers should be
more predictable to ensure that employees understand them.

According to some researchers, it is important for managers to adapt their
leadership styles to the organizations in which they are working. Media organizations move managers through various positions and holdings with a
great deal of frequency. Managers who are able to understand their new environments and adapt their styles to fit the environments are generally
viewed as most successful in an organization. We will discuss these issues
more carefully in Chapter 7 as we examine cultural issues and leadership.

Systems Approaches

A third area of modern management is the *systems approach*. Scholars
call it a systems approach because it deals with management from both
macro and micro perspectives. In other words, systems approaches look at
the actions and activities of the entire organization and how they relate to
the organization's goals and then decide what is best for the organization's
operations.[16]

These system approaches are based on a variety of assumptions but are generally defined as inputs, production processes and outputs. Inputs relate to the ingredients necessary for the creation of a product, labor, capital, equipment and other expected raw materials. Each is necessary before the organization can produce anything. If the organization wants to own a television station, management must first secure an FCC license and then build, buy or lease property and equipment and hire the appropriate people for the appropriate positions in the organization.

If the station intends to have a news operation, this process is even more complex. Now management needs more than a transmitter, a few tape machines, computer servers and programs; the organization now needs field equipment, cameras and studio equipment. The investment is often double or triple the amount needed for an operation without a newsroom. In fact, many cable networks operate without traditional studios and lease studio space for short periods of time only when it is beneficial.

Production processes are the actual performance of the work to be done. If we continue with the television station example, production processes are the creation of commercials, news programs and entertainment programs from the raw materials acquired in the input phase when needed. The work involved in the creation of the product is extremely important, and in media management, it is frequently overlooked or played down. Media operations spend a great deal of time and effort in securing the personnel to run operations and a great deal on the marketing of those products but often have tremendous expectations from the working environment while failing to understand the workings of the process.

The final part of the systems approach is output. Output represents the finished goods and services provided to customers. In television, this includes the daily dose of news stories and network feeds as well as locally acquired programs. In radio, it is the music or talk programs aired that fit a particular station's format. In a newspaper, it is the number of hard news stories, photographs and feature stories prepared for the publication. It also includes the printed form, or in today's workplace, the multimedia stories.

Organizations examine these functions both internally and externally. It is crucial to understand that systems theories and models include the external environment in all of their approaches. Systems theories recognize that organizations cannot operate in isolation. Significant studies show that one of the surefire ways to fail as an organization is to ignore the world and the processes creating external pressures on the organization.

Managers cannot control the external environment, though many try. The graveyard of the marketplace is littered with the "bodies" of managers who ignored the conditions of the changing environments around them. Media managers, struck by today's need to change to survive, are looking at their external environments. Those ignoring the changing environment or believing their operations are somehow different from those around them will join those in the organizational dumpster sooner rather than later. Media managers ignoring convergence or believing it is a fad are among this group.

Many of the dynamics of uncertainty that organizations face are due to environmental factors. Systems management approaches recognize that external factors exist, and they work to add those factors into the mix. The overall effort now comes down not simply to producing a product, but to understanding the opportunities and constraints that the external marketplace is putting on the decisions to make and market those products.

Organizations often try to alter their interdependence on their external environments in one of two ways; first, they may try to acquire and absorb other entities that may or may not compete with them, and second, they may try to reach agreements for cooperation in such a way as to create mutual interdependence between the organizations.

Much of the media concentration taking place today through mergers and hand-changing of companies is due to a need to recognize what industry competitors are up to in the marketplace. Mergers, acquisitions and other management activities leading to interdependence and cooperation among competitors will be discussed in a later section.

Total Quality Management (TQM)

A fourth area of the modern management school is total quality management (TQM). In total quality management, managers face two component tasks; the first is using strategies to deliver the best possible products while looking for ways to continuously improve every part of the operation of the organization.[17]

In TQM, management implements and leads the movement, but employees are responsible for the quality. Used effectively, TQM helps organizations maintain their competitive edge. In theory, TQM is exceptional and, if utilized properly, would work well in a newsroom setting. Unfortunately, TQM is one of those theoretical processes that has already been driven amok in the United States.

In a journalistic environment, TQM would have reporters and photographers as well as producers and production personnel involved in providing the best product possible for their organization. Taken together, individual performances would be based on the contributions employees make to improve the product. Employees would essentially be required to tell managers what is needed to improve their products, and managers would respond by making those changes to ensure improvement. Regrettably, quality usually requires investment, and television and radio stations as well as other media firms are wary of over-investing. Broadcasting can be an extraordinarily expensive business. When recommendations come from employees who require increased expenditures, the suggestions are often ignored. The costs involved in upgrading the components that lead to improving the production of the final product simply overshadow the desire to improve quality.

TQM therefore is frequently very frustrating, particularly when employees believe that management is openly soliciting ideas for change, only to turn around and ignore those ideas. Ignoring or downplaying employee suggestions will lead to low morale and the expectation that the company is uncaring. Managers often think they are doing the right thing by soliciting advice, but if the approach doesn't receive favorable responses, employees will think management is just offering up the corporate line and that management doesn't care what they think.

The truth is that it's just too expensive to upgrade products continually. Managers report to CEOs and other executives, all of whom report to stockholders. Most stockholders are more interested in a return on their investment than they are on how the company does its business.

The Working Environment

To this point, we have been discussing the management function from a generally theoretical level, with little discussion about the individual contributions and work from the employees. This section begins an examination of the ability of people to work with one another and various factors and issues that come into play in that work environment. The first questions individuals need to ask themselves are "How do I work?" and "How do my working preferences influence my work with others?"

These questions appear simple, but how they are dealt with and how managers attempt to create a systematic method for working with employees makes for a complex relationship. Each individual is imbued with a certain set of personality traits, what management and human resources people call predisposition factors. These factors are communication behaviors that are created from an individual's intrapersonal organizational experience.

Predispositions are personally-held preferences for particular types of communication situations or behaviors. They usually are an outgrowth of an individual's personal needs and are based on individual motivations; past experiences; current information that individuals have about their jobs, co-workers and organization; and the individual's perception of his or her communication competency. For example, predispositions for oral communication have been found to be related to occupational choice, job satisfaction, productivity, advancement and job retention.

These predispositions have led to researchers identifying three areas of preferences among workers and supervisors: communication apprehension, leadership and conflict preferences, and communication competency.[18] Communication apprehension is probably the best known of these three employee preferences. When students have difficulties in class, they are often tested to determine their level of reluctance to speak up in class. Communication apprehension is the measure of the level of anxiety an individual faces and overcomes when communicating with others, generally in a verbal fashion. Every individual has a level of reluctance regarding communication. For some, it is triggered by conflict. For others, speaking before a small group of five or six people may trigger high levels of anxiety. Some people may be incapable of talking to other individuals even in a one-to-one situation.

Although people tend to talk collectively about the shyness of others, communication apprehension is a much more complex condition than simply being shy. Shyness is often overcome through training and acquired self-confidence. True communication apprehension is generally more difficult to change. Communications scholars have written a great deal about the conditions surrounding communication apprehension, and a great deal of exploration on the issue continues.

Leadership and conflict preferences are factors relating to an individual's perception of what leadership means and his or her desire to lead others. A great deal of variation exists in how people approach these skills or preferences, particularly in dealing with conflict. Conflict preferences range in individuals from those people who show an absolute avoidance to dealing with serious disagreements or differences to those who relish the thought of a peer battle. Leadership skills tend to moderate the behaviors that are counterproductive in conflict situations.

Many scholars define leadership as the ability to lead others through visualizing how to complete a task or solve a problem at hand while understanding the needs of workers. Individuals with leadership skills have a knack for collaboration and use compromise as a substitute for conflict. This often leads to an expectation that conflict and leadership are at opposite ends of a performance continuum; however, leadership may on occasion foster conflict to help individuals within a workgroup understand and realize the expectations for the tasks before them.[19]

Those people unwilling to enter conflicts or those unwilling to forego their own ideas for the ideas of others are rarely good leaders. They may have good management skills in ensuring that projects are completed on time and efficiently, but they generally do not have a shared vision of the workplace with employees. This often leads to high stress, low creativity and high turnover in workgroups where managers are not capable of creating a shared vision.

The third aspect of communication preferences deals with communication competency. The issue of competency refers to an individual's perception and understanding of how to create influence in his or her organization. Higher levels of communication competency are generally associated with an individual's knowledge, sensitivity, skills and values regarding the organization.

One example of a high competency level would include an individual understanding how layoffs or downsizing would be beneficial to the financial safety of the overall organization even though the individual was potentially a victim of the downsizing. Additionally, these people would be able to communicate those issues clearly to others within the organization and likely would be able to generate support for the move.

Sensitivity, punctuated by an ability to see all sides of an issue and how that issue would influence others from employees and managers to shareholders and other stakeholders, is a critical component of communication competency. Individuals with highly developed skills in writing and speaking are generally among those who fit well into roles needed for communication competency. Interestingly, communication competency and communication apprehension tend to offset one another in a management sense. Managers with well-defined communication preferences, low levels of apprehension and high levels of leadership and competency remain among the most-valued managers in an organization.

Value, Perceptions and Selection

For more than fifty years, researchers have been attempting to examine how people relate their working environments to their personal systems of values and beliefs. A great deal of literature has begun to illuminate the human mind and its relationship to the workplace, but a great deal of work is left to be done. We will begin this section with an overview of this literature and how these issues are evolving into today's media workplace. We will continue this line of thinking throughout Chapter 7, where we examine power and leadership in an organizational context.

Values are the stuff of philosophy. How we build and live our lives and how feudal states and nation states evolved are all part of the discussion of the philosophy of values.[20] From the dawn of man's seeking to understand itself, philosophers periodically have developed sets of values that attribute themselves to the actions of those of the time. These value systems have evolved into a set of systems that now are entrenched in modern life and have led to the development of ethics as a study area in philosophy. Journalism has a particular affinity for dealing with ethical issues; for that reason, we will discuss the value systems that have led to ethical canons that help describe how individuals, groups, organizations and even nations behave.

Prominent Ethical Systems

The study of ethics requires a great deal of background and understanding into the nature of mankind. We will not endeavor here to bring you into a complete understanding of the mechanisms that lead people to act the way they act. Instead, we will attempt to draw your attention to the most significant ethical systems currently under study. By identifying those areas, we will be better able to understand how people choose to lead their lives and better able to define management parameters that help people in the workplace. For simplicity's sake, this section examines ethics through a historical lens, situating the ethical system development into its place in time.

As Greek civilization flourished between 400 and 300 BC, people were finding new ways of discovering how they believed they should live their lives. Some believed that living a life that reflected the potential starkness of nature put them into close proximity with their gods. These people often wore roughly-woven clothing, ate very meager meals and deprived themselves of many available conveniences. Some were even known to practice self flogging. They would travel about various Greek cities, flailing themselves with whips across their backs; some even attached rocks and thorns to these whips. The goal was to create pain so that they could better understand the pain that the earth bore through living with mankind.

At the other end of the spectrum in Greek culture were those who indulged in all sorts of behaviors based on submitting themselves to all forms of pleasure. These people engaged in all forms of immorality and decadence. If you have seen the motion picture *Seven*, you will have heard of the seven deadly sins. These sins are often what you see in the depictions of motion pictures set in that period. To these folks, life was one big party.

Aristotle, one of history's best-known philosophers, believed both excess and denial wrong. He explained that virtue and happiness come from living a balanced life. Aristotle thereby developed one of the first recorded forms of ethical philosophy, the Golden Mean. The Golden Mean was based on the expectation that a life well-lived was one in which neither depravity nor excess ruled one's life. Instead, this ethical belief system called on individuals and groups to balance their lives. To live a good life, in Aristotle's view, was simply to avoid extremes. He saw life as a great gift that could be fostered and developed only as human beings opened their eyes, pursuing virtue while avoiding what was to him "excellence . . . destroyed by excess or deficiency, but secured by pursuing the mean."[21]

Several hundred years later, the rise of Christianity in Europe led to the extension of value systems tied to one of the primary tenets of both Christianity and Judaism. This was the concept of love. Obviously, we are not talking about romantic love, but rather a variety of principles that evolved from this notion, including "do unto others as you would have them do unto you" and "love they neighbor as you love yourself."[22]

Sometimes this love is expressed through the principles laid out in the Bible's Old Testament and the Ten Commandments. Although there is a great deal of distance between ideas surrounding the belief that "thou shall not kill" and loving your neighbor, the ideas are similar. A closer commandment might be the one that requires people to "honor thy father and thy mother." At any rate, this set of values became known as Judeo-Christian ethics.

Aristotle's balanced moderation and the Judeo-Christian ethics were the foremost western philosophical value strategies for more than a millennium as European values and philosophical development were controlled by religious groups throughout the region. Eastern philosophies and religion hadn't entered into the Western psyche and didn't begin to impose themselves into value system discussions until the twentieth century. Still, following the Dark Ages and the Age of Enlightenment, new philosophies and ethical systems began to rise. Several of these are noteworthy for discussion.[23]

The Categorical Imperative was crafted by Immanuel Kant. Kant was a German philosopher who based his writings on what he called one's moral "sense of duty."[24] He wrote that individual actions should be based on those acts that are acceptable to all members of society. The Categorical Imperative is based on the process of ethical decision making rather than the outcomes of what would be considered morally defensible to most people, so if you are acting in a way that society embraces, you are on the correct path.

Utilitarianism was developed by John Stuart Mill. This is the concept of working to develop an ethical sense or a moral compass that is designed to create the greatest good. Decision making is very outcome-derived; it is expected that the outcomes will benefit the group, a concept often used in describing the activities of a democracy.[25]

Egalitarianism is the work of John Rawls and argues that everyone must be treated equally and fairly when individuals form ethical judgments. Rawls introduced the term "veil of ignorance." Rawls believed that we are able to eliminate the greatest number of biases if we wear a veil that separates us from discriminatory acts.[26] In other words, ignorance is sometimes helpful. This has its benefits in some decision-making situations, but if followed too closely, it may lead to making those decisions in a self-imposed vacuum. Still, the biases are thrown out, creating a positive benefit.

Relativism was best described by John Dewey and Bertrand Russell.[27] Relativists believe that what is best for one is not necessarily best for another, even under similar situations. In this system, each individual decides what is best for him or her based on individual concerns and viewpoints and not on the predispositions of others. This has given rise to the study of situational ethics in the business and media environment. Relativism too is dangerous, particularly in a journalistic sense. Several recent journalism scandals in which reporters used fictitious or improper sources for stories come to mind as facilitating the individual at the expense of the public's information needs.

Social responsibility theory grew out of the U.S. Congress' Hutchins Commission report on the freedom of the press during the 1940s.[28] This theory is based on concepts surrounding good intentions. It is frequently used when discussing news reporting. Social responsibility theory acknowledges that although journalists may make errors in their reporting, their stories are generally constructed based on good intentions. Much of our law regarding libel and the legal concept of careless and reckless disregard for the truth grow out of this ethical tradition.

The process of ethical decision making is often referred to as deontological ethics. This process is based on the assumption that established principles guide decision making. The outcome of those actions, often the result of decisions based on a set of prescribed principles, is considered the study of teleological ethics. Therefore, theories of ethics may be either process-based or outcome-based. Kant was a good example of deontological thinking, i.e., if the process is undertaken correctly, the outcomes will follow a logical and correct course. Judeo-Christian ethics and the Golden Mean also fall into this category.

The others fall into outcome philosophies. In outcome-directed philosophies, the idea is that it doesn't matter how "good" or moral the process is if the outcome fails to help others—the process of taking the "right" or correct action has failed.

Practicing Practical Ethics in Convergence

So what does all of this have to do with managing media through these tumultuous times? Natural conflicts arise over the ability of the media to serve the market and marketplace. It is helpful that we understand the ethical nature of both as we try to serve them.

Practically, ethical concerns can be broken into a variety of broad categories. From broadcasting decisions about the form of appropriate news and information programming to building and maintaining firewalls between editorial and advertising departments in newspapers, ethical positions are crucial. The storm that descended on the *Los Angeles Times* when management sought to use the news pages to openly promote private business enterprise led to the eventual sale of the Times Mirror Company to the Tribune Company. This is an unusually stark reminder that simply owning a news operation shouldn't allow management to ignore or underestimate the public's power to force reform.

Convergence opens a veritable Pandora's Box when it is the basis for shifting an organization's responsibilities away from high news production standards to a more profit-driven environment. In news, concerns for the ethical behavior of the organization are paramount. Organizations must create policies that bring philosophies into concrete practices and include specific methods for dealing with a variety of issues. Some of those concerns require

- ensuring the truth and accuracy of presented material over deadline pressures.
- protecting non-involved members of the public.
- eliminating or limiting conflicts of interest.

- ensuring confidentially of sources.
- hardening the firewall between reporters and advertisers.

Today's media managers are often confronted with making decisions that challenge their personal morals and values. The level of intensity of those concerns from ownership will manifest itself differently at all levels of the organization. Where possible, managers should try to work for organizations with clearly established codes of conduct and ethics. Although most major companies and broadcasters have these credos established, there are varying degrees of acceptance and adherence to them.

How should we look at implementing plans to allay those concerns and conflicting interests? Ethical decisions are made easier when an organization has clearly outlined a course of action for converged companies. To make the standards credible to all employees, organizations need to

- clarify the values of the organization.
- develop an organizational mission statement.
- create a code of ethics.
- develop an official ethics program and enforce it.

Mission statements should clearly state the goals of the organization and how those ends are to be met. Managers also need to clarify the values of the organization unless mission statements reflect the organization's true values; otherwise, a code of ethics will be seen by employees and outsiders as pandering.

A written code of ethics, generally in an employee handbook, is a good starting place. It should outline how employees must act on the job and how they should act away from the job in situations when they represent the organization. These rules can prove valuable to creating a mission statement.

Writing a code isn't enough, however; organizations must develop ethics programs and train employees to understand what those values mean. Written codes must not make lofty statements that raise more questions than they answer, and all organizations should frequently retrain reporters, editors and talent in appropriate versus inappropriate behavior.

Conclusions

Management approaches continue to evolve as organizations and the workers who represent them become more sophisticated in both individual and organizational needs while better understanding the nature of work. News operations are challenged at all levels as convergence becomes a reality of the workplace. Employers need to facilitate the development of newsroom workers by developing programs that will encourage their development and cross-platform interest.

Creating a solid ethical structure is one way to ensure that employees know that the standards of ethical conduct remain unchanged despite the evolutions occurring in the workplace. Careful consideration of the development of employees, coupled with these sound ethical standards, will help ensure that converged news operations move toward the future in a fruitful manner.

Still, organizations themselves often create issues and conditions that fail to foster positive development of human resources. Chapter 5 examines those issues and organizational styles more thoroughly.

Exercises

1. Talk with a manager at a radio or television station in your area. Try to determine his or her mindset on management decision making and then write a short paper evaluating that management style.
2. Meet with a reporter at a local newspaper or television or radio station or with an Internet reporter. Discover how he or she views the management of his or her operation. Using this information and the material presented in this chapter, determine whether the management style at the operation is effective.
3. If possible, find a converged news operation in your area. Talk with reporters and editors to see if they believe the organization is working in the converged environment. Write a paper about four pages long outlining the issues and concerns you found at the organization.

CHAPTER 5

Understanding Organizations

Dealing with work is one thing; understanding how the workplace operates beyond the confines of one's own work area is another. In Chapter 4, we looked at the evolution of work through its theories and management structures and how those theories apply to mass media. In this chapter we turn more to the actions of organizations and how people fit into those organizations on a collective level to ensure that they are working in a way that makes sense to the traditions and cultures (which will be defined later) in which they find themselves.

Not unlike the evolution of management theories, the evolution of organizational theories crosses a number of perspectives. Early research into organizations focused on behavioral perspectives of how people worked. These areas, developed through organizational psychology and general management philosophies, dominated workplace evolution. Behavioral views developed from research using experiments and observational scientific techniques that tested worker skills and adaptability to various jobs.

In the past 40 years, interpretive views that incorporate actions based on organizational meaning and symbols have come to play a role just as important in investigating the field. Communications, sociology and anthropology scholars have all used symbolic or interpretive methods for research.

More recently, two other schools of thought—critical and post modern perspectives—have been useful in investigating the relationships of people and their organizations. Management ideas based on these schools of thought, or ways of viewing reality, have been synthesized from an organizational perspective by several authors. Syn-

thesizing these approaches results in the creation of various perceptions, each looking at organizations and how they are managed.

Bolman and Deal, following the work of numerous other scholars,
characterized the variety of views of reality as "frames." Although the use
of the term in communications may be somewhat problematic because of
framing and framing theories, some relationship between the areas and the
definitions are useful for our purposes. The four frames described by Bolman and Deal were structural, human resource, political and symbolic.[1]

We will examine all four areas (Table 5.1), particularly as they contribute to our knowledge about organizational culture and communication
and their applications to media organizations. These frames will also be
useful in Chapter 7 in our discussion on power and risk.

Table 5.1. Organizational frames: process of communication behaviors

	FRAME			
	Structural	Human Resource	Political	Symbolic
Organizational Metaphor	Factory or machine	Family	Jungle	Carnival, Temple, Theater
Central Concepts	Rules, Roles, Goals, Policies, Technology, Environment	Needs, Skills, Relationships	Power, Conflict, Competition, Organizational politics	Culture, Meaning, Metaphor, Ritual, Ceremony, Stories, Heroes
Image of Leadership	Social architecture	Empowerment	Advocacy	Inspiration
Basic Leadership Challenge	Attune structure to task, technology, environment	Align organizational and human needs	Develop agenda and power base	Create faith, beauty, meaning

Source: Bolman and Deal, 1998.

Note: Each frame provides its own set of characteristics, providing direction in dealing with organizational activity and change.

The four frames are based on the historic development of organizational theories and approaches to work and multiple levels of interaction through communication processes. Each frame contributes significantly to our knowledge. These frames also allow us to consider how we work with other people and how they work with us.

As you can see from the table, structural frames are derived from early management research basing organizations on factory or machine metaphors. This develops through systematic rules, roles, goals and policies that evolve into an organizational social structure. The goal is to attune the structure to the task.

Human resources frames are derived from family metaphors embedded in the organization. This approach allows the evolution of the organization and the workforce based on needs, skills and relationships while empowering the group through effective leadership. Challenges are expressed through aligning those human needs with the needs of the organization.

Political frames are based on a jungle concept. Here, the emphasis is on issues of power, conflict and competition in the jungle of the working world. Leaders are seen as advocates, and their challenge is related to creating a power base and developing an agenda that is useful to themselves and others.

The fourth frame is symbolic, and the metaphors are wide ranging and based on the development of the organization through metaphors such as carnival, temple and theater. Here, metaphors are actually descriptors of the organization at work. The concepts are based on culture, meaning, rituals, stories and ceremonies that exist within the organization. Leaders are seen as providing inspiration, and the challenges for leadership are to create faith, beauty and meaning through those inspirational images.

We address these four frames so that you might be able to assess the form of working environment you find yourselves in and able to work to determine how the frame will suit convergence. We will return to a discussion on these frames later, but first, an overview of organizations and systems within those organizations is needed.

Media as Organizations

Sociologist Amatai Etzioni said, "Our society is an organizational society. We are born in organizations, educated in organizations, and most of us spend most of our lives working for organizations. We spend much of our leisure time playing and praying in organizations. Most of us will die in an organization, and when it comes time for burial, the largest organization of all—the state—must grant official permission."[2]

Organizations are considered living things, generally because they are subject to and influenced by the people who work as a part of the organization. Another concept that adds to the organism metaphor is that organizations are always dealing with the ongoing necessity of change. The term was taken from science because organisms are alive, not inanimate or static.

All organizations exhibit some characteristics that researchers term as similar in nature. Four factors define virtually every organization: formality; hierarchy; lack of the ability to form extended close relationships; and being long-lived, generally longer than a human lifetime.[3]

Formality applies to the creation and existence of policies, goals, procedures and regulations. Depending on the type of organization (or its organizational frame), it will use these functions differently, but all organizations will display certain levels of each.

Hierarchy, of course, deals with who reports to whom. Even the most fluid and symbolically based organization will have some degree of hierarchy. It is in the portrayal and execution of that hierarchy that the organization's factor style is identified.

Size is generally a distinguishing feature in the third characteristic—the inability to form close relationships. Most organizations will, when new, have opportunities for people to work closely and create a large circle of people within the organization that they know well. The larger the organization, however, the more difficult it is to extend those relationships beyond one's work area; there are just too many people to know them all. By this definition, some television and radio stations wouldn't really fit an organizational model, but for the most part, they do.

Organizations generally are developed to last a long time. NBC, CBS and ABC have been around longer than most of the people who were there at the beginning. Younger organizations such as News Corporation will remain after the deaths of their founders.

Media organizations have many similarities to other organizations but also have a number of qualities that make them unique. Media organizations exist based on an expectation that the organization will produce information, sometimes information that will transform society. How information is created and transferred for use by consumers has been the subject of numerous articles, and media organizations themselves have been researched by scholars in a variety of fields.

Applying old tools to media may not be appropriate. In Chapters 6 and 7 we will explore two very different ideas applied to media: creativity in Chapter 6 and risk and power in Chapter 7. For instance, some research suggests that highly creative people are more receptive to change through proactive mechanisms. Before we investigate these concepts, however, we must establish a foundation in the operations of organizations themselves.

Managing Media Organizations

Most media management research takes its cues from general business management structures. The thought is and has been that managing people transitions easily from one business typology to another. In *Media Management: A Casebook Approach*, the authors recognize that team building is an important activity in creating positive work strategies in media organizations. The authors discuss the three stages of group development, orientation, dissatisfaction and resolution.[4]

Powers and Lacy modeled four groups of factors involving job satisfaction among television news employees. Those factors include leadership, individual factors, market factors and organizational factors. In addition, each factor influences how journalists perceive the success of their organization and the goals that are embodied in successful workplaces.[5]

Powers and Lacy noted that the most important factor seemed to be leadership behavior. In newsrooms where news directors took a human relations approach and developed positive relationships with employees, there was a higher sense of job satisfaction. My research has found that reporters held their managers and editors in higher esteem in instances when those managers worried about the satisfaction of their workers. The implication in that study was that the concern for employees showed through in the actions and activities of the manager.

Redmond and Trager point out that "Human nuances and individual perceptions of reality ebb and flow within the interactions of the social beings of which groups are composed. Media organizations are even more complicated because of the combination of mechanistic and professional aspects to the activity . . . as well as the inherent difficulty of managing creative people."[6]

Zavonia and Reichert examined the issues of workflow and its impact on the evolving environment of visual journalists in the converged workplace. They examined the Web site created by a joint venture between *The Dallas*

Morning News and *The Fort Worth Star Telegram*. The authors point out that although research has examined the technological and educational factors in converged platforms, little has been done about workflow or decision making. They found that the majority of activity in online publications is done without clear communications from hardcopy counterparts. In the instances when communication and decisions were shared, the authors termed those activities as anomalies.[7] If we are to believe that a converged environment is coming, then the Zavonia and Reichert study points to the likelihood of serious problems in the converged workplace in the future.

Each of these studies reveals components of organizations that fit well into the Bolman and Deal set of organizational frames. The results tell us in general terms, however, that frames based on either a human relations or symbolic approach likely create the optimum working environment for journalists. If the Zavonia and Reichert study is a typical example of newsroom organization, however, then most news organizations remain systematically embedded in structural frames. These frames work well when organizations are being absorbed into other organizations, but they do little to help reporters, editors, photo personnel and others adapt.

With convergence, a conflict is likely between old and new or different organizations and organizational adaptation. Very little research is available to help us with determining how these differences influence journalists, but there is a great deal of research on how mergers (a construct with similarities to convergence) influence work in general.

Management and Mergers

Studies of recent merger activity may help the examination. Chan-Olmstead (1998) defines mergers as a combination of two corporations in which only one corporation survives. Instances of consolidation occur, according to Chan-Olmstead, when two corporations join to form a completely new company.[8]

It is noteworthy that mass media, whether buying, creating its own, or entering into cross-platform agreements with other media, is fundamentally moving in a direction that fosters merger-like conditions. In most merger cases, uncertainty creates a volatile environment. Worker barriers go up as work place practices are closely scrutinized. Examining research in this area will assist in determining which issues are applicable to the mass media and will help discover if they are important barriers to ownership and convergence issues.

In *The Human Side of Mergers and Acquisitions,* author Thomas Legare differentiates between organizational "fits" and "mis-fits." Legare points out that not every member of an organization is poised to carry out a new mission.[9] This is not a performance issue, but a readiness issue. Some people simply hesitate when change is presented to them abruptly, yet Legare reports that the ultimate success of reorganization (or as in most media cases, integration) rests with the people.

Legare writes, "If these human resources issues are not resolved, they can result in the turnover of key people, people refusing assignments, performance drops and morale problems." According to Legare, one of the most common causes of these transitional problems lies in the lack of adequate integration planning, which he says creates an analytical vacuum that will result in conflicts and, frequently, seemingly irresolvable dilemmas.

Argyris suggests that organizations create their own defensive routines in a "skillful action that inhibits individuals, groups, inter-groups and organizations from suffering embarrassment or threat and at the same time prevents individuals from reducing the causes of the embarrassment or threat."[10] In other words, when change enters the workplace, finding ways to practically instill new organizational activity may reach a standstill. The organization and its workers reach a standoff as each side stages ways to save face and protect itself. In Chapter 6 we will specifically examine how one approach to convergence leads directly to this outcome.

Workers, regardless of their organizational place, generally work to feel safe. Rules and specific plans for the future help create a sense of understanding (thus safeness) in individuals. Changing the rules and the workplace conditions may overwhelm expectations of safety, creating a higher level of dissatisfaction and anxiety in workers.

Simply put, defense mechanisms tend to be activated by individuals when they enter periods of anxiety and uncertainty (and today's environment seems a good fit). People often resort to making decisions based on perceptions rather than facts because they are unable to cope with change. These perceptions lead to the acceptance (or sometimes generation) of information that has been extrapolated from sources that may not be accurate, which in turn leads the individual to act in ways that may be counterproductive to both the organizational goals and the individual's own job safety. In other words, individuals may act in ways in which they believe they are protecting themselves when they are in fact placing their jobs at risk because others do not share their perception of change. In a period of extensive change like convergence, these defense mechanisms are often disruptive as employees seek to protect themselves rather than take risks.

Organizational Culture

If culture is a determinant, it must be examined at other levels. Defining organizational culture has been an ongoing exercise for at least the past 40 years. Researchers have scrutinized culture from a variety of perspectives, but three areas—traditional management perspectives, organizational psychology perspectives and organizational communication perspectives—may be most helpful in this discussion.

Traditional management research looks at culture in organizational terms with descriptions of overarching themes and attributes and their contributions to organizational understanding. Organizational psychologists tend to view cultural actions from the perspective of the individual, and a great deal has been written about organization-person fit. In this area, researchers examine how the individual contributes to or accepts the organization's culture. Organizational communications runs the gamut and places emphasis on the unit of need at a specific level of analysis—i.e., individual, group or organization—but all three are keyed into the interrelationship of the organization's culture and the individual—only the view is shifted.

Every organization is its own creation of perceptions, values and hierarchy, and each has its own formal and informal sense of identity. What Kurt Lewin described as group and intergroup "life space" controls the organization's ability to deal with issues of satisfaction and dissatisfaction.[11] Where dissatisfaction cannot be attributed to others, Argyris suggests that the members are predisposed to either covering up the situation or bypassing it altogether. There is evidence that cultural incompatibility is the greatest cause of reduced performance and nonresponsiveness to organizational goals.

Nahavandi and Malekzadeh used early organizational research to explain the process of what has been termed acculturation. They examined cultural problems in merging organizations, identifying three types of cultural evolution: integration and assimilation, separation, and deculturation.[12]

The authors identified integration as the process of two organizations seeking to work together while preserving their own cultures. They noted that this often led to structural assimilation but did little to assist in cultural or behavioral assimilation. Assimilation was identified as a unilateral process in which one group willingly adopts the identity and culture of the other; the adopting group's culture simply disappears.

In separation, one group or organization attempts to preserve its own culture and practices by remaining apart from the other members of the organization. In these instances, there is minimal communication and the groups tend to continue to operate independently.

Finally, there is deculturation, which involves losing cultural and psychological contact with both one's group and the other group. In instances when this happens, the individuals involved become outcasts from both groups.

Other researchers have examined organizational attractiveness factors in determining how they might integrate. The research shows that in instances where both groups had deeply held and compatible values that were held highly by both, the merger led to integration.[13] When the second group held the first organization attractive but also had a low opinion of its own values, the mergers ended in assimilation. Conversely, when the second organization found the first organization unattractive but held its own values high, there was a great deal of separation. In the worst of scenarios, when an organization found the first organization unattractive and held its own values in low esteem, it found itself in a situation of deculturation.

Some people see organizations as socially constructed. Organizations are the result of the coming together of various meanings to produce what is seen. Media organizations under a socially constructed umbrella could be defined as organizations assembled from the need of those in the organization to create and distribute messages informing others of the actions of those who are observed.

Organizational culture could be broadly defined as everything that constitutes "organizational life." Weber said that "man is an animal suspended in webs of significance he himself has spun . . . culture [is] those webs."[14]

Three specific areas require examination in this context: values, structure and organizational climate/openness. Values can be defined as either enduring or transitory in organizations. Dose defined values as "evaluative standards relating to work or the work environment by which individuals discern what is 'right' or assess the importance of preferences."[15]

Rokeach defined values as "an enduring belief that a specific mode of conduct or end-state existence is personally or socially preferable to an opposite or converse mode of control." Still other researchers examined the "value fit" between individuals and organizations. In those studies, value was in the eye of the beholder.[16]

The composition of organizational culture surrounds the behavior and nature of human action within an organization. Certain acts and actions will always be considered appropriate; conversely, other actions will be viewed as inappropriate. An expectation of appropriateness exists and extends to all organizations. Structure may also show itself through organizational hierarchy and the emphasis on centralized or decentralized decision making. The degree of centralization often is a component of organizational climate.

Organizational climate is defined by Poole and McPhee as the "spirit of the organization." It is the atmosphere surrounding the activities of the organization.[17] Most of us understand the notion of climate. It is the organizational climate that influences the behavior, though rarely the beliefs of individual employees and managers. Organizational climate is based on factors such as safety, ease of training, realistic expectations of workers and openness to change and criticism.

Generally, climate is viewed at the surface. A high level of awareness by individuals of their organization's operation and how each individual fits into that organization is essential. Where awareness is low, the organizational climate is often reflected in a constrained atmosphere, the result of uncertainty by organizational members. Factors of change and organizational climate are intrinsically linked.

The Changing Workplace

Change, by its nature, puts the expectations of safety and awareness at a disadvantage. The degree to which an organization embraces openness to change is likely an outcome of the interrelationship between values, culture and climate. In instances when organizations have been open in the past and organizational members feel there is a continuation of accurate and reliable information and actions, a greater degree of acceptance to change will likely exist.

Understanding how these concepts fit into the changing journalistic workplace is extremely important. Pavlik notes that newspapers have been called the "editor's medium" and television, the "producer's medium." He now calls the Internet the "journalist's medium." In convergence, this means that authority is shifting from one level of work to another.[18]

Reporters, editors and the supervisors charged with making convergence journalism a reality are finding a great deal of dissonance in the workplace today. Organizations and people unwilling, uncertain or just plain fearful of change may soon be left behind. Regardless of one's long-term view of these changes, it is likely that convergence journalism will be disruptive to the process of collecting and presenting news and information.

On the one hand, convergence is a dynamic and fascinating prospect. In the trenches, where experiments already are underway, however, it often has been a nightmare. These problems can develop in a variety of organizational corners all because of the differing styles of journalistic content and presentation. Convergence journalism asks reporters to provide material in a form that many are not trained to provide. It is outside of their training and comfort zones.

One news organization, finding the shift to convergence a major disruption, has slowly begun the process of replacing recalcitrant managers with others who believe the future of news organizations lies specifically in converging content platforms. The changes are taking place much more slowly than the top managers had expected, but the changes are taking place. Recognizing the need for organizational agreement is just one more consideration in the quest for adopting convergence.

Another organization is using the promotion process to lift people away from the organization's convergence "fulcrum." This frees the newsroom from one sort of disruption but may create other issues in the loss of experience or understanding of local issues. Neither of these approaches overcomes the underlying differences between the print and broadcast platforms.

A variety of forces therefore can be viewed as barriers to successfully progressing through convergence.

Organizational Movement

Until now, the emphasis of this chapter has been on explaining organizations and how culture and climate influence decisions regarding change. Those factors were then examined through the lens of competing news operations that would or could be asked to converge into a single media outlet. Now we look to some potential approaches to overcoming these obstacles. It should be remembered that a great many more obstacles occur as well and are the focus of later chapters.

At this point then, the principal issues seem to be management readiness, employee readiness, value structure differences between the merging groups (even when the groups remain physically separate), organizational attitudes (both in culture and climate) and issues of structural/relational differences.

The tension resulting from these unanswered questions raises the complexity of group/organizational integration. Each of these is a major threat to successfully meeting the challenges of change.

Management readiness and employee readiness are two sides of the same coin. Managers who are ill-prepared to cope with the stress of change in the move to a converged news environment will increase the level of stress among employees who are being asked to work in a new cross-platform environment. Although eliminating stress is likely impossible, improving management readiness will reduce the power of stress in the transition phase. Readiness is an issue of training, but not training in the traditional sense; although managers and employees must be trained and made comfortable in their new platforms, they must also be trained in working under new conditions.

This means that training shouldn't be limited to advancing the skills of the managers and the practitioners but should include a process for identifying the individuals who will most easily adapt to the new strategies and placing them in the forefront of the changing activity. In the near term, this may be disruptive to the traditional hierarchy of the newsroom, but it will be essential for long-range success in the convergence process. These frontline managers who understand, adapt and adopt the converged process will provide a more confident source of new structure for employees.

Most news organizations proceeding with technological convergence have examined the issue of management and employee readiness at superficial levels. The selection criteria used to identify cross-platform managers and workers have frequently focused on singling out people who are talented in one area and pressing them into service in the cross-platform environment. The thinking has been that creative people who write well should be capable of adapting their talents to multiple platforms. Although this is partially true, proceeding with convergence and using talent as the primary criterion may actually undermine the process. The training process therefore should identify managers and employees who are not only flexible and competent in cross-platform reporting/writing/presentation, but who are interested as well.

Defining value and attitude differences between converging news organizations are measurable activities. Content analysis procedures would be useful in defining the embedded organizational values and attitudes of the converging news organizations. Once differences are discovered, what remains a challenge is developing a process for overcoming those value and attitude differences. Employing a variety of persuasive techniques would likely help, but organizations would need to ensure that they were monitoring value change at both superficial and deep structure levels.[19]

Of serious concern is the difference in organizational factors similar to those advanced by Bolman and Deal.[20] Where one member organization is structural, say a heavily hierarchy-dominated company, meets a functionally open and team-oriented organization, the ability to overcome these problems will be difficult. Structure dictates how one organization perceives itself, while a lack of structure guides the second organization. If there is a perception in the membership of one group that the other group is too rigid (i.e., a heavily traditional environment) or too lax in behavior control (as with a team-based or circular management system), neither group will respect the other. Attempts to incorporate the dominant management tradition for both will generally prove disruptive to all. There is some indication that adopting a new management style that encompasses neither of the previous frames will function more appropriately than either existing frame. Unfortunately, most of the managers in a new organization will come from the existing organizations, which will preclude full adoption of a new frame. Because organizations generate these frames over a long time, changing approaches is again difficult.

The age of the organizations is likely to play into the ability to create a new organizational culture as well. There is also the perception of age. Newspapers tend to think of themselves as enduring providers of information. In most instances, community newspapers are able to trace their publication dates back more than 100 years. Television stations are the "new kids" in the media picture. Few stations or broadcast organizations are more than 50 years old, and many are only 25–35 years old. This tends to skew the view of newspaper editors and reporters toward an attitude that they were "here first" and " do it best."

These cultural definitions are embraced in both the value and structure of the newspaper industry. In one contentious meeting of television and newspaper editorial staffs, one news director blatantly accused the newspaper of trying to undermine the convergence efforts. There was little evidence to show that either media outlet was working against the project, but the frustrations poured out over the managerial decision-making process that is traditionally slower and more layered in the newspaper environment. Decisions simply take longer to make at newspapers, and that process is a culturally acceptable approach in those organizations.

Conclusions

Organizational research provides us with a significant ability to examine how media organizations will work in a converged environment. It is essential to understand that a variety of competing management and cultural frames are at work in broadcast and print newsrooms and that each will serve to create tensions between the groups. Before any true convergence activity may be undertaken, it is vital that these differences are not only recognized but also put to a variety of tests to ensure potential organizational compatibility. In the near term, upper management should undertake other actions to make the convergence opportunities as viable as possible.

Media managers embarking on convergence activities should work to create an organizational value shift among the participants of the upcoming enterprise. Those individuals should be identified among organizational risk takers and from those who share similar values at both an individual and corporate level. They should write well, be easily cross-trained, and should be targeted for inclusion before the undertaking is announced. These people must be trained prior to the launch of the converged activities.

Once individuals have been identified and trained for the convergence activity, the organization(s) must undertake a well-designed plan of action to foster understanding among all employees and managers. These activities should be planned to discuss the new platform from both positive and negative vantages. Reporters are well trained in misspeak and will understand when actions and words are at odds with one another.

Organizations must take care *before* the launch to identify those who will view the activity negatively. These people should be engaged where possible in thoughtful discussions about the future of the field. At the same time, these staff members must be reassured that they will be exempt from cross-platform activities if they have no interest in convergence.

Where possible, the organization should launch convergence in small markets. If that isn't possible, beta units could be created within the organization; however, management must take care to insulate these people from non-risk takers who might try to scuttle the new venture.

Regardless of approach, individuals who are identified must be specifically and thoroughly trained for the convergence activity. A number of convergence operations have been undertaken in the United States, but few have dealt with training convergence journalists adequately, and they generally have failed to make appropriate investments in the people who will lead the convergence revolution.

Ongoing communication is essential for everyone working in the cross-platform environments. Value and attitude discrepancies will pose serious risks to the undertaking if communications are not complete, accurate and forthcoming. Corporate myths regarding the competing platforms should be discovered and either exorcised from the lexicon or marginalized by consistent and frequent information to all employee groups.

Managers also should avoid the "nuance dance." When information is not ready for dissemination, managers shouldn't engage in the "I'll let you know later" habit. Because convergence requires a high degree of change, managers need to be open about the speed at which those changes take place. Sometimes this creates a communications vacuum. Honesty is the best approach to answer questions. If you don't know the answers to questions, tell employees and other managers that you don't know. Information is power; it should be used wisely and in information-intensive organizations and should be used often.

Several points should be understood by those undertaking converged news environments: 1) identify and train good reporters, 2) hire slowly and thoughtfully for the new organization, 3) make the time and investment to create an excellent product, 4) have patience, 5) evaluate constantly and consistently, 6) avoid quick fixes when problems arise and 7) use a "best practices" approach throughout the evolving organization.

A key component of change and the integration of diverse units in the media could lie in reorienting creativity among news professionals. Creativity, which is discussed at length in the following chapter, is a function of journalism, regardless of the platform from which it is practiced. Some current and past efforts aimed at creating an environment that is open and transcends existing cultures have failed (or have sputtered endlessly); all of these efforts have hinged on bringing convergence into the current workplace.

During the 1980s, when mature businesses began to feel the first pangs of long-term neglect, the companies found that the cultures existing in their organizations continued to pull toward the legacies created by the past rather than move forward with potentially beneficial prospects for the future. Many of these organizations simply ceased to exist. A few looked at the dynamics of their organizations; identified individuals who were capable, competent and innovative; and created new ventures for these people.

At least a dozen companies from diverse industries recreated themselves by moving "off campus" to develop new mini-organizations that could be successful without interference from existing cultures. Some news organizations have done this, but more need to look at this approach. Where offsite development of new endeavors is possible, media organizations should look for opportunities to create new, converged sites to build an audience and then bring the products back to the existing environment.

The '80s spawned a cultural shift in the industries of many nations, leading to the creation of incubators and small startups that could be controlled by the company but allowed to develop and expand on their own. These incubator sites also created a fertile training ground that allowed the workers, once retrained, to be placed in the older organization to foster internal change.

One of the key activities in the United States today is the attempt by media companies to move cross-ownership into small markets. Although that thinking has not specifically been applied to turning these small activities into incubator or training areas, it would be logical to do so. Media in the United States has a long-standing tradition of using smaller holdings to feed talented individuals into larger systems. Network television has used its owned and operated stations to develop talented anchors and reporters since the early '70s. Newspaper groups have brought along talented reporters and photographers by allowing them to learn their industry in smaller markets and move into larger markets.

If convergence is to be culturally acceptable without facing the division and antipathy seen in the deeply entrenched and more culturally intractable large markets, small-market development makes sense. It should be investigated vigorously. For instance, a large-market newspaper could team with a local cable channel (or buy rights to time on a cable system), create a 24-hour news channel and bring employees from both print and broadcast into the neutral environment. These individuals would work for the converged operation and would not be staff members of the newspaper or broadcast outlets within the community. Creating a separate environment in which to immerse reporters and train them as converged staff meets the opportunities of multiple-platform approaches to journalism while avoiding the pitfalls of deeply divisive cultures.

The organization would be able to use the resources of the parent company to ensure that the effort could succeed. This approach is similar to that used by the Tribune Company with its Chicago Tribune and CLTV cable news operation. The difference is that the separation is complete and the staff provides content on all platforms, even to the creation of its own newspaper (perhaps a weekly) that would compete with the heavy hitters in the market.[21]

The difficulty with this process, however, is that it takes time. Most media companies have not fully recognized their impatience with the process of adapting and adopting convergence. How to best create new environments aimed at accepting change in a "timely" fashion remains a question that needs to be answered. Adapting the creativity factor and overcoming journalistic skepticism are possible, but manipulation should be avoided at all costs.

Finally, convergence is here to stay. Anyone who believes that "old school" journalism thinking will suffice for the twenty-first century is sadly mistaken. What needs to be understood is that convergence is neither an end-all or be-all—it is simply the next step. Managers who plan on using convergence only for a more efficient operation likely misunderstand the nature and power of this emerging tool of information. The New Media workplace will indeed be new, but managers and media owners should understand that technology is not the most significant addition to the journalistic toolbox; it is rather the ability to conceive and deliver effective audience reach, effective journalism and effective public understanding. If the focus remains on efficiency, that viewpoint may ultimately be ownership's undoing.

Exercises

1. The author seems to believe that small organizations are better at adapting than larger organizations. Do you agree or disagree? Explain your position.
2. Should convergence be left to the decisions of media ownership, or should others be involved in the decision-making process? For instance, should the FCC or some other government agency require local public hearings when companies ask to adopt convergence (like cable television franchise agreements)?

CHAPTER 6

The Creativity Factor

Hundreds of books and articles have been written about how to manage people within organizations; however, only a small percentage of them deal with the interrelationship between management and creativity. Creativity as a term has been used in a range of management and communications scenarios. A variety of definitions have arisen out of the resulting literature, so we must situate our definition. Because all people exhibit certain levels of creativity, how creativity is defined, used and operationalized becomes an important issue. For this book we will stay close to our journalistic roots and define creativity within a more limited sphere— its outward expression by people both individually and collectively. That expression may be through writing, photography or even in layout and design, but the point is that it is a function of our journalistic output.

Creativity and the factors that direct its realization have been investigated by organizational communications, organizational psychology and general business research scholars. The overall approach has been to see how creativity influences the workplace as well as how it influences work performance. During the mid-twentieth century, research on organizational creativity was focused generally at the individual level. Within the past decade, the amount of research at the organizational level has expanded dramatically.

Although research on creativity is moving forward, crafting theoretical models (we'll do a bit of that here) and looking for the factors that influence creativity, there are people who believe that a better way is simply to do what works. Some organizations have followed unconventional approaches while others have brought in consultants to design a more "creative" environment. Depending on the organization, a high likelihood exists that the implementation of any plan for creativity will fall short of its goal without considering all of the consequences of change and the organizational tension created by changing the work environment. We will discuss organizational change in Chapter 7, but for now we should simply understand that its significance cannot be underestimated.

It is important to note that creativity is intrinsic to the output of journalists and is not just an aspect in the productivity or output of their news stories. In other words, both content and context characteristics of creativity exist where journalism is concerned. Other professions may exhibit similar qualities—MIS programmers or engineers discover and implement new ways to advance social development. This book is being written via a large text program on an operating system that was created for public consumption and use. Without the program's development, we would still be writing on electric typewriters. Still, the creative output of these individuals in their organizations was developed first and foremost to create profit for the organization. The software developer may have received a bonus for getting the code or programming to market quickly and with few errors or "fixes." The nature of the business is readily known and seldom debated.

Although journalists certainly work for profit-making companies, it is the owners who think first about profit, not the journalists. Breaking a major scandal or political development or developing a top enterprise or investigative story will certainly test a reporter's creativity; however, it is unlikely to show up as a bonus in the journalist's next paycheck. The reward is in the writing and reporting; it is in the social responsibility taken by the reporter to do the job in a way that helps others better understand the world around them.

Obviously, we are talking about journalists at the individual level, but much of what is discussed at the individual level extends throughout the editorial sections of news departments.

By job description, journalists should be creative people. Whether crafting a story that takes a reader on a journey through someone's life or editing a poignant moment between a parent and child, journalists, regardless of their primary platform of work, look for creative ways to inform. The types of stories that reporters write and the functional relevance of those stories to the general public are direct results of the creative process. So how should we define creativity? That question brings us back to the organizational researchers.

Organizational researchers define creativity as the act of "doing something for the first time anywhere or creating new knowledge." Others define it as "generating new and useful ideas." Pop culture and business writers tend to define creativity in terms of "innovation, leaps of logic, and breakthroughs" for the purpose of advancing the ideas created.[1]

Journalists would likely define creativity at multiple levels. Those levels would stretch from the creation of new word formations (turning a phrase) to finding new story ideas in unusual places. They would place curiosity, intuition and observation in the mix for defining creativity.[2]

Realistically, at the individual level, creativity is all of the above. It takes place at multiple levels and is a process. Interestingly, although creativity has been studied at the individual level for more than 50 years, little general agreement exists on how it works or how to foster its development at the organizational level. We will first briefly examine creativity at the individual level and then spend more time on discussion of creativity at the organizational level. Insights gathered from a variety of sources will then be added.

Individual Creativity

Earlier, we noted that everyone has some capacity for creativity. Some authors feel that the primary influences to increasing creative output exist within the environment of the person seeking to be creative. How creativity manifests itself is also a function of the individual's training and education, his or her lifestyle and family background and his or her general intelligence. For some, the question isn't "are they creative?"—it is more general in nature and seeks to find ways to access that creativity.

For years, a number of authors have put together some well thought-out ways to get in touch with the individual side of creativity. Gamache and Kuhn discuss the creativity infusion and how organizations needed to foster an "infusion of creativity" to help employees. The authors differentiated between creative managers and those who are managers of creativity.[3] Creative managers generate ideas and innovations on their own, but they are few and far between. Managers of creativity facilitate their work groups to be innovative by providing them with the proper resources and support to bring an idea to fruition; in the arena of capitalism, that means profitable ideas.

In the media, Redmond and Trager point out, media professionals often have a higher need for self-actualization and believe that their field is a "calling."[4] Noting this, they say that it is important for creative personalities to feel appreciated and that creative personalities will provide higher-quality work when they believe they are respected and central to the operations of their respective organizations. The authors also point out that for these journalists to perform at their highest levels, there must be an openness and a sense that their ideas and the risks associated with those ideas are worth taking.

Ideas and innovation are important on a number of levels. Jack Fuller, president of the Tribune Company, puts it this way: "You have to permit people to believe they can make decisions, be wrong and survive—that they don't have to be perfect, because innovation is an imperfect process."[5]

Tom Johnson, former chairman and CEO of CNN News Group, fears that media organizations are becoming too rigid: "And I fear that so many of our [media] bureaucracies don't enable creative people to flourish."[6]

In media terms, creativity and productivity are interrelated; one does not have one without the other. Because output is not measured in column inches or stories written, it is measured in terms of lead stories and major headlines. There is an old saying in the news business; "You are only as good as your last story." This is a belief that crosses both print and broadcast news cultures. It is the way news people think.

So what are some practical and theoretical ideas regarding the individual and fostering their productivity/creativity in the journalistic workplace? Understanding what makes people productive is among the most complex areas in management.

From a practical standpoint, a review of a variety of sources boils down to an interesting laundry list: All ideas are equally important, workers should have freedom to explore their ideas, they should be encouraged to develop their creativity through open dialogs with managers, and coworkers and managers should work openly to remove organizational impediments from the workplace. Lists are relatively simple to put together; making them work is much more difficult, as we learned in the last chapter. Convergence will pose even greater threats to the open environment of creativity. We'll look at those issues in a moment.

Although this book isn't specifically intended to be prescriptive or fully scientific in its approach, some issues are better defined by looking at them in a more formulative manner. One alternative that I have developed over the course of the past several years deals with the relationship between an individual's ability to be creative or productive and the factors that influence that productivity. It should be understood that organizationally, these factors form a triad starting with the individual and extend through the conditions within the organization, and the conditions outside of the organization relate directly to the individual's working life.

Individual components of productive and creative work (p/c) include the individual's ability to do the work through skills (s), aptitude (a) for the work, incentives (i) (both positive and negative) to do the work, and the general conditions under which the work is performed (w/c). These attributes have been examined in various literatures and may be expressed as

$$pc = s + a + i + wc$$

While these components are part and parcel to assuring that the individual is properly assessed in their work performance, it should also be noted that a variety of factors may lead to disequilibria on the part of the individual in the workplace. Several factors that contribute to these disequilibria include environmental situations (both within and outside of the workplace), individual aptitude, and the perceived value of the actions or production being undertaken by the individual. This may be expressed as

$$px = e/1 + e/2 + e/3 \ldots + pv$$

p/x categorizes productive or counterproductive actions by the organization, while "e" identifies environmental factors not directly associated with working conditions, "a" is again aptitude and "pv" is perceived value to the organization.

Taking the two equations together will allow us to calculate the practical level of an individual's ability to be a productive and creative influence in the organization.

$$pc(op) = (s + a + i + wc)(px)$$

"pc" again represents an individual's productive creativity, while "op" represents individual productivity based on the approach of the organization. Skills (s), aptitude (a), incentives (i), and working conditions (wc) again represent the individual's overall creative ability while "px" represents the expressed relationship between environmental factors and perceived value by an organization. "px" may be either positively or negatively correlated to its individual components and thereby sets the direction in which the individual's creativity is operationalized within the organization.

Finally, we should remember that people change as they develop. They mature at different rates, and creativity has a way of living a life of its own. Those who write for a living know full well that every day is not equal at the fountain of creativity. Managers and organizations would do well to remember that as well.

Organizational Creativity

Eisenberg and Goodall discuss the need to balance creativity and constraint within organizations. Their perspective on technology—ultimately the backbone of convergence—is that organizations need to be positioned to deal with the artifacts of technology as they employ them. They refer to four conditional views of technology in the workplace including utopian, dystopian, neutral and contingent.[7]

The utopian view would hold that "information technology serves to equalize power relationships at work by bridging time and space, thereby improving both productivity and work life." Convergence would likely extend this idea to conditions beyond the workplace. Proponents would see this as an equalizing power relationship in the marketplace that improves productivity and frees individuals in their work life at the same time.

Dystopian views would extend to the opposite end of this spectrum, assuming that the introduction of new technologies such as convergence will benefit only the economic and empowered elite. Those with this view would see convergence as an opportunity for owners to downsize, increase work loads and generally lower or alter work skill requirements. Eisenberg and Goodall report that these individuals often are viewed as extremists, or "luddites," in the organization who long for a "simpler" time.

The neutral view, again according to Eisenberg and Goodall, would take no position on technology. They believe that the influence of technology on individuals has been overstated and that "people are people" and will continue to work and perform in expected ways, regardless of the technology.

The contingent view of technology is, according to the authors, the best supported view at this time. Research has examined the issue of technological innovation in the workplace, and the belief is that the use of technology will be based on the context into which it is adopted.

Contingent view research has dealt generally with measuring the influences of the technology on workplace issues (How do CRT units contribute to health hazards? Is poor work station design a contributing factor to productivity where headaches, eyestrain and low back pain seem to be prevalent?). The area has also studied how employees react to the potential for on-the-job surveillance. Some companies measure keystrokes on the computer and evaluate productivity through that measurement. Others check Web site usage and monitor email.

But does this have an influence on convergence? Certainly, the contingency position makes the most sense in convergence. Conditions within the workplace allow for managers to evaluate the workplace conditions before convergence is implemented. How is communications technology viewed? Does the organization have a plan or understand the implications for adopting a converged work environment?

Key questions arise in determining whether management's position is similar to the employee workgroup's position. If management has a utopian view while workers take a more dystopian view, problems will likely exist with adopting new communications technology. In convergence, if adaptation and adoption require both groups to cooperate as smoothly as possible, the goal of the news organization should be to reach a contingent level of understanding—that context is of utmost importance.

Organizational Convergence and Creativity

Information organizations reaching a point where they are expecting to implement or join a converged environment must first recognize how that adoption process will affect overall news operations. Although most managers have observed a strong understanding of the implementation of innovative technologies, they have generally been less understanding in their desire to bring employees and work groups into the mix.

Drazin, Glynn and Kazanjian created a multilevel model of examining organizational creativity.[8] Their study examined the tension between two large work groups: technical staff with computer systems responsibility for an organization, and the managerial staff charged with implementing the technology delivered by the technical group. A key component in the examination of this company's organizational creativity was how that activity took place over time.

The point of the study was to attempt to move research in organizational creativity from two-dimensional studies to multiple levels of analysis. They envisioned their model as providing opportunities to examine creativity in organizations over the long haul. They measured the effects of a variety of variables, but their goal was to create a model that showed the process of creativity among competing work groups in an organization over time.

Drazin et. al. viewed the system in such a way that crises were at the focus of the organization's changing environment. Crises were accounted for across the timeline, and the influence of each crisis allowed the organization to view creativity over time. Other authors and organizations, including Price Waterhouse in its "Paradox Principles," have developed similar models based on performance.[9]

These models afford an opportunity for development and adaptation into a journalistic environment. News organizations are under constant pressure to prepare new and innovative information for the public. Journalists, as noted earlier, should, by definition, be creative.

If the time-based models produced by Drazin, Price Waterhouse and others are adapted to news organizations, we can substitute variables and create models that explore individual ways in which convergence is adopted in organizations.

Convergence has been defined very clearly from a technological viewpoint, and definitions for convergence, as those noted in Chapter 3, are beginning to clear its definition in creative news- and information-dominated environments. We can therefore use an adaptive model to explain the potential effects of convergence on creativity in news organizations.

Convergence as Crisis

Depending on the age and embedded values of a news organization, any major change in its organization may be defined as a crisis in the making. Where crises take place, organizations often find ways to systematically protect themselves from the potential crises-bound changes.

In Figure 6.1, the potential for newsroom, and hence, creativity crisis, is shown through a "forced convergence" model. Adapting the Drazin et. al. timeline, creativity in this model is expressed as a learning activity. Here, it is shown through its outward expression of projects and news stories. Technology, a fundamental tenet of convergence, is shown as "technical learning." Individuals in a newsroom are required to learn new skills. Learning requirements in this instance are increasing in a very compressed timeframe, thereby creating a crisis within the organization.

This model shows how the swift introduction of convergence influences the organizational behavior of those involved in the process. News and information workers may at first encounter confusion, fear and an inability to articulate their concerns to management. When forced environmental changes are made, the result is diminished creativity.

This particular model does not discuss the length of time that it takes for the organization to adapt to change. Organizations adapt to change in a variety of ways. In this forced convergence model, the time will be dependent on variables ranging from the size of the organization to the organization's communication styles with work groups to the perception of employees on the reasoning for the changes.

Prior to the implementation of convergence "change agents," creativity moves rather steadily from technical creativity and learning to creative jour-

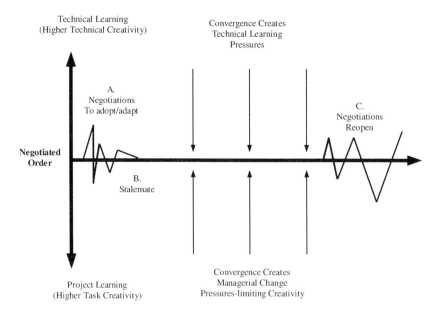

Creativity & Convergence
<u>Forced</u> Newsroom Adaptation

Figure 6.1. Creativity and convergence: *Forced* newsroom adaptation.

nalistic output. Organizational adoption and learning take place at a generally accepted, expected and systematic pace prior to implementing convergence.

Implementing a forced convergence model initially stops the creative process in all directions; organizational shock sets in. This is a reaction to a variety of surprise factors. The most serious of these factors is the imposition of new learning conditions—conditions which may initially overwhelm individuals. Regardless of the organization's warnings and preparations for convergence's implementation, most people won't respond to the changes until events force them to view the changes as both real and organizationally required.

The length of time in which creativity is suspended depends on the adaptability of the organization and its determination to do so. The time factor is important because the organizational learning timeline will influence management decision making about convergence. If convergence takes what management believes is an inordinate amount of time for adoption, or if the learning is treated as a deceptive act by the groups expected to adapt, the organization may abandon convergence. If learning is viewed as too complex, this also may lead to abandonment of the process. Eventually, the organization passes through the realignment phase, and creativity is reinvigorated as inhibiting factors are removed, redefined or simply unrealized.

Based on these expectations, three technical learning components of organizational change should be viewed as extraordinarily important before deciding how to implement convergence.

1. Recognize that technical learning takes place over time. That time will be dictated by the management style of the organization and its acceptance and fostering of risk taking by newsroom personnel.
2. Adopt technical learning only as needed. Individuals will ignore technology that does not show direct application to their lives.
3. Integrating new technical skills into the workplace is essential for the successful introduction of convergence (or any culturally driven change).

Extending this discussion to culture is the focus of the next chapter. For now it is important that we examine other, less dramatic, approaches to adopting convergence.

Convergence through Evolution

A second approach to adopting convergence is through organizational evolution. In this instance, the leadership of the organization views the disruptions of forced convergence as too risky to adopt in their organizational system.

In an evolving environment, technology and output are implemented in ways that are compatible with organizational expectations. For instance, the organization may adopt new technologies by increasing its Web presence and requiring reporters to understand the differences between Web-based journalism and print or broadcast journalism. This model does not generate specific requirements for learning the skills needed to actually perform the information-creation tasks associated with the new technology, but rather is an approach to reaching an understanding of the technology among all news employees (Figure 6.2).

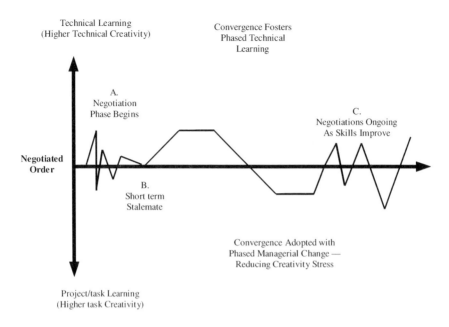

Technical Learning
(Higher Technical Creativity)

Convergence Fosters
Phased Technical
Learning

A.
Negotiation
Phase Begins

C.
Negotiations Ongoing
As Skills Improve

Negotiated
Order

B.
Short term
Stalemate

Convergence Adopted with
Phased Managerial Change —
Reducing Creativity Stress

Project/task Learning
(Higher task Creativity)

Creativity & Convergence
Evolving Newsroom Adaptation

Figure 6.2. Creativity and convergence: Evolving newsroom adaptation.

In this environment, creative output is encouraged, and news members are encouraged to learn and use the new technologies. The understanding is that convergence will be an ultimate goal and that partnering with another platform is expected in the future. That future will begin as an estimate but will evolve into a concrete requirement.

Again, the time period for implementation is based on the makeup of the organization, its energy levels directed toward convergence, and the level of resistance encountered in getting employees to face the learning process.

Implementation takes place over time and may begin with partnering activities between the platforms. Here, the emphasis would be on creating cooperative environments in stories that were likely to be considered non-threatening and did little in the way of compromising existing newsroom values regarding competition and proprietary issues. Technological

change would shift back and forth between slowly accelerating requirements to more-specific learning requirements as the platform cooperation
increased.

Creating a Balanced "Tight Wire"

A third approach to adoption is balanced in its recognition of convergence needs and traditional organizational values. In this model, pressure
exists to adapt and agree to convergence, but adaptation isn't required immediately. Although learning is required and timeframes are fixed, individuals are encouraged to learn new techniques and are provided
opportunities for learning, adapting and adopting the new system. Organizationally, requirements shift back and forth between implementation
and learning phases. In this view, shown in Figure 6.3, creativity would be

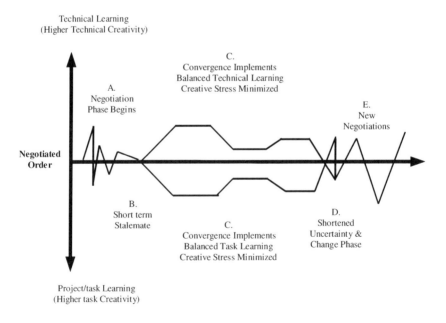

**Creativity & Convergence
Balanced Evolution**

Figure 6.3. Creativity and convergence: Balanced evolution.

expected to increase in a somewhat balanced fashion across the technology and information output planes.

In a balanced approach, the emphasis is on coordinating the technological learning and creativity function with the news and information learning and output function. This model adopts attributes of the forced model and the evolving model. Generating material across platforms is the expected eventuality of this model, and a time frame for the implementation of the process is set in advance. Once the organization has adapted to the new environment, the organization returns to its more short-term traditional learn-adapt-adopt time sequence for creativity.

Model Advantages and Disadvantages

Each model has advantages and disadvantages to selecting its approach for implementation. On the side of advantages, the speed of implementation is evident in a forced-convergence model. The rewards brought about through competitive surprise and new marketing advantages are evident. Economies of scale are able to be quickly implemented, and the organization is placed in a position in which it begins the monitoring process very quickly.

The disadvantages in a forced model, however, may offset the advantages. For instance, a company may impose convergence by relocating newsroom employees to a new facility and either combining or placing the newsrooms contiguous to one another. At the same time, new work requirements may be imposed on all platforms, requiring them to work together. This swift move may result in environmental backlash. The backlash may range from disruptions in long-term innovative and creative output to outright employee flight, all due to workplace uncertainty. Organizational risks in forced convergence will likely be highest among the three models. Companies implementing this model need to be aware of those risks and assess the potential disadvantages against the advantages of rapid implementation.

Evolving convergence places much more emphasis on preparing employees for organizational change than does the forced model. Here, the advantages are likely to include less disruption to work output, expectations of inclusion in the overall change and adoption process by workers, and greater feeling of organizational continuity as once-competing platforms are trained to understand and work with one another. The goal is to lessen the pressure for organizational change and therefore create an atmosphere in which the organizational culture can evolve and adapt to the new platforms being introduced into its system. The evolving model allows organizations to cross-train employees and work toward undermining cultural biases between platforms.

The disadvantages to evolving convergence are less disruptive to the traditional organization but may make the organization more susceptible to outside influences. Organizations taking the evolutionary approach are looking to implement convergence over a very long time. That period may be as long as five to ten years and as short as three to five years. Some evidence indicates that attempts to change organizational culture in a short time frame (fewer than five years) bear little fruit. Culture is deeply embedded. Change comes slowly.

Additionally, competitors will be able to view convergences tactics and take action because convergence is a very public form of organizational change. Competitors will be able to fashion their own alliances with other platforms, offsetting potential market gains by the evolving convergence organization. Technological changes also may be introduced more rapidly than anticipated, forcing the organization into a retraining mode even before initial training is complete.

The balanced model attempts to control for the disadvantages of both the forced and evolutionary models; it recognizes the importance of organizational culture to the well being of the company while understanding that adapting with some speed is necessary. The goal is to keep moving forward without losing market advantage. Hence, it is a balance between the needs and constraints of organizational culture and the expectations of the marketplace, but this model is also fraught with disadvantages. Moving too quickly in one direction will tip the scales to disadvantages seen in the other models. Expecting that adaptation and adoption can take place more rapidly than is organizationally possible may lead to employees leaving for other opportunities or retreating into minimal performance standards. Moving too slowly may allow competitors to seize advantages in the marketplace.

Regardless of the model selected, organizational leaders opting to move into convergence need to better understand how their organization works. News organizations have not spent enough time understanding the uniqueness of their position and have avoided discussing creativity as their primary product; nor should they assume that they understand their organization or the nature of their employees without careful research and an understanding of the expectations that employees bring to a news and information workplace. Leaders must learn. Some of the factors in organizational learning are discussed in the next section.

Ways of Adapting

Organizational learning is an evolving area of management, organizational psychology and organizational communication research. Coupled with discussions of change management functions, we may be able to evaluate convergence in the workplace in a more appropriate manner.[10]

Organizational learning has been variously defined, but for our purposes, a good normative definition is that it is the ability of an organization to respond to uncertain environmental conditions via a thorough and critical examination of its organizational premises and assumptions. This is accomplished by evaluating ongoing and evolving routines and then responding to organizational needs by changing those routines (where needed) systematically.

This means that an organization that is actively learning is keenly aware of the changes taking place within and works to create ways of completing organizational objectives without reaching a point of organizational crisis. Although some definitions of organizational learning are quite a bit more complex than this and include a large number of variables, we will use this straightforward approach for our discussion on convergence.

Management culture has a great deal to do with how organizational learning takes place. It should be understood that organizations have both overarching cultural expectations and suborganizational or group-level cultural meaning. These subgroups contribute to the organization based on their in-group assumptions and beliefs about the workplace.

Shein examined three organizational subculture types while attempting to determine why some companies learn how to adapt to marketplace conditions more rapidly than other companies. Schein applied his conditions to specific job types, but some generalities exist.[11] For the most part, Shein saw organizational managers as having perspectives that were local- or unit-based, task-driven and job-specific, or emotionally-distanced with depersonalized opinions of employees.

These limiting characteristics generally inhibit organizational learning, which requires a systematic outward look at the organization. To Schein, organizational learning is impeded by a systematic lack of understanding among various levels of many organizations. He proposes to discover ways to create mutual understanding between organizational areas in order to open organizational learning.

Other researchers point out that the complexity of change, its surprise initiation, the ambiguity of communications and the potential for (or at least concern for) deception all contribute to limiting learning. So how can organizational learning take place in a changing environment?

We briefly examined the concept of organizational learning in Chapter 5. Gherardi reviewed the current state of understanding in organizational learning and concluded that organizational learning is a complex activity: "[R]esearchers have located learning at various positions along a continuum with adaptation to the environment at one extreme . . . and the autonomous elaboration of thought at the other."[12] She notes that it is not necessary to situate oneself at either end of this spectrum but that understanding the range of learning activities points to its organizational complexity.

Organizational knowledge is also fundamental to understanding the organizational learning process. Some researchers would view organizational learning as actually accessing some cognitive level, but others believe that simply confuses the issue and tends to send organizational learning back to an individual level of understanding, inappropriately simplifying the complexity.

Organizational learning to some is a set of conditions or processes that tends to change the knowledge level of the organization. This may be either good, creating new and innovative approaches to understanding of organizations, or bad, finding tools to put up roadblocks to understanding. Utilizing organizational learning therefore requires an in-depth understanding of the knowledge and history of the organization. Developing these through a cultural lens is an expected artifact of the literature.

According to Schein, "The most intriguing role in culture management is one in which the leader attempts to develop a learning organization that will be able to make its own perpetual diagnosis and self-manage whatever transformations are needed as the environment changes."[13] Schein goes on to say that organizations, despite change, must create a culture for learning and adapting to changing environments. To him, a learning culture must assume that the world can be managed and that it is appropriate for humans to be proactive problem solvers. He lists a number of conditions that must be understood and managed, ranging from human relations to time frames. He notes that rewards should go to those best serving the organization during the changes.

Organizational change, knowledge and learning all contribute to our understanding of how to handle the move into convergence for news organizations, but how do we bring two or more disparate news organizations together? We need to deal with forces of change coupled with cultures that are situated at different points on the organizational spectrum—organizations that have different values, attitudes and understandings of their working worlds. Before we can bring them together, we must understand how they are different. Fortunately, assessment tools already exist.

Differences, Value-shifts and Risk Takers

Defining value and attitude differences between converging news organizations are measurable activities. Through a variety of quantitative and qualitative methods, we are able to determine the general "attitude" and culture of an organization. What remains a challenge would be developing a process for overcoming those value and attitude differences. Here, a variety of persuasive techniques would likely help, but organizations would need to ensure that they were monitoring value change throughout the structure of the culture.[14]

Of serious concern are the differences in structural and relational functions. Where the structural differences are fundamental—say a heavily hierarchy-dominated organization versus a functionally open and team-oriented organization—the ability to overcome these problems will be difficult. Structure dictates how the organizations will work together. If there is a perception in the membership of one group that the other group is too rigid (i.e., a heavily traditional environment) or too lax in behavior control (as with a team-based or circular management system), neither group will respect the other. Attempts to incorporate the dominant management tradition for both will generally prove disruptive to all. Some indication exists that adopting a new management style that encompasses neither of the previous styles often functions well. Unfortunately, most of the managers in a new organization will come from the existing organizations, which will preclude full adoption of a new style.

The age of the organizations is likely to play into the ability to create a new organizational culture as well. The perception of age is also different from an organization's chronological age. Newspapers tend to think of themselves as enduring providers of information even when they are relatively young (fewer than 35–45 years in existence). In most instances, however, community newspapers are able to trace their publication dates back more than 100 years. Television stations are the "new kids" in the media picture—few are more than 50 years old, and many are only 25–35 years old. This tends to skew the view of newspaper editors and reporters toward an attitude that they "were here first" and "do it best." These cultural definitions are embraced in both the value and structure of the newspaper industry. In one contentious meeting of television and newspaper editorial staffs, one news director blatantly accused the newspaper of trying to undermine the convergence efforts. Little evidence existed to show that either media outlet was working against the project, but the frustrations poured out over the managerial decision-making process that is traditionally slower and more layered in the newspaper environment. Decisions simply take longer to make at newspapers.

As discussed earlier, we must therefore overcome the differences to ensure that the organizations are able to converge. This is accomplished through value shifting. The organizations must first find common ground, then develop values based on common perceptions, knowledge and culture. From there the organizations need to embark on an organizational learning scheme that will bring the groups closer together rather than keep them apart.

Media managers embarking on convergence activities should work to create an organizational value shift among the participants of the upcoming enterprise. All members have a vested interest in their own organizations, but some will be more likely to take risks where they see opportunities for personal growth, development and rewards. Individuals should be identified among organizational risk takers and from those who share similar values at both an individual and corporate level. They should write well, be easily cross-trained, and should be targeted for inclusion before the undertaking is announced. These people must be trained prior to the launch of the converged activities. How to accomplish the needed training without creating a cultural viewpoint that some employees have been "chosen" while others have been excluded presents a set of issues in and of itself.

Price Waterhouse developed a series of materials leading to the generation of what has been termed the "Paradox Principles."[15] The first of these principles requires providing a strong sense of stability to create positive change. Stability, according to the authors, provides the anchor for substantive change where workers might otherwise fall into periods of despair. News organizations have had mixed successes with creating a strong sense of stability in their journalistic operations.

Ongoing communication is essential for everyone working in the cross-platform environments. Value and attitude discrepancies will pose serious risks to the undertaking if communications are not complete, accurate and forthcoming. Corporate myths regarding the competing platforms should be discovered and either exorcised from the lexicon or marginalized by consistent and frequent information to all employee groups.

Finally, managers should avoid the "nuance dance." When information is not ready for dissemination, managers shouldn't engage in the "I'll let you know later" approach. Information is power; it should be used wisely, and in information-intensive organizations, it should be used often. Where managers are uncertain of answers to questions being posed, they should be willing to simply say they don't know, particularly when traveling through perilous times of reorganizing and cultural shifting.

We should remember that this chapter was about creativity—protecting it, growing it and making allowances for it during learning and change in the organization. In Chapter 3 we looked at several actions that should be understood by those undertaking converged news environments, and we should review them here. These individuals should identify and train good (creative) reporters who share the values of the changing organization, hire slowly and thoughtfully for the newly evolving organization, take the time and investment to create an excellent product (allow creativity to take hold in changing times), have patience, evaluate constantly and consistently and avoid quick fixes when problems arise.

Conclusions

This chapter has examined creativity in media organizations at both the individual and organizational levels. While strides are being made at the organizational level, a great deal of work is left to be done. At least for now, some of the fundamental concerns are being addressed.

At the individual level, creativity is more psychology than organization. The complexities are enormous. For instance, think of individual creativity in the following context. Creativity is a very large sphere. The very center of that sphere is the zero-point for creativity. From there, moving outward, is a three-dimensional curvilinear timeline forming the outer ring of the sphere. Arranged around the various time points is an individual's creativity. Now we see how creative an individual was at various times in his or her life.

Connecting the points, we would see a line that soared, circled, stopped and inched along as it made its way toward that outer ring. This represents our so-called ebb and flow of life. Creativity would be tied to environmental factors such as the workplace and home life. Individual characteristics would include some of those mentioned earlier, such as aptitude and education. Couple these factors with all of the various psychological factors from fear to competition to ethical belief systems. The variables seem limitless.

At the beginning of this chapter we pointed out that this chapter's emphasis would be on the outward expression of creativity by journalists. Although some discussion has been made about selection and orientation at the individual level, the true emphasis should likely be at the organizational level, where monitoring can take place on an overall basis. At this level, we can begin to use summative variables that will allow us to moderate some of the wide fluctuations found in individuals. This shifts the emphasis to fostering creative activity through the environment of the total organization. Control and consensus will remain a struggle, but one with boundaries that are more easily understood.

Organizationally, optimizing the stability of the work environment therefore remains important to minimize the potential for resulting backlash in our news and information organizations. Convergence obviously creates a problem for maximizing this stability. If, as some believe, convergence is a "car wreck," then the job of managers is part traffic cop and part organizational planner. Realizing this ahead of time allows managers to employ change management tactics and develop strategies that will diminish the backlash.

For Further Reading

Bolman, L.G. and Deal, T. E. (2003). *Reframing Organizations: Artistry, Choice and Leadership*. 3rd ed. San Francisco: Jossey-Bass.

Burke, W. W. (2002). *Organization Change: Theory and Practice*. Thousand Oaks, CA: Sage Publications.

Eisenberg, E.M. and Goodall, H.L. (2004). *Organizational Communication: Balancing Creativity and Constraint*. 4th ed. New York: Bedford St. Martins Press.

Exercises

1. Creativity is an interesting concept. This book looks at it from the standpoint of journalists. Are there other ways to look at creativity? How could that creativity be expressed? Explain.

2. Do you believe that creativity is a component of management that should be examined separately? Are journalists any more creative than any other group of people? Explain your answer.

CHAPTER 7

Power, Risk and the Management Process

Earlier chapters in this book have dealt with the basic outlines of how work is accomplished and its application to journalism and convergence. Much of that material is based on applying theoretical concepts to the journalistic workplace.

This chapter is designed to shift the focus of discussion from managing work to evaluating factors that either enable or disable work productivity in the converged newsroom environment. Two of these management factors, power and risk, deserve an in-depth review of their application to journalism and particularly convergence. These factors are particularly important because of the relationship between convergence and change and the role change plays in attempts to incorporate convergence in newsrooms.

Change may either facilitate the development of convergence within the organization or disable efforts to converge, thereby rendering the workplace a living nightmare. Careful consideration of the complex nature of relationships, both individual and organizational, is essential in understanding how the workplace—particularly the journalistic workplace—really works.

To examine work in the field of journalism, as well as journalists and their response to convergence, we will make two assumptions. The first is that resistance to convergence is not about simply resisting new technology or work schemes, but the fulcrum of a complex set of expectations (often presented as demands) by those performing converged journalism tasks. The second assumption is that resistance is also about power and the risks associated with change.

Work—more of it—without appropriate or just compensation is often the cry raised by those who oppose integrating convergence into their daily lives. Others have raised doubts about the ability of reporters trained in one platform to perform well in other platforms. These arguments have become so well defined that some news organizations are already backing off in their commitments to convergence.

I disagree with both assumptions. Writers who write well are capable of writing in any style, period. Reporters who gather information gather information; there are no platform differences in the need to gather information, only a difference in how that information is presented and used. Those who have attempted to stall the implementation of convergence based on issues of individual talent or abilities are doing so because it does not fit their personal perceptions of the workplace; it has little to do with their abilities, though it may have a great deal to do with their skills. The reluctance to incorporate stylistic changes into their work routines is not about doing more work but about attempting to assert the personal power that they have over the work they are doing currently.

The assumptions we are making will not be well received by a number of people in the journalistic workplace, but they are accurate. The arguments against change are based not on the perception of what these individuals believe workplace should be. Those perceptions are based on training and values ascribed in the culture of the workplace. Resistance, when developed systematically by a group and validated through existing culture, will stop change, but only temporarily.

Resistance to change, however, is not (as *Star Trek* fans have learned) futile. Resistance serves to place a form of checks and balances on the organization as it moves into the adoption of changes in the workplace, hence the use of a fulcrum as the metaphor for resistance. Managers who remove those who resist change may be damaging the culture and the climate of the organization. There are better ways to deal with resistors. We will examine methods for incorporating different opinions into the converged workplace later in this chapter, but first we must set up a foundation for how these influences are based on power and embedded in organizational risk.

Journalism and the Nature of Power

Perhaps a bit of history will help clarify why many journalists have been feeling so much additional pressure in the workplace. Many mid-career reporters joined newsrooms in the early 1980s. At the time, newsrooms were undergoing another dramatic shift in their cultures; they were becoming "corporatized."

During this period, large corporations were buying newspapers, television stations and radio stations (putting many radio news operations out of business altogether) and reordering the priorities of the working environments in the newsrooms. Rules were changing. Newsrooms moved from being rather wide-open enterprises where individuality, communication and interaction were prized to becoming models of corporate operations. Deadlines and competition still were esteemed, but the emphasis shifted to fulfilling the need to join the corporate culture. Teamwork, and not individuality, became the mantra. The outcome of this focus was to shift the interest away from the individual reporter.

Journalists were treated just like everyone else in a corporate environment. Rows of open desks and information sharing were replaced with mini-cubicles and no-smoking signs. The hierarchy of cubicle wall height showing your position in the pecking order slowed communication between levels. In addition, as these organizations attempted to cut costs and increase efficiency, the focus of news output shifted from reporters, who were often well paid, to lower-paid copy editors at newspapers and producers and assignment desk staff in broadcasting who rarely left the newsroom.

This shift changed the physical culture of newsrooms and, to some, the nature of news altogether. For instance, in the late 1970s and early 1980s, newspaper reporters generally started on the overnight police beat, picking up reports and covering what crime took place in their designated city, county or region. Copy desk editors were primarily grammarians who reviewed reporter copy for the basics. They rarely changed sentence structure or meaning. A somewhat larger force of senior editors and assignment desk personnel kept younger reporters on the "straight and narrow." These senior positions were held by former reporters who had been in journeymen positions but for various reasons needed to be off the beat. They managed story length for the layout editor and did a fair amount of rewriting as needed. Their goal was to ensure accuracy and tone that was consistent with the story's needs.

Corporatization changed the basics of newsrooms. For the most part, mid-level and senior editor positions were eliminated in major cost-cutting efforts. These editors were generally "bought off" through early retirement packages. Many were simply fired as downsizing took place. More copy editors were hired as entry level workers, and their responsibilities increased. Reporters faced much the same fate as senior editors.

Some newspapers, through cutbacks, lost a substantial portion of their corporate history and culture. By the late 1980s, police beat reporting was no longer an entry level position but was rather considered a step up from the desk and an enviable beat to cover.[1]

Much the same happened during this period in television broadcast newsrooms. Reporters, always more expensive than producers and desk assistants, were not replaced when vacancies occurred, and others were simply fired. More stations hired writers, who were even cheaper than producers or assignment desk personnel. The result was to diminish the number of television reporters on the street. Now, 20 years later, many television newsrooms in growing markets still have fewer reporters on the street than they did then. Changes didn't stop there, however.

To keep pace, many colleges and universities shifted their course offerings in journalism from reporting (often seen as tradesman's work) to writing (a somewhat loftier and supposedly nobler calling). Throughout the 1960s and 1970s, journalism educators had fought a pitched battle with other academic fields who believed they were not worthy of inclusion in the domain of higher education. The shift to writing and the emphasis on becoming "professional schools" aided in trading academic *persona non gratis* status for academic solvency.[2]

The changes also served to disenfranchise young journalists just entering the professional field, however. Their college mentors, often from what is now termed the "green eye shade" camp, were replaced by younger faculty members holding coveted doctorates in journalism and related fields. Many of these younger faculty, however, had little real world experience. Newly anointed journalism graduates who had entered the field with one set of expectations were suddenly faced with a new set of requirements. They couldn't even find solace in their alma maters because educators also had embraced the changes.

This fashioned what is today a large mix of mid-career, desk-bound information purveyors who still want to be reporters, all while fewer and fewer field jobs are available. Most have learned to keep their places in the organization, have made peace with the changed expectations and work hard to meet the needs of the workplace. Still, they are suspicious of organizational change; they have been throttled by lost expectations and lower salaries in the past. Many of these journalists still long to "break out" of the newsroom.[3] Convergence does not appear to be a solution to their situations, only a continuation of corporate pressures to work harder for less reward. The environment for developing risk as a positive component of the culture does not exist. From the standpoint of power, these mid-career professionals have a great deal of informal power, which also inhibits risk taking by other organizational members.

Mumby suggests that "organizations are not neutral sites of sense making; rather they are created in the context of struggles between competing interest groups and systems of representation."[4] News organizations are replete with these competing interest groups, as the 20-year "evolution" of the field points out. Journalists have a belief system that is based on a set of values generally instilled in them through education, experience and workplace interaction. In addition, policies exist in the journalistic workplace that foster the continuation of those values and promote the actions that conform to those expectations. Organizationally, this develops into a power structure that is, at a minimum, two-tiered.

Managers must understand the nature of the power structures in their news organizations so they can ensure that the implementation of change agents such as convergence are received in a manner that creates the least amount of resistance but enough resistance to help the organization properly evolve into a converged system.

Knowing this, it is important that we understand that power is a two-edged sword; it both benefits and hampers organizations. Foucault said, "We have to stop describing power always in negative terms; [as in] it excludes, it represses. In fact, power produces; it produces reality."[5] From the viewpoint of journalism and convergence then, power must be examined in ways that negotiate the needs of the workplace and reconcile those needs to organizational needs. Understanding the nature of power and its importance in the politics of an organization is essential. Politics and power exist in both structural and sub-structural frames in all organizations. These frames are based on the notions discussed in the previous chapter, where we noted that organizations are living arenas that host a complex set of individual and group interests.

Workplace politics are the outward expressions of embedded power factors. Individuals and groups "play" politics, but they play their political games very seriously. Bolman and Deal cite five propositions that contribute to creating and understanding the nature of the political frames in organizations:[6]

1. Organizations are coalitions of diverse individuals and interest groups.
2. Enduring differences exist among collation members in values, beliefs, information, interests and perceptions of reality.
3. Most important decisions involve allocating scarce resources—who gets what.

4. Scarce resources and enduring differences make conflict central to organizational dynamics and underline power as the most important asset.
5. Goals and decisions emerge from bargaining, negotiations and jockeying for position among competing stakeholders.

These five propositions may be seen through a variety of lenses in newsrooms. News departments, whether print or broadcast, are rarely well off financially; therefore, internal competition for these resources creates organizational differences even when many values are shared.

Because technology is a key component to convergence, an example in allocation of funds makes sense here. For instance, a newspaper newsroom preparing to convert to digital photography loses its budget for material replacement because computer software is desperately needed to link the newspaper and television newsrooms. From a cost standpoint, this may appear justified to management, but the photography unit in the newspaper will likely contrive an organizational story about the shifting of resources away from "their" (i.e., the newspaper) needs to the needs of a competing platform (even in a converged operation, most units have difficulty removing the notion of competition from other platforms). If the computer software also helps link the television reporters to the newspaper's archives, the story is given further credence without technical justification. In fact, the newspaper's entire editorial staff may feel that resources were allocated away from their work environment without reciprocal assistance; this is then viewed as a political disadvantage among the newspaper's staff.

From a power standpoint, those who have conditional or informal power and influence will likely use the incident against management to show how the newspaper platform is being undermined in its ability to perform its mission. Management will view the software purchase as a shifting of resources, not the abandonment of the newspaper's switch to digital cameras. Nevertheless, workers will portray the changes in their own culturally learned way that a competing platform is siphoning away much needed resources.

Conversely, in television, the small number of field reporters may limit their ability to produce information in a manner satisfactory to the newspaper. This results in an under-representation of work produced by television journalists in the pages of the newspaper and reconfirms the fear of losing resources. Meanwhile, the television journalists will feel disenfranchised as their print counterparts withdraw and will believe the print reporters just aren't interested in allowing broadcasters into the "ivory tower."

Both of these scenarios are based on false assumptions, but both have been used in U.S. news organizations to undermine the adaptation and adoption of convergence. We must remember from the discussions in Chapters 4 and 5, however, that reality is based on perception; therefore, regardless of the facts, the perceptions create the reality, energizing these misconceptions.

The political atmosphere in news organizations is based on criteria generally ignored in traditional management literature. News managers recognize its existence but seem to center attention on how journalists should focus on the greater good of providing information to the public. These days, there is a great deal of organizational talk about "craft excellence." This is a similar notion, and although journalists will openly embrace the philosophy, they will privately joke about a new "vision" that has little to do with their working conditions or the "real world."

Traditional management and some organizational research seem to view journalists no differently than workers in other professions. Because the output of journalists consists of creative works organized on the pages and screens of their respective organizations, however, it is important that we view them differently. Their output collectively represents the *direct* overall product of the organization—information. The product's conversion takes place primarily through the technology. A skilled reporter's output will look much the same in the pages of the newspaper or on air as it did when the reporter released it to the organization's editors. Few other products have so little conversion from input to output. So what difference does this make?

From a power standpoint, those with the strongest journalistic credentials, even if they have no organizational leadership roles, will have substantive organizational power. This power comes from both internal alliances and external prestige. Unlike workers in most organizations, journalists meet and deal with the public daily. Where the journalist is well received, informal referent power is ascribed to the journalist; therefore, despite what appears to be an organizational hierarchy in newsrooms, this is a somewhat mythical hierarchy, and the true organizational leadership may lie with "non-empowered" workers. Often referred to as formal and informal circles of power, the acknowledgment of multiple levels of power within news departments is crucial.

This emphasis shift from formal to informal power creates a great deal of pressure on news organizations to embrace unofficial but institutionally empowered journalists in attempts to move forward with converged media efforts. In this instance, Bolman and Deal's understanding of organizations as coalitions creates a paradigmatic fit for developing journalistic consensus among those with unofficial power.[7] Individuals and groups with unofficial power have insular objectives while also holding resources that differ from those with formal power (i.e., external public approval). Managers and leaders with formal power must find ways to meet or negate the inward-looking objectives of informal power leaders to bring about consensus from the coalition. When these needs are recognized and met, management is positioned to negotiate its way into a settlement situation that potentially produces a win-win situation.

Win-win situations are often considered a sign of weakness by traditional managers, but with creative people, as shown in Chapter 6, they are necessary to minimize the destructive influences and promote the positive influences of change. Keeping creativity high while inviting serious change to the organization requires a delicate balance between organizational needs and individual/coalition needs.

These changes cannot take place through talk alone. Management must provide both protection and rewards for those who accept change. For journalists, this means better pay, fewer stories, cross-training facilitation and acknowledgement that converging journalists are organizational leaders.

Before entering into any negotiations with potential coalitions, the organization must understand how power is distributed within it. Alderfer recognized what were termed "overbounded" and "underbounded" systems.[8] Overbounded systems are characterized by a tight rule within the organization. Often, the political players in these organizations are forced underground, and leaders may have difficulty identifying them because those selected for unofficial power are protected by their coalition.

Conversely, in organizations where underbounded systems are prevalent, management may find the groups highly vocal and hostile toward proposed changes. In these instances, the organization needs to both identify the power players and find ways to deal with them effectively. If the power players are opposed to change and unwilling to participate in the workplace evolution, they must be neutralized in terms of the messages they deliver to other members of the group. This may be a simple process or one of great complexity.

Either way, negative factors need to be dealt with before the group gains a larger consensus, creates a stronger coalition and begins to create discord informally. However, management must take care in its approach to dealing with informally empowered employees. Typically, main-line organizations tend to find ways to destabilize the coalition. Destabilization might lead to firings, wholesale realignment of assignments and reorganization. The news industry, with its products so dependent on creativity, will generally find this approach unwise. Dismissal should be the least-favored approach. Negotiation is a more reasoned approach in newsrooms, though some news managers have used isolation techniques to bring reluctant staffers around to the corporate way of thinking.[9]

Management tends to approach conflict from one of two directions. In the first representation, conflict is considered a normal function of change, and in the second approach, conflict is considered the result of poor development of competency techniques among manager groups.

From the standpoint of good newsroom management practices, it seems that working from the first set of assumptions is better. In this setting, blame is not assessed, but solutions are developed for incorporating the appropriate changes into the newsroom. Where convergence is concerned, the change techniques remain experimental, and a key component would be to ensure that change is undertaken while minimizing individual or group risk. We will discuss this point further once we have moved from a discussion on change to one of management and employee risk.

We should also note that a great deal of research indicates that in properly evolving organizations, conflict is considered both inevitable and helpful. From this point of view, managers are able to view conflicts in ways that allow groups to identify problems for the larger organization. This approach allows management to identify potential solutions to the problem and take action to restore consensus before initiating major changes.

Still, conflicts need to be controlled, particularly where the source of conflict is organizational change. Bolman and Deal describe conflict as evolving in one of two ways: in either an unorganized "street fight" fashion or one set up as an "arena." The street fight is characterized as an event without rules, in which individuals get hurt and feelings run deep for years, often leading to difficulty in bringing change to fruition.[10]

The arena views conflict differently. In the arena, there are rules, referees and spectators. The goal is negotiate a peace that results in "forging divisive issues into shared agreements." In the arena, issues are worked out to move from the status quo to a position that embraces change, perhaps not in a way envisioned by either group, but in a way that welds one set of evolving ideas together with existing values and ideas.

Convergence provides the news industry with its greatest conflict in more than a century. Newsrooms across the country are being asked to change; some 60 cities already have at least two news organizations in their communities working through either partial or full convergence agreements.[11] While the FCC grapples with the legal and societal implications of these evolutions (which will be discussed extensively in the next chapter), the business of news is moving forward to embrace convergence.

Change? Now what?

Tucked inside all of the rhetoric about convergence and the need for the news industry to change is another area that needs to be both assessed and addressed—that of risk.

Why should a perfectly well-trained and competent print journalist want to be on television? Why should he or she write for the Internet? Indeed, why would a well-paid, highly visible broadcast news reporter want to write newspaper copy? In general, these people are very comfortable with their current situations. The expectation that they would be willing to embark on a new converged career, potentially jeopardizing their current reputation, is difficult to conceive. For most, the answer is "no thanks, I'm fine." Enter the much maligned, but frequently necessary, status quo. Don't shake the boat. Don't rattle the chains. Things are going quite well.

Countering the status quo and initiating situations in which comfortable people assume higher levels of risk is tantamount to picking the street fight we just discussed. Moving journalists to a converged environment is possible only when substantive rewards exist at the other end. The questions from journalists become "You want me to take these enormous risks? What are the potential rewards? (And they had better be good!!)"

This is where convergence and the news industry run afoul of one another. For the most part, the news industry has embraced convergence from the standpoint of economies of scale. Through the appropriate melding of materials and people, news organizations believe they will be better able to provide long-term services to the public. Some have built monuments to convergence through new news facilities. Others have improved equipment and brought about a shared environment for journalists. Some have even worked to overcome cultural issues such as those discussed in the previous chapter. Still, individual issues exist, and chief among those is risk.

Unfortunately, few news organizations have actually dealt with the issues of risk from the standpoint of the journalist. After all, owners tend to believe that if they will take the risks to upgrade materials and facilities (e.g., through increased investment), journalists should be willing to take the necessary steps to ensure that newly merged platforms work. This is a very wrong-headed view. A few examples already have begun trickling out of convergence efforts to show just how wrong-headed this approach has been in the effort.[12]

Media owners and upper management had expected movement into convergence to create enough anxiety among journalist groups to lead to some leaving the workplace. Most managers, however, were unprepared for what became a wholesale exodus from several newsrooms around the country. The imposition of strict policies requiring new hires to embrace a convergence philosophy also hampered replacement recruiting in some shops. In these instances, management failed to recognize the extent of fear arising from risk in the media marketplace.

Nevertheless, techniques are available to help journalists embrace risk. The trouble is that it is rarely effective in the largest of news organizations because the larger the organization, the more difficult it is for owners to provide rewards substantive enough to outweigh higher risks. In other words, a journeyman reporter who has consistently broken stories, won awards and is generally known and respected by the public has little interest in embarking on a new adventure. These journalists are also among the highest-paid staffers in the local newsroom and often among the highest-paid in the country. What would qualify as an appropriate reward to someone at the top of the profession?

The Nature of Risk: Takers and Avoiders

Risk is such a pervasive notion in organizational literature today that it generally is assumed and accounted for in the process of discovering new management techniques. Consequently, a variety of definitions of risk exist, but generally, those definitions incorporate situations or issues associated with risk. For our purposes, we will define risk as the process of identifying and utilizing skills and ideas beyond the scope of everyday individual life requirements. In this definition, skills may be identified as human, technical or physical. Regardless of type, the acquisition and implementation of new skills means that an individual must step out of his or her ordinary routines to make use of these skills.

Nearly 20 years ago, Gamache and Kuhn reported that "creativity and risk are inseparable, so the element of risk is typically highest in the entrepreneurial startup of an innovative idea."[13] The authors also note that doing anything new entails some degree of creativity and, consequently, risk. Convergence is just such an idea, and risk is essential to its success. Still, Gamache and Kuhn add, risk aversion is pervasive in any organizational culture unless cataclysmic events are underway.

The expectation that people will deliberately avoid taking risks is, according to Jackson, tied to our deeply held instinct for survival.[14] In organizations, this translates into our desire to survive in the current job place. Additionally, humans are known as group, or socially-based, animals. Fear of exclusion from the group fosters risk aversion. Bringing change to the journalistic workplace, then, first requires that the organization devise ways in which to overcome risk aversion.

Eisenberg and Goodall report a tension between getting things done according to rules and organizational goals and properly communicating those goals in a way that develops consensus.[15] Businesses, as profit-oriented organizations, are interested primarily in reducing costs and maximizing returns for shareholders. As noted earlier, this emphasis on the bottom line is essential to generating profits (or occasionally maintaining current profitability), but still is disruptive to workers who are trained to maximize their performance based on quality and not quantity.

Maximizing individual performance also may require increased investment that companies are unwilling to provide. With journalists, where we have noted that their outputs are essential to the overall profitability of the organization, this creates a paradox leading to unfulfilled expectations. In convergence activities, this discontinuity may further disrupt the workplace. The question becomes one of how to get journalists to take the necessary risks associated with convergence while not creating gaps of unfulfilled expectations.

Various approaches offer potential solutions to this question. As discussed in *The Paradox Principles,* stability is an important commodity for organizations in change.[16] Risk without stability places the same potential for despair and disillusionment as change; therefore, one approach would be to foster risk-taking attitudes while ensuring that a safety net was in place for the employees willing to step out. Nevertheless, before this discussion on risk gets too far ahead of itself, we must discuss the attributes and advantages of risk taking from the journalists' vantage point.

Changing Change

More than 50 years ago, social psychologist and communications scholar Kurt Lewin developed Field Theory.[17] He said that people exist in a force field of competing interests and that individual behavior is an interaction between a person's needs and personality and this force field. How the individual perceives his or her position in this force field determines the actions he or she takes in response to those needs. Lewin later expanded on his work to include driving and restraining forces. Driving forces are those used to push an individual toward a new behavior, and restraining forces are those that inhibit new behavior. Lewin used strong supervision, pushing behavior change as an example of a driving force and entrenched group norms as an example of a restraining force.

Several other researchers have expanded Lewin's work. Argyris is among the best known of those researchers and has spent more than 30 years advancing Lewin's theories.[18] Lewin saw organizations as social systems. Argyris noted that problems within these social systems often arise when messages from those in authority are at odds with the actions taken by those in authority. Argyris notes that this leads to mistrust, lower commitment and poor morale among employees. Argyris believes that espoused values are the key to understanding the behavior of employees.

When an organization's espoused values mesh with its actions, Argyris believes there is a greater level of congruency within the organization. The greater the congruency between words and actions, the fewer the expected tensions between management and employees.

Dozens of models that focus on the relationship between management and employees can be examined; however, the topic continues to be risk. How are values related to risk? The direct correlation is one of trust. A news organization that tells editorial department workers that the organization is changing in positive ways but then proceeds to force reporters into assignments in which they have no background or knowledge and little interest places the employee, and the organization, at a disadvantage.

Schein believes that risk is associated with the emotional strength of leaders.[19] In his view, risk asks individuals to give up cultural elements and replace them with other elements that they may not be inclined to adopt. The risk results from the individual's fear of the unknown and the potential that he or she will be worse off after adopting the risky element than before the risk element was sent his or her way. Schein explains that the leader must have the emotional strength to help forge the way through the unknown.

Having asked individuals to give up one cultural element, leaders must identify and define replacement elements. It is imperative that they have the courage of their convictions and the strength of those convictions to assist in creating the new cultural element. As noted previously, culture and elements of that culture are enduring; this places a great deal of pressure on the leader to produce elements of change that are organizationally acceptable but also meet the organization's needs.

News management needs to understand that any change involves cost. Those costs are in much more than facilities and equipment and are most visible in people. Eisenberg and Goodall report that organizations that treat their people as their most important commodity are also the most profitable.[20] Eisenberg and Goodall noted that other research had shown that using "high performance practices" improved employee output, increased the rate of return and resulted in a drop of more than seven percent in employee turnover.

High performance practices are defined as those practices that include employee empowerment, extensive training, extensive information sharing, pay for performance, self-managed teams and a "purposeful reduction in attention to status differences." The authors also cite three critical components to effective organizational communication. The components are targeted selection, performance management and training and development.

Eisenberg and Goodall say that too many organizations bring unqualified or unprepared individuals into the organizations, thereby setting them up to fail. Targeted selection requires implementing a process that allows prospective employees to know immediately what is expected of them. Likewise, managers are able to make certain that requirements of the job are specific and concrete.

Through performance management, employees are tracked and given specific feedback on how well they are performing and meeting the organization's expectation of them. Without a system, according to Eisenberg and Goodall, managers go by their gut feelings, which generally may not be based on the realities of work.

The impact of training and development cannot be underestimated in the organization. Today's workplace is evolving dramatically, and training just to help employees keep pace is invaluable.

How do these actions relate to convergence? Interestingly, because news has been corporatized, it is important that we understand that creative people have generally been poorly put through their paces in understanding how their work matters. This leaves a vacuum that bases performance on poorly constructed ideas such as an individual's last best story. The motivation is to present information, not even to present it more completely or appropriately.

Convergence is a training opportunity, but training has not been the emphasis of most media organizations. Several newspapers have adopted a "talk-back" training program for their reporters. This program is reportedly designed to help these individuals perform in front of a camera. Is that the most valuable contribution a print reporter can bring to television? At the same time, television reporters have been given columns and told to write newspaper-style pieces. The result is that newspapers tread on the "personality" of the television journalist while television draws only on the "expertise" of the newspaper journalist. In neither case are the journalists learning how the other platform operates; they are kept on the periphery without becoming adept at the new platform.

No wonder the risks seem too high.

This approach also ignores the Internet journalist, who may have a handle on both ways of reporting but is considered inconsequential to the older platforms because he or she has established neither personality or "expertise." Why would anyone want to take the risks when the rewards are based on nothing that will definitively show up in your work?

Convergence as Organizations

Eisenberg and Goodall make several exceptional points regarding organizational development.[21] Each remains critical to the adoption of convergence, not as platform transfer, but as a new attitude and news paradigm. They note three concepts of human endeavor:

1. People still want to be inspired. It is important that we understand that people still work to gain meaning in their lives. Nearly every journalist enters the field looking for opportunities to help society. The emphasis today in journalism sometimes seem to be focused less on "shining the light of truth" on issues and more on entertaining for readership and ratings' sake.
2. People are more likely to support something they helped create. Journalists feel empowered when they are part of the vision to bring information to the public. When they are brought aboard a converging operation and the appropriate resources are given to them, they will perform at exceptional levels.
3. Actions still speak louder than words. Nonverbal behaviors will always generate more meaning than stated goals. No matter how inspiring the message, if the organization does not believe in supporting the message, the opportunity to develop will fail. Journalists already know this. They are skeptical, and management must be clear in its support and promotion of convergence.

If we are to expect journalists to take risks, to realign their power bases and take extraordinary steps to move out of their original training, then it is incumbent on those involved in convergence's development to take seriously the needs of those who will develop the next level of journalistic endeavors.

Where to Go from Here

For already-discussed reasons, I believe that the implementation of most convergence activities should happen in small- to medium-media markets or, as discussed earlier, in incubator environments. Rewards in these markets may be developed in ways that are consistent with a reporter, editor, photographer or designer "growing" to the next level. Although this approach raises the alarm among some, it is a more natural progression from a management perspective. Issues arising from small-market convergence of media properties, including possible ramifications for regulation, are discussed more thoroughly in Chapter 8.

Although the best approach appears to be to begin in small- to medium markets, where does that leave major markets already in the process of converging, and how can the proper positioning of risk lead to improved attitudes about convergence? Several of these converging operations have opted for temporary chaos; others have backed out of the fray. Regardless, these situations are such that for media managers in organizational churn, it is time for implementing strong risk-assessment programs while maintaining a willingness to hold on to long-term goals in the face of short-term crises. Risk assessment and plans to both encourage risk taking and overcome risk avoidance are critical to overall planning.

Conclusions

News organizations that ignore power and risk activities in their cultures will ultimately pay the penalty of poor response and performance as they attempt to move to a converged environment. Convergence is not a cheap route to new audiences; rather, it is an expensive route to new avenues of journalism.

Convergence must be viewed as valuable and desirable within the organization. This viewpoint must be expressed by providing adequate rewards for those who risk their careers by joining the convergence movement. It also must protect these individuals from the existing culture and help them to move the organizational culture to the next level: convergence acceptance.

In markets where this is impossible, a variation on convergence is possible through the creation of a stand-alone, incubator-style media organization that is fully converged from the outset. Again, attention should be paid to the rewards of joining the new media team. There should not be pressure on those involved in the media incubator to contribute to the bottom line. The emphasis should be on cross-platform performance and the development of journalistic excellence across these platforms. The nature of these organizations will be that ultimately, they compete with the parent organization and may supplant its operations as it grows . . . or be integrated back into the larger news organization to ensure the influx of talent and prepare for overall convergence.

Convergence activities will not be accomplished quickly. An appropriate timeline is likely to be longer than five years, perhaps even 10 years, but the motivation is to develop and harness a new and practical method of delivering the news to an ever-growing and ever-divergent populace. The public is already transferring its media habits to Web-based services. Media companies that look to creating and attracting these new audiences now will be much more positioned for profitability in the future.

Exercises

1. Examine the relationship you have with friends, with professors and at work (if you are in the workplace). Where would you place yourself in the power structure of each group? Remember, power is about a lot of things, not just who you think is powerful (though perception is part of it).
2. What sort of risks have you taken to get ahead in life? How do you view risk as a part of your own psyche?
3. Has anyone around you used his or her power to avoid or take risks? Explain.

CHAPTER 8

Regulation in an Evolving Media Environment

In June 2003, the U.S. Federal Communications Commission (FCC) rescinded a set of 30-year regulations that had kept the lid on one last area of media ownership . . . the cross-ownership of newspapers and broadcast outlets in the same market. The rules, somewhat firmly established in the mid-1970s, were a constant source of concern among media conglomerates. To owners, the rules reflected an outmoded way of thinking, the belief that people could only get their information in limited ways. They argued that with cable, satellite and the Internet, there were dozens of alternate information sources and that the rules were simply there to inhibit their ownership efforts.

To consumer advocates, who feared that issues and voices in the media would be driven by investors and not by the public at large, the rules were just and appropriate. With the narrow 3–2 FCC ruling, the changes saw media owners, after decades of maneuvering, finally getting their way. But no sooner had the FCC ruled than consumer groups headed to court and Congress to block the relaxation of the rules. At press time for this book, the issue continued to rage, unresolved.[1]

The battle between ownership concentration and the cry for more independent media voices is an old one. That cry will only continue to gain strength as information and entertainment organizations, seeking to improve their economies of scale, go on further buying sprees.

Media ownership across the globe, and particularly in the United States, has undergone sweeping changes since the beginning of this deregulatory period. From the beginnings of deregulation, undertaken in the 1980s, to its full-blown anthems of the 1990s, the mantra of "less is better" in a regulatory sense has created a fervent and dramatic shift in how we view mass media. From station ownership levels to cross-ownership and market concentration caps, the way the media looks today is vastly different than it looked two decades ago. Rules that set up strict boundaries for broadcasters, telecommunications companies and satellite providers fell by the wayside at an ever-quickening pace.

In the United States, as well as elsewhere, the changes, although driven to some extent by a national frenzy to deregulate everything from airlines to electricity, were strongly influenced in the media by the revolutionary advancements in technology available for the delivery of entertainment and information. As government moved away from its traditional role in media, it was supplanted by a marketplace vision. That vision has not borne the competitive fruit once envisioned, and those facts will be discussed further in a later section of this chapter.

Simultaneously, the global media market, particularly in Europe, has been evolving at a pace likely to be viewed as faster than its evolution in the United States. Although the United States has embraced the notion of technological advancement, there has been only sporadic agreement on how that advancement should take place. Consequently, as U.S. competitors bicker over the resolution of HDTV sets and the standards for digital delivery (not to mention how digital signal divisions should be allocated for programming), other nations quickly resolved (or ignored) those issues and moved forward into the discussion of information delivery itself.

Convergence has been more systematically embraced in Europe than in the United States.[2] In a regulatory sense, convergence has had fewer difficulties in Europe, perhaps because the nation states of the European community provide more media per capita than the media outlets in the U.S.

Additionally, media in the United States is bound to a large extent by a common language. In Europe, half a dozen languages serve to act as artificial borders for the governing entities. This allows each nation state to have a distinct national media and access to what might be termed as supra-media content from other nations. The information is available from many national sources but is readily recognized as belonging to another.[3]

First viewed from a technological standpoint, convergence has come to define the future of information delivery across the globe, including the United States. Convergence also has constructed a new set of realities for journalists. The divisions between "old" media and "new" media are melting away. Before we address its interrelationship with various media interests, however, we should discuss federal regulation and the Federal Communications Commission.

The Federal Communications Commission

The Radio Act of 1927 created the first true regulatory agency for commercial radio broadcasts in the United States. Earlier legislation had parceled out the airwaves but hadn't set up licensing policies for individual and commercial use. The Radio Act created the five-member Federal Radio Commission (FRC) to oversee the licensing of all broadcasting stations in the U.S. The act also fashioned and codified, for the first time, the notion that broadcasting would operate in "the public interest, convenience and necessity." At the same time, Congress gave radio First Amendment status, meaning that government could not censor the programming content of radio stations. The tension between what constitutes operating in the public interest and what constitutes a breach of a station operator's First Amendment rights has been the subject of countless court cases in the past 80 years.[4]

Congress had not expected the FRC to exist beyond several years, but it soon became apparent that issues beyond licensing were going to take up a substantial portion of the Commission's time. By 1932, new initiatives were underway to more technically regulate the telephony industry.

The Federal Communications Commission succeeded the FRC with Congress' approval of the Communications Act of 1934. The 1934 Communications Act brought radio, telephony and all other communications activities under the regulatory aegis of one governmental group.

The public interest debate throughout the history of the FCC has resulted in an undulating set of rules and regulations that have both supported and confounded broadcasters, depending on the issue at hand and the time and political mood of the country. The election of Ronald Reagan as President in 1980 began a persistent move toward deregulation in all U.S. industries, including broadcasting and telephony.

By the time Congress passed the Telecommunications Act of 1996, deregulation had reached a state that caused key members of Congress to began calling for the abolition of the Federal Communications Commission. The reasoning was based on the free market belief that the marketplace could police and take care of itself. Clearly, the purpose of the 1996 Act was to create a deregulated broadcasting and telephony industry. During the first several years of the act, telephone, cable and broadcasting giants tentatively moved toward consolidation, but in recent years that movement has ended. Still, the major broadcasting and print industry companies, in which information and entertainment are primary activities, continue to consolidate. This is creating an atmosphere in which the developments in converged media properties are taking the forefront.

Division of Labor

So while the battle lines are drawn, how do the realities of the evolving workplace align themselves with future regulatory activity? When regulatory activity was high, journalists were well positioned in one platform or another. As noted in Chapter 3, the training was specific to the expected platform in which the journalist would work. From a regulatory point of view, these divisions were set up to keep media ownership at bay and ensure community voices access to the airwaves. Media existed, to many in Congress and the early versions of the Federal Communications Commission (FCC), to perform in the public interest and essentially to reflect the interests of mainstream America.[5] Journalists were the first line of attack in the arena of public interest. By the late 1970s, broadcasting operations were producing detailed diaries of programming based on interviews with community leaders, those in both the majority and the minority. These interviews, called "ascertainments," were conducted to ensure that their local constituencies were being served. The FCC required that these reports be filed annually and that the "standards" of good community citizen and reflector of community issues be a part of the job.

In broadcasting, journalistic standards of performance rested on the ability of the broadcaster to understand and react to issues in the community. The driving force behind covering certain stories rarely had anything to do with the interests of the broadcasters but generally reflected the concerns of the elected and selected "leaders" within the community or listening/viewing area. This approach ensured that a great deal of benefit would come to officials poised to tout their own issues. Not surprisingly, each year, many broadcasters would select a series of issues from the ascertainment studies for major coverage to make certain the FCC's definition of public interest was met.

In good markets where broadcasters took their jobs seriously, these stories constituted only a portion of the news generated that could be positioned as performing a public service. In less ambitious stations, the ascertainment led the news coverage, and broadcasters became mere cheerleaders for public officials instead of critics of public performance.

As with most government requirements, regulators can never get too much of a good thing. From the open-ended and generally useful interviews of the late 1960s and early 1970s, the ascertainment evolved into a government boondoggle. Filling the time of broadcasters with more and more questions, more and more forms, more and more tidbits of information, the government got more information, but at a tremendous cost to broadcast news. By the late 1970s, ascertainments had become an onerous and useless burden. With a backlash from broadcasters, the ascertainments began to lose favor, and the requirement was repealed in the 1980s.

Taking place at the same time was a shift in emphasis. Early FCC regulations had been based on the "trustee model," in which regulators oversaw the interests of the public through the broadcast licensing procedures. In 1979, heralding a major shift in policy, the government declared that a marketplace philosophy would replace the old model. The FCC also said that regulation is necessary only when the marketplace fails to protect the public interest . . . not simply where there is the potential for marketplace failure. The trouble was that no one defined what that meant or what could trigger a failure of the marketplace.

By the end of the Clinton administration, coverage of public interest issues (other than crime) in television newsrooms was only a shadow of its past, and in the few remaining radio newsrooms, nearly non-existent. In fact, the regulatory concerns for journalistic and public interest voices in radio diminished to the point that by the entrance into the twenty-first century, fewer than half the radio stations with news programming in the 1970s still carried their own news at all. Instead, they relied on news services like the Associated Press and the local newspapers for much of their information. Independent newsrooms in radio, once expansive, were all but dark.

Deregulation in television news, to date, has produced mixed results and has proceeded at a more cautious level. Owners have attempted to create regional news operations, but with limited success. Local news on television is a visible, viable force. Radio had been heard, but not seen, and radio news was seldom missed because all music stations, CDs and audiotapes competed against news operations.

As the twenty-first century dawned, new regulatory models were rolled out by politicians and regulators. At the FCC, the prevailing philosophy under Chairman Michael Powell has been that less is better. As a philosophy, it remained under the radar screen of most members of the public until convergence and cross-ownership issues smacked into traditions based on free access and multiple voices in the marketplace.

In June 2003, following nearly two years of review, Powell announced that cross-ownership rules would be seriously relaxed and market concentration of television ownership could reach a 45-percent penetration in a market. The FCC chairman based the decision on both political and regulatory expectations. Media owners had argued throughout the process that under the Telecommunications Act of 1996, prohibiting cross-ownership was no longer valid or legal; that issues regarding voices were not relevant, due to increased market penetration from competing information providers; and that the marketplace was the appropriate mechanism for ensuring that media ownership remained competitive in individual markets.[6]

Consumer advocates joined forces to stop the Fall 2003 implementation of the new rules. They countered that the media companies were reporting information from a biased and obviously vested-interest point of view. They reported that the "so-called" competition would be short-term as media conglomerates swiftly bought up competitors; that the discussion of new competitors was inappropriate and invalid because those "new" competitors were generally owned by the major media companies; and that voices would be curtailed and media owners had not shown evidence to the contrary.[7]

Congress rolled back both rules. At press time, the issues remained unresolved, though it seemed that the concentration rules would fall back to a negotiated 39 percent. Cross-ownership and convergence remained in limbo, awaiting a creative approach to help both the public and media owners.

Seeking Solutions

The tension created between the public and its concerns over access and voices versus the owners and their concerns over models of efficiency and profitability has not diminished. A variety of scholars have discussed and advanced ideas on resolving the issue, but resolution will need to be based on an understanding of the complexities of balancing the competing interests.

Van Cuilenberg and McQuail have examined the evolution of media regulation in the United States and Europe.[8] They believe that communications regulations and access to media by the public must be managed in such a way that they work together:

> [T]he main goal of any communications policy can be described as that of securing the free and equal access to a social communications system that diversely provides for the information and communication needs in society.

In a context of technological convergence and increasing market competition, communications policies are likely to be primarily policy for access.

An expectation exists that access to the airwaves is, in part, guaranteed to the public. How that takes place should obviously be regulated. Van Cuilenberg and McQuail note that policy has evolved through two periods since the mid-1920s, and they believe that a paradigmatic shift is underway in the creation of new policies.

In the first wave of policy development, the emphasis was on designing regulations that would appropriately parcel out the airwaves. Content was examined very little. In the second wave, with the assignment of licensing under control, the regulatory arena moved into discussions of content. The third wave is yet to be defined and is the result of the conflict (or tension) that continues between the public and the businesses that own the media outlets.

The primary discussion regarding regulations always centers on broadcasting and telecommunications. These two areas have long been considered limited access resources, unlike newspapers, where the adage was always that anyone who had a press could start a newspaper. The tremendous costs of starting a newspaper today may dissuade some from that argument, but still the issue is not the printed press but those who use the airwaves. Van Cuilenberg and McQuail developed a model that expresses the current state of regulation and its expected need to move toward centering on public interest issues (Figure 8.1).

Van Cuilenberg and McQuail see convergence as a principle actor in the need for this yet-to-be-defined regulatory arena. Balancing the competing factors is of critical importance to the authors, but they still believe that access is the key to ensuring that any lasting policy is useful and responsible.

Legal scholar C. Edwin Baker sees media regulation as a function of democracy because "Democracy embodies the equal right of each person to participate in matters of self-determination."[9] Baker notes four sets of values in the way these participatory approaches are organized: Elitist Democracy, Liberal Pluralism, Republican Democracy, and Complex Democracy.[10]

Each approach brings significant artifacts to regulating media, and a full discussion is unnecessary here. Baker believes that the Complex Democracy model serves the public best when creating rules and regulations to govern those who have the self-determination he described earlier.

Complex Democracy recognizes the interrelationship between the need for self-determination, or individual rights, and the need to carry out group

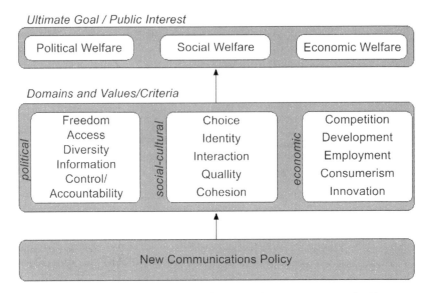

Figure 8.1. Phase III (1980/90–now): An emerging new communications policy paradigm.

activities that may hinder one individual's right of self-determination to the benefit of group rights. The complex view "assumes the reality and legitimacy of bargaining among groups over irreconcilable conceptions of the good, but also hopes for discursive development of common conceptions of aspects of the good."

In this context, there is recognition that although differences exist, the moral or rightness of something comes first, then the discussion regarding the differences in philosophy. Moral value will always supersede the individual or group need. Still, that leaves a great deal of room for discussion, and the Complex Democracy model attempts to handle that through a process of negotiation or discourse. Complex Democracy, according to Baker, seeks a political process that promotes both "fair partisan bargaining and discourses aimed at agreement."

From a regulatory sense, then, this method recognizes that there is little in the way of a "rightness" or "wrongness" between parties, only a difference. The regulatory body is then poised to help the differing factions find a resolution or common ground on issues.

Media requirements in a Complex Democracy include performing somewhat conflicting functions, respectively highlighting the diversity of thought of those who would normally be in competition for the limelight. This is an exceptionally difficult approach for many to embrace.

Baker notes that the dominant groups popular at any given time tend to control the expression that is considered most appropriate. This places expression that is not in the dominant current mainstream as "the paradigm of 'unreason'—sometimes dangerous, and at best an arousing, offensive diversion."[11] But Complex Democracy would find these "outliers" as necessary components of appropriate discourse. These differences of opinion would be needed for the dominant group to continue its internal discourse in a manner that was appropriate.

Given the current climate in Washington, where sides argue defiantly until the bitter end and often create little positive result for society, a model of regulatory reform that embraces Complex Democracy could pave the way to solving future regulatory problems. Rather than place sides at loggerheads, all parties agree that they disagree, but seek to move forward to a negotiated position that works for the general (though not infinite) good of the parties involved.

Another Approach

Where should we be looking to create a new or revised regulatory system for convergence? Most policy models designed focus on a systematic national approach to regulation. Television policy has essentially applied to all markets since its inception, and the only general differences in radio regulation pertained to broadcast power differences (day-timers, high-powered, etc). Earlier television licensing was based on either a VHF or UHF license, but this was part of a systematic plan based on national policy. That trend has continued.

Eric Easton believes that a reevaluation of copyright law at the national level will assist in aiding the integration of converged media into the marketplace. He looks primarily at the Internet and its inclusion as a component of television and newspaper convergence.[12]

Van Cuilenberg and Verhoest defined six modes of communication and information delivery systems to properly view the changing information marketplace.[13] They believe that by examining modes of distribution, exchange, proliferation, registration, editing and packaging, we can properly identify the level of integration of a communications company. By unbundling a variety (convergence would fit here) of activities, the authors believe, the marketplace would become more transparent.

Van Cuilenberg and Verhoest also believe that any policy system must be based on a service regulatory system rather than one assigned to evaluating media through technology. This approach has some promise, particularly in its desire to move regulation away from a system based on technological delivery and into a system based on how it functions (interrelates) with the general citizenry.

Still, national models may be fraught with problems where convergence is concerned. Although convergence does take place and certainly exists at the national level, where ownership concentration is apparent, it also has a strong influence on the content of information delivery at the local level. Because of this, it seems that a two-tiered model may work better. It would create a scenario in which the media are organized via their ownership at a national level but reviewed and regulated specifically at the local level. Delivery of information takes place on multiple levels, thus creating a need for a division of regulation.

Based on this ideal, the following diagrams should begin to show how a system could be achieved. First, we must recognize that any regulatory system in the future should encompass a paradigm that embraces some aspects of all major philosophical viewpoints involved in the regulated system. The process must speak to many voices. What this means is that the free market influences who believe strongly in Adam Smith's "invisible hand" concept must be instrumental in any process.[14] It also means that those who believe in a pluralistic form of republican democracy must be equally invested in the plan. Free market forces are opposed to any regulation from the government, believing that government intervention stifles the marketplace. Republican democracy believes that the will of the people is paramount and that free markets or business must take all aspects of society's needs into account to work properly; hence, regulation is a good thing.

Complex Democracy systems would argue that both sides should seek common ground. But what if that common ground is not apparent? How would these forces, these concepts that are at odds with one another, reconcile their differences sufficiently for that common ground? Currently, the push-pull relationship creates more difference, not commonality. When these opposing forces are pitted against each other, the resulting tension tends to end in a stalemate rather than a lasting solution. Yet, there should be some mechanism available that will at least appease the free-marketers while protecting and recognizing that the public and society are part and parcel to any public "good" on the horizon. Failing common ground, we must seek methods for balancing the tension among philosophies.

In this scenario, it is recognized that although the parties have individual goals, the best outcome for the general "good" and the regulatory climate is one that brings the forces into balance or equilibrium. Graphically, we could look at this much like a normal curve ,in which the sides of the curve remain constant and the mean level of agreement is the approximate middle of the curve. This places most issues and people in an equalized state. Individual views exist, but for the most part, they are gathered relatively closely around the mean.

Let's explain this a bit further. What regulation needs to do is understand that the goal of each population is drastically different from other population groups and that a specific solution will never satisfy all groups; therefore, any regulatory form must accept and be designed around the tension that takes place between the groups. In this case, we are determined to place the tension in a position where no group has an advantage or disadvantage in the marketplace of ideas or in the presentation of those ideas. Organizationally, the regulations must be structured to distribute tension among all sides to produce the needed equilibrium (Figure 8.2).

By creating various fundamental measurements, we can monitor the fit of the curve to the public. In other words, we can extend the old term "the goodness of the fit" from statistics to the more normative world of people and ideas. This might not be a popular stance when current factions appear to be satisfied only when they reach a winning situation, but it must be recognized that winning may result in the ultimate loss of the organization or group's goals.

Acknowledging this tension creates a somewhat different model of administrative government than current trends taken in regulatory activity. The role is not as controller, but as arbiter between the forces of the marketplace and the needs of the public or citizenry. In this scenario, the government regulatory body would rarely make new policy but would instead balance policy based on the values of competing forces. The difficulty in this form of regulation is that few regulatory bodies operate outside of political predisposition. This path requires that government not choose between alternatives; instead, it must balance the two (or more) competing interests.

This approach is much more legalistic in nature than current trends that politicize the landscape for the tenure of one administration or another and draws not just from the nature of recognizing that tension exists but also

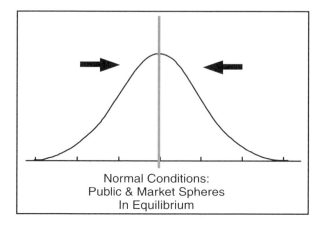

Figure 8.2. Equilibrium curve. This is a form of stasis; neither side is in control of the overall market. The equilibrium results in a balanced and thorough approach to competitive factions.

in recognizing that the competing interests have at least some level of correctness in their desire and need to exist. Much as the U.S. Supreme Court established a "balancing test" for First Amendment rights when government and press interests were in conflict, regulatory agencies would face a similar requirement when balancing the voices of the citizenry against the needs of business.

A balancing approach also reinvigorates a Federal Communications Commission that today often finds itself making policy rather than implementing policy approved by Congress. Policy making should not be the direct role of the FCC, but much as the courts are not technically in charge of making law yet somehow manage to do just that, the FCC and other agencies would not originate policy but would balance interests in such a way that policy making occurred.

Why is such a radical departure needed? We only need to look at convergence to provide us with appropriate reasoning in moving regulation into a new arena.

Regulating Convergence

As of late 2003, the Federal Communications Commission and the Bush Administration had continued the process of undoing more than 45 years of regulation. Chief among the latest measures scheduled for undo-ing was the limitation of cross-ownership, or the ownership of both a newspaper and television station in a single market. Cross-ownership rules, imposed in 1975 (see Chapter 2) had forbidden ownership of tele-vision properties by a newspaper in a single market. Media owners have long fought for repeal of the rule. About 40 cross-owned operations, most in small markets, were grandfathered into the rules to lower the possibili-ties of litigation at the time. Convergence has brought the discussion back to the fore.

As noted in Chapter 2, the FCC relaxed those rules in mid-2003, but Congress stayed the implementation of the rule change until further hear-ings could be held. As of publication, those hearings were incomplete. Still, cross-ownership (and subsequently, convergence) is a classic case of competing interests needing to be addressed in a way that is beneficial both to the public and to the marketplace.

From a balancing point of view, the first requirement is to determine how the issue/policy change would create an imbalance between the com-peting forces. In the case of cross-ownership, opponents contend that voices will be lost if owners are allowed to hold both a broadcast and print news operation in a single market.

Media owners, particularly broadcasters, argue that without the changes, the television newsrooms will go dark. News is expensive; it is sometimes a money-losing operation and generally increases legal costs and the overall risk of doing business. The owners argue that without change and with the absence of news in a broadcast forum, the public will have already lost part of its voice; hence, cross-ownership would bolster the station's news operations, increase its resources in a cost-efficient manner and keep it in business. However, this results in an emphasis on the marketplace that may allow advertisers to control content. Because viewership is tantamount to increased advertising revenues, the expecta-tion would be that advertisers would gear television shows toward a least-common-denominator approach to avoid risk and maximize advertising dollars to pay for the programming. News would become caught in the same web, pushing an emphasis on avoiding anything that viewers might not "enjoy." The alternative would be to close newsrooms. Figure 8.3 shows how this would look. Satisfaction would be a function of advertis-ing, not viewer needs.

Opponents of market controls would then counter that owners would close news operations simply to create a self-fulfilling prophesy, just to make their point. These public interest groups would argue that the rate of

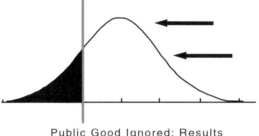

Advertisers dictate
Programming. Con-
sequently shifting to
a state of disequilibria
since emphasis on
bringing messages
that are market based
rather than public in-
terest based.

Public Good Ignored: Results
in least objectionable
programming

Figure 8.3. Marketplace disequilibrium: Disequilibrium when the emphasis
is on the public good and not driven by market forces. Although
programming may be improved in quality, competitive forces will create
financial strain for the broadcaster and may result in termination of services.

return in media properties is disproportionately high when compared with
other companies and should not be a consideration. To them, media owners should absorb the costs and keep news out of the revenue picture. To
the "citizen voice," broadcasters would be required to include local newscasts in their programming. This, of course, would be part of their public
interest requirement . . . even though that requirement has been under-
played for more than a decade.

If the public interest model is allowed to control the marketplace, however, the result is likely to be unfavorable in an overall view of media, particularly news, as well. Figure 8.4 shows that skewing the regulatory
activity toward the public interest view might be cause for concern in
keeping media outlets profitable. News as an operation of a station or corporation could become more expensive without creating additional benefits.

The competing positions seem irreconcilable, yet the positions are very
real approaches when seen through the lenses of current competing interests. To reach any agreement has, to date, met with acrimony from both
sides, but a balancing system would require the FCC to examine the issues
involved in each case and make a case-by-case judgment call on requests to
converge media properties. The FCC would be required to balance the divergent interests. Simply put, the FCC would need to examine all of the positions (and the artifacts surrounding those positions) to make a decision.

For instance, it is true that media companies, on average, fare much better in their gross profits and rate of return on investment than other indus-

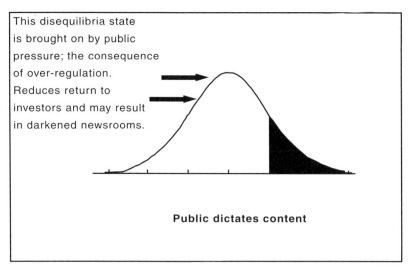

This disequilibria state is brought on by public pressure; the consequence of over-regulation. Reduces return to investors and may result in darkened newsrooms.

Public dictates content

Figure 8.4. Public view disequilibrium: Money for nothing, reduced viewership. Disequilibrium brought about when advertising forces are in control of the programming products. This results in short-term audience gains and improved profits but will result in long-term audience erosion and subsequently end in financial failure for the organization when advertisers fail to contribute to buoying programs with low ratings.

tries. But they also take a great deal of risk. These risks exist in a business environment where competition has created pressures that have fractured traditional media organization.

Cross-ownership and convergence allow a company to use economies of scale to produce information products, thus lowering the organization's overall level of risk and improve its profitability. Would or should the FCC, in allowing cross-ownership to take place, also require an assessment of the public's information needs? Are there ways to make the public generally less concerned about the fact that there are fewer voices in the community? Would gathering and dissemination best accomplish meeting that requirement?

Regulation, Market Size and Cross-ownership

I believe that mechanisms exist to create such a balance between conflicting interests, although this book isn't positioned to go into great detail.

What if the FCC, in allowing cross-ownership, increased the organization's public interest commitment in the market where the cross-owner-ship took place? Here, the FCC could require the organization to carry additional local news or occasional documentaries or it might even require the reinstitution of the hated ascertainment studies to ensure that local news truly deals with current issues (albeit some easily-created short-form version would be less onerous, though no less divisive).

To borrow a term from the logging industry, increased regulatory re-quirements would certainly keep the cross-owned company from "clear cutting" the media landscape. The gist of the argument then is if you want cross-ownership and ultimately convergence, what are you willing to pay to get it?

Balancing principles rarely make either side happy. It is doubtful that a company would go cheerfully into an agreement that would increase its responsibilities to regulators, but the temptation to own both a newspaper and television station in a single market (or some other significant combi-nation of media properties) might make owners more sensitive to creating a mutually beneficial arrangement.

A second, but no less important, issue in cross-ownership and conver-gence is the potential impact on other media outlets in the market where cross ownership takes place. Although newspapers pack an information wallop in most communities, most Americans still say they get their news from television.[15] The resources brought to the table through the newspa-per would enhance the broadcast news operations at all levels. It would amount to creating a strong competitive edge.

In a balancing sense, the FCC would now need to examine ways to recreate balance from the imbalance brought on by the cross-ownership. This time, however, the balance is about the marketplace and not about voices (although some solutions may influence voices). One solution would involve the methods currently used to determine radio ownership in a market . . . the concept of market share.

Using market share as a controlling factor in cross-ownership and con-vergence is fraught with its own set of difficulties. In casting market share as the deciding factor, we must first decide how it would be used, what constitutes appropriate market share and how many other media organi-zations would be included in calculating that share.

As a concept, market share could be based on the division of total rev-enues produced in a market by all broadcast units (in this case, television) versus the revenues of the broadcast outlet involved in cross-ownership. This percentage would be based on the assumption that no one outlet would be allowed to control the market. This percentage could be as low as 20 percent and as high as 45 percent. The size of the market and number of television outlets, cable franchises and other media would create the determining factors in the control of the market's revenue share.

Several scenarios are possible if the cross-owned media outlet reaches a revenue penetration above its determined earnings threshold. Among the potential methods used to control market share are creation of a second cross-owned operation, increased public affairs requirements, public interest programming control or off-loading revenue in the forms of penalties that would perhaps be used in some other area (funding Universal Service comes to mind). The first two options are more useful to both the public interest and the marketplace. The last two alternatives amount to a punitive action that would not be viewed favorably by most media organizations (or me).

Creating a second cross-owned operation could take the form of another newspaper-television converged operation, a television duopoly, a cable news/broadcast operation or some mixture of radio, television, cable and print outlets that differ from the primary cross-owned media operation. The goal with any of these alternatives is to create additional competition for the major cross-owned and converged media organization.

Increasing public affairs programming is somewhat self-explanatory. The result of adding to the public affairs requirement would be to increase the costs of the news operation for the broadcast outlet. It would likely require additional staff and produce shows that were less profitable than entertainment programming. The converged group would then find itself in a position of airing more television in the public interest while bringing revenues back below the established threshold.

Obviously, each of these ideas is based on speculation, not on hard evidence about how each of these operations could or would work in the real world. The effort here is simply to put additional ideas on the table. Remember, the focus of this section is on creating balance and finding effective ways to implement convergence and keep it working. The alternative is to confound what may be a significant development in media organizations in the U.S.

If media organizations are willing to deal with the prospects of some additional controls, albeit perhaps self-monitored (except for market share determinants), then the potential exists to institute measures that will keep broadcast newsrooms not only viable but thriving and upgrade the level of news while protecting voices. It is not a plan, simply a series of ideas that need to be examined.

Convergence and Global Media Regulation

In the United States, free market principles seem to be the controlling agents in producing the environment in which the media operates. Deregulation, in earnest since the Reagan Administration, is taking hold in the United States. According to Ó Siochrú and Girard, the influence of trade and marketers on the media now supercedes control by governments.[16] The emphasis on marketplace issues today is overshadowing the issue of operating in the public interest. The citizen as a force in democracy is being replaced by the concept of business as citizen, and what business needs is good for the public (or so goes the premise).

Interestingly, this concept is moving outward and taking hold globally. From Japan to Russia and even in the Republic of China, marketplace control is being seen as an appropriate object and direction to dictate regulatory activity. Where then lie the boundaries between economic or market control and societal control? From a global perspective, the issues revolve around innumerable variables, with nation wealth coming into play as surely as global needs. Let us take a look at conditions and two organizations tied to the United Nations that shape the attitudes of these divergent groups: The World Trade Organization (WTO) and the United Nations Educational, Scientific and Cultural Organization (UNESCO). Both agencies, first discussed in Chapter 1, are independent members of the Economic and Social Council of the United Nations. From there, all similarities end.

The World Trade Organization was established to end international barriers and tariffs to trade. Ó Siochrú and Girard call WTO the most powerful global trade institution ever created. WTO was created in 1995 and replaced the GATT (General Agreement on Tariffs and Trade), an organization created as a temporary agency in 1947 but that lasted nearly 50 years. The WTO now manages the GATT agreements. There are 143 member nations in WTO, and that number is subject to change.

WTO has been immersed in controversy since its inception. Viewed by many as a way for the largest and wealthiest nations of the world to control the smaller nations, many people and organizations are wary of the global implications of such an agency. Some of those groups have been behind the protests that have marred the WTO annual and committee meetings around the globe. Philosophically, the higher purpose of the WTO is to create an environment in which the marketplace will allow all people access to a wider variety of goods and services. Small, economically unstable nations and consumer-based groups have a different view.

They see WTO as a way for the wealthy nations to impose their technological and financial will on others less able to "defend" themselves.
Clearly, the "truth" is in the eye of the beholder.

Generally, large wealthy nations and large globally-operated corporations want few controls over their communications forms, and only then to
ensure that the technologies being utilized transfer easily from company to
company and nation to nation. The argument that less-wealthy nations
need more support seems rarely heeded by media megaliths. Societal
need-based regulation is seen as counterproductive, and hat the marketplace will likely bring advances to the less advanced, given time. Large
nations and media corporations work closely with the WTO to reach the
accords they need to overcome national barriers to improving their global
positions.

At UNESCO, the issues are vastly different than those at the WTO.
Where mass media is concerned, WTO interests are driven by seeking
ways to improve marketplace conditions and create incentives for bringing the world closer together on communications policy. UNESCO technically is charged with helping find ways to create world peace. The
agency was among the first organizations chartered following the creation
of the United Nations after World War II. UNESCO's membership includes 190 nations, and its operations are interesting by the standards of
many other organizations. Unlike the WTO, in which the wealthiest members wield the greatest influence, UNESCO members have occasionally
been known to stand up to big media and big money.

In the late 1970s and early 1980s, UNESCO's membership created a
"treaty" calling for a New World Information and Communications Order
(NWICO). Among the provisions of the treaty were requirements that major nations (and their media) essentially would fund the creation and upgrade of media and technology in less-developed nations and that those
states would be fully in charge of those media developments. Many of
those nations were not democracies, and a central tenet of U.S. involvement in any media development was its democratization. U.S. media owners as well as a few in Europe and Japan were furious over UNESCO's
attempts to secure billions of dollars in aid without oversight of those supplying the money. The differences became contentious, and in 1984, President Ronald Reagan essentially withdrew the U.S. from UNESCO
membership.

The move by the U.S. stunned some of the UNESCO members. Great
Britain joined the U.S. in 1985. Without the United States, the largest single
contributor to UNESCO's budget, the agency became much less active. The

agency kept alive its NWICO hopes, but when the leadership changed in 1987, NWICO was pushed to the backburner. For years, the sides agreed to disagree. UNESCO finally allowed its NWICO position to fade away, and the United States rethought its membership. The U.S. finally rejoined UN-ESCO in October 2003.[17]

Both UNESCO and the WTO help shape communications policy globally, but neither has a direct connection in creating those policies. That is specifically because telecommunications policy, with few exceptions, remains firmly in the hands of the nation states and is not likely to change.

Some would argue that this lack of international control is counterproductive. UNESCO issued a report in the late 1990s calling for nations to "consider" implementing policies that would establish and promote radio and television space for "community, linguistic, and minority services." The statement was a tepid version of a draft report created nearly two years earlier when UNESCO sponsored a commission looking at media concentration and global ownership of the airwaves. Apparently they were beginning to understand the pressures of the marketplace that had led to issues with the United States and others.

On the other side of the coin, the World Trade Organization sits in a position to create a great deal of control over the global activities of media, and clearly, the goal is to allow global media and global media concentration to thrive.

Policies, particularly those dealing with technological issues, require some consistency at a global level to ensure a semi-seamless approach to the use of products globally. The WTO is positioned to facilitate those developments along market-driven lines. That position has not come easily.

Throughout the 1980s and 1990s, several organizations and nations had fought to create policies that would open media markets globally and contribute to an overall structure for the media marketing of technology, services and products. When WTO supplanted the GATT, it was in a position to take on many of those activities. The result was that most nations belonging to WTO signed the Agreement on Basic Telecommunications (ABT). The policy liberalized a number of areas, allowing for a more transparent approach to telecommunications policy globally. Most nations have continued to set limits on foreign ownership and have kept their national policies in place, but the fact that the agreement was signed showed a significant move toward consideration of the existence of global media.

The International Telecommunications Union

A section on global media regulation could not end without a brief discussion on the International Telecommunications Union (ITU). The ITU, established in 1865 following the invention of the telegraph, helps set standards for the production and use of telecommunications equipment, allocates satellite positions and facilitates tariff sharing agreements between telecommunications providers. It was the first truly international agency and has, from time to time, worked well in setting communications policy.

Since its inception, the ITU has been challenged. One of the greatest challenges has been to negotiate with companies that create proprietary equipment that is generally beneficial to multiple nations simultaneously. Obviously, corporations seek to gain the greatest advantage when their products and patents are on the line. ITU has been the agency charged with attempting to reconcile those differences. Historically, ITU has worked well, but not always quickly. Corporations and nations are slow to act in ways that may not seem to benefit them directly.

Even when agreements are apparently completed, dangers arise as individual companies argue over standards. Some of the arguments have delayed the introduction of technological innovations for years. The nastiest of arguments often happen in the United States, where competing large companies use their political clout and moneyed voices to influence policy (or sometimes prevent the implementation of policy). In satellite service, digital signal conversion and even high-definition television, the United States has lagged years behind other nations because of internal corporate bickering over standards.

The United States was the eleventh nation to begin offering satellite service directly to consumers, more than a decade after its offerings in Japan and Europe. HDTV sets in America have required multiple inputs because the U.S. hasn't been able to settle on a single HDTV standard.[18] Televisions range from a 480 progressive scan range to 1080 interlaced or progressive scan. Most Americans are incapable of understanding the difference because televisions are marketed in ways that obfuscate the real applications of the products.

None of this is the responsibility of the ITU, but the examples point to some of the differences that frequently interfere with the adoption of and adaptation to new technologies.

Conclusions

Regulatory issues both in the United States and globally will continue to create challenges for the converged workplace during the next decade. As media companies continue their attempts at cross-ownership and work toward further consolidation, an expectation exists that nation states will counter to offset their growing power.

The shape of the response remains uncertain. This chapter has posed one alternative that proposes creating an equilibrium state based on the marketing power of media units in their respective local markets. Overall media concentration may be a somewhat moot point. If localism is used as a barometer for gauging the power of a media company rather than its national revenue structure, the scenario shifts away from concerns over concentration and national voices to one of market sensitivity and local voices. Because the national media, whether dealing with information or entertainment, is already relatively concentrated, the focus should shift to local markets.

Regardless of the regulatory tactics taken by the United States or other nations, a place for convergence exists in the media marketplace. Journalism and its ability to get information to the public should not be constrained by simple market structures at the national level. For media power to inure to the people, that power must begin at a grassroots level; therefore, any system that includes a local component will be better than systems that attempt to create a non-evolving set of rules at a national or potentially international level. Keeping the playing field level is of utmost importance if convergence is to be allowed to move forward. Otherwise, serious constraints and regulations are inevitable.

Further Readings

Aufderheide, P. (1999). Communications Policy and the Public Interest: The Telecommunications Act of 1996. New York: The Guilford Press.

Napoli, P. M. (2001). Foundations of Communications Policy: Principles and Process in the Regulation of Electronic Media. CressKill, NJ: Hampton Press.

Ó Siochrú, S. and Girard B.(2002). Global Media Governance: A Beginner's Guide. New York: Rowan and Littlefield.

Questions

1. Review testimony from the Federal Communications Commission hearings on cross-ownership. Choose one owner and restate their position on this issue. What is the response from consumer groups? Use specific testimony (available at www.fcc.gov).
2. Having read the previous chapter, do you believe that a global media policy is possible on cross-ownership or media concentration issues? Justify your answer with material not in the book.

CHAPTER 9

Beyond the Newsroom

Throughout this book, the emphasis has been on the placement and management of journalists in a new and intriguing frontier generally called media convergence. However, newsrooms do not operate in a vacuum. To understand the overall workings of news media and the environments in which journalists work, a brief look at other aspects of media is required. In this way we hope to bring context to the overall understanding of converged media and how media work.

Although the heart of any newspaper and many television stations is in the news department, the brains of these organizations are generally locked in other areas frequently referred to as profit centers. The work in these departments is often ignored by journalists as they work on their daily stories, but it becomes very important on at least one or two days a month: payday. While the altruist wants to ignore the money side of journalism, the pragmatist understands its necessity.

The profitability of a media operation relies on a complex interplay among information delivery, customer satisfaction and advertiser acceptance. Regardless of the operation, the advertising departments, their sales staffs and the production side of the business are as important as the news gathered by journalists. The jobs aren't always pretty and the pressure is always on to make money, but publications and stations don't stay on the streets or air very long without profitability.

If convergence truly takes hold, what will be the shape of media in the future? How will advertising and public relations find their places in the future? How will converged media be promoted? Can ratings systems survive? If the media is going to change, what is the outcome on marketing plans and lines of profit?

We already have some guidance in these areas. It seems that some transformation is likely as media becomes a truly integrated, multi-platform activity. One of my colleagues, Dr. Marie Curkan-Flanagan, at the University of South Florida is convinced that the way to reach people with information in the coming decades is through interactive games. To her, the ability to reach younger audiences must be coupled with interesting activities; if information it isn't interesting, younger audiences will go away. Dr. Curkan-Flanagan believes that the current reliance on media being fed to consumers is a key reason that audiences are growing smaller in television and that readership is stagnant at newspapers.[1]

Enter the interactive arena. Curkan-Flanagan believes, as do others, that interconnectivity is the key to convergence. Information is included in the interconnect, and games are a way to engage the mind and not let it be simply pandered to by big media. "Linking" and "click throughs" get us there.[2]

Schrage notes that "Wherever there are audiences, there will be advertising." News is about finding an audience. Games therefore have the potential of presenting information within the information package.[3] This approach to journalism would not be as overt as the sponsored games envisioned by some in which McDonalds creates a Ronald McDonald game that plays on the next version of Game Boy or X-Box.

Instead, this version would be provided in a more subtle way through information-based Web sites. Part of the game scenario for news is wrapped up in the expectation that people who want information on a particular subject are willing to travel about the Web to find it. If the news hub presents the issue but also supplies multiple links on the issue (which is already becoming customary), then some of those links could likely be provided by advertisers or at least through corporate information sites.

For instance, automobile manufacturers could create sites that are historically accurate about the birth and development of America's fascination with automobiles. The site could include quizzes that show close-ups of various automobile parts such as grills and taillights through time and then ask the participant to name the car and the year in which it was produced. Points would be allotted and rewards offered for answering the questions correctly. In the meantime, the participant is learning about automobile history.

This is advertising clothed in a thin layer of fun. I have advertising colleagues who believe advertising should always be first about fun and then about selling goods and products. The key to this approach is that the writers and the message creators are working for the client who produced the game. The game is linked to the news because it is germane to the story the reporter has written. The potential for Web sites incorporating these functions is phenomenal.

While these sites are focusing on products and activities belonging to a profit-seeking organization, they also may provide information in a straightforward, non-positioned way. Interestingly, this likely makes the preparation of the information a function of public relations rather than advertising. In this setting, public relations practitioners would create, write and prepare the games, and advertising would place and promote those games.

To date, most public relations practitioners have avoided discussions of their role in a converged media operation. The previous game is just one example of how public relations could be tied to both information and advertising. Just as organizations would create informational games about products, they would also create informational games about the organization, its leaders, its history and its manufacturing or service capabilities. The companies recognizing that creating these games provides a public service while helping the company position its overall image and corporate face are those who will win early in the converging media environment.

Generally, public relations practitioners view their organizational role as that of the corporate conscience and information provider. They are the managers of the corporate image. They oversee the notion of ethical informational behaviors. They deal with various audiences and work to create information specifically tailored to answer the needs and questions of those audiences. This is why their positions in the organization are so important. It is also why they should be providing the games for converged news operations.

Let's take another example: anthrax. Not a popular subject in the United States these days, but one that gets everyone's attention. A hospital, medical center or pharmaceutical company could develop an interactive teaching Web site that includes information on various strains of anthrax, shows the user how anthrax works on the body's central nervous system and asks questions about the potential danger of anthrax in one's home or community. Because the risk of anthrax exposure is really quite low, the site could serve to allay fears about anthrax. It would put the issue back into perspective.

Every position paper ever written by an organization where that paper still has currency is a potential Web site and interactive game. Training materials and community services activities from fire prevention to baby-proofing a home are ripe for Web-based games. Because the links are practical and helpful, they could be picked up readily by the media. If traditional media is in transition, it is only logical that those organizational functions dependent upon media change as well.

Professional public relations organizations like the International Association of Business Communicators (IABC) and Public Relations Society of America (PRSA) could develop clearinghouse servers with topically directed links to various sites. This would offer the media choice, thereby helping to ensure the ethical appropriateness of the link.[4] If the organizations were reluctant to move in this direction because of internal political concerns, entrepreneurially minded practitioners could build their own clearing sites and charge fees to organizations for listings. Important to this would be some sort of vetting service to ensure the reliability of the information. Once vetted, the information would be open for access and available to the public and news organizations.

Providing online vetted information meets the public relations objective of providing information to news media but fails to meet the proactive posture many organizations would prefer to take. That would require a more traditional approach to making news contacts, but the vetted source would help the overall effort.

Some experts believe that the Internet began changing public relations nearly a decade ago. *Salon Magazine* carried an article that showed how public relations professionals were working to deal with the troubles of accelerating headlines. Stories that once took days to get out now reach millions in a matter of minutes.[5] This, according to Nicholas Stein, results in the need for "mindshare," the ability to get the right kind of attention in the midst of competitive ideas and products. As the acceleration continues, it will be important for practitioners to form new methods for reaching audiences and discovering ways in which they are different from other audiences.

Advertising Tools

Back on the advertising side, there would be a need to create new tools that brought the surfer to a custom-tailored Web site. Perhaps some advertising games could be built into the informational games. It would be appropriately labeled by a color-coded link that immediately told participants that some advertising was part of the link. Advertising uses persuasive skills in exceptional ways, and the ability to develop games that are low-keyed, interesting, yet positioned for marketing would likely receive hits and ultimately mean that messages were received by the viewer.

Schrage notes that high-end financial institutions could build sites around expert, custom-calibrated investment advice. In the end, the possibilities are limitless, and the expectations are naturally high.[6] Advertising would need to study message types closely and create multiple Web sites to reach the targeted audiences. Certain tags and presentation in certain types of stories would dictate which advertising site the individual was able to click to. Creating a targeted message is a central focus of the advertising arsenal. Once an individual was at the site, the "sale" could take place based on the usual functions of need and creativity in the creation of the advertisement or its game representation.

Interestingly, although these tools may make advertising more fun, the hottest advertising tool today is the purchased search engine ad. In 2003, marketers spent nearly $2 billion on two-sentence search engine ads. The figure, according to the *New York Times*, is expected to grow to $2.8 billion in 2004, a 47 percent growth in one year.[7]

The beauty of these ads is that they are the result of a search initiated by the potential customer. Customers are finding their way to create their own form of targeting by the types of goods and services they are seeking. Corporations are more than happy to oblige. Search engines will produce lists of hundreds, if not thousands, of responses to inquiries from users.

Risks in Cyberspace

Still, Internet advertising and information efforts have not, to date, yielded the profit expected from corporate management. The collapse of the so-called dot.com revolution in 2001 was the result of investments not meeting expectations, but it appears that a recovery is finally on the way.

Part of the problem with the dot.coms of the '90s was their lack of positioning in a true marketing environment. The efforts had little organization, a great deal of leveraged financing and entrepreneurial individuals who knew a lot about the Internet but very little about marketing. On the flip side, some companies knew a great deal about traditional marketing but little about the Internet or the psychological mechanisms that influenced its use by the public. These problems were coupled with several others; most serious among them was that if the market can't find you, there is no market.

Many of the so-called brick-and-clicks—companies who tried to maintain an Internet presence with their existing traditional retail outlets—found it difficult to bring in new customers.[8] Independent retailers, expecting strong customer use on the Web from existing name recognition, were surprised when the public didn't show up.

The search engine approach is overcoming those early shortfalls. Both Google.com and Yahoo's Overture.com are growing in online sales traffic. Moving beyond the simple subject-defined search engines, the companies now fall into the newly lucrative "paid search market."[9]

In these dot.com markets, advertisers pay a fee to be listed on the Web sites' search engines. Listings are then generated based on the fee paid to the search engine. Search locations on the list are determined by the fees paid by the company for its products or services.

Google and Overture are only two of the companies that have survived and even thrived. Ebay.com and Amazon.com also are successful operations, although they too have certainly had their financial ups and downs.

One of the keys to success of all of these companies has been that they are really gatekeeper services. Loaded with keywords and links all pointing in the direction of various Web sites, these companies bring products to people who are searching for something that meets a specific need.

Amazon.com is technically a clearinghouse for reselling everything from books to movies to computers and office equipment. Ebay.com is another kind of clearinghouse helping hundreds of thousands of people worldwide exchange goods through the oldest form of barter in the world . . . auction bidding.

These approaches, coupled with a conscious effort at satisfying customer needs, have led to the successful operation of their companies. Recently, the CEO of Ebay.com was a guest on *Oprah*, a certain sign of success and cross-platform market positioning.

The turnaround for Internet advertising is well underway; the *Los Angeles Times* recently reported total Internet advertising of more than $6 billion for 2003. That figure jumped more than 40 percent from 2002. Today, more than 140 million Americans use the Internet.[10]

The outlook for Internet advertising again appears to be bright. We've heard all this before, but it now seems that technological capacity and understanding is catching up to advertiser needs. The world of advertising also is getting a "feel" for how the Internet works. Those factors taken together likely will continue to fuel Internet sales growth efforts.

The "Death" of Advertising

Some writers believe that advertising will die when people move to converged environments for their news and entertainment. The point they make is not that advertising will die *per se*, but that it will change to reflect the needs of consumers rather than the marketing desires of advertisers.

These researchers believe that, because the public will not be using appointment television or generally picking up a complete newspaper, traditional advertising will disappear, and big media with it. Many expect that the days of the expensive and very slick television ads may be a thing of the past, resurrecting themselves only in times of very strong consumer commitment to a program like the Super Bowl.

Randall Rothenberg, writer for *Wired Magazine*, notes that it is the very measurability of the Internet that will set the tone for marketing and advertising for the future.[11] Rothenberg believes that media today use suspicious forms of measurement, including Nielsen's broadcast rating system and Simmons readership measurements for newspapers. He sees these systems as flawed because they use samples that are too small and extrapolated out too far.

With the Internet, Rothenberg believes that marketers will eventually flock to the Web simply because they will be able to find out what sells and find it out in ways they can understand. Rothenberg thinks that too much big media is and has been a cause for great concern but that it has been driven by big advertising. To him, less advertising spending will result in better marketing to consumers, i.e., less hype and more product information.

If Rothenberg is correct, how will television programming be influenced? Programming could tumble as surely as a jet liner caught in a wind sheer. Advertising has driven the ability to provide much of television's quality programming (along with its drivel). How would revenue sources be derived in a realigned programming universe?

Technology in television programming already has put together the ability to place products in shows and then label the products on the digital medium. Pointing a remote at the product on the screen and then pushing a scan button could allow the viewer to access the product on a Web page tied to the television screen. The effort essentially pauses the television show while the viewer looks at the advertisement for the product. Once the viewer either orders the product via the Web link or returns to the show, the program takes up from the point at which it stopped. Embedding product codes into the program is a relatively easy prospect and is already underway in some experimental markets.[12]

The real difficulty here is in getting the viewer to pay attention to the product without distracting from the program underway. That will require some clever and subtle writing and production techniques beyond the scope of this chapter.[13]

Journalism and Advertising

How can traditional media companies learn from these successes and experiments? First and foremost, the media must use their existing platforms to promote their multiple operations. Most news operations are already deeply committed to this cross-promotional activity. For both newspapers and television, it allows viewers to read and see more information on particular stories. It also takes people to other branding areas of the organization.

Only in the past decade or so have managers in journalism operations talked about branding efforts. These branding efforts fall clearly in the lap of advertising but are often linked directly to the newsroom's activities. Management training in journalism was generally limited to understanding personnel issues (not human resources), EEO and discrimination problems, and financial management of the operation. Branding was left to others. Bottom-line pressures have moved upper-level news executives into the broader fight for brand recognition.[14]

Slogans, logos and strong colors are central themes in promoting both broadcast and newspaper outlets. At one time, those themes were simply passed on to the news department by management. Today, news managers take an active role in helping shape the look of the newspaper and television station. Cross-platform promotions and advertising on other regional Web sites extend these brand images.

From another point of view, news media could use Internet search engines to effectively sell stories with embedded advertising just as retailers are doing. This process already is underway, but many newspapers, television stations and Internet news services imprint the stories only with their brand. In most instances, this means the media company is paying for its brand recognition with no financial upside to the investment.

Because of this limitation, many newspapers and magazines have gone to a subscription-based information service whereby subscribers have full access to content but free surfers only get "newsbits." This works well for large, well-known organizations but is less profitable for smaller news operations.[15]

Other news groups are now placing well-written persuasive ads in their story-based Web pages. This allows the news organization to offset the cost of the news stories and still offer the story to non-subscribers. Because most Internet users are not specifically interested in ongoing news copy, it makes sense to offer more access through embedded advertising. The trick is to match the advertising with the story. Some feature stories lend themselves to targeted advertising more easily than hard news stories.

Researching this section of the chapter brought up a number of stories, but it also brought up advertising for everything from laptop computers to the Atkins Diet. Although the ads were well written and placed, the targeting seemed off-center.

The upside to this sort of advertising is that it is both measurable and can be targeted. Companies will know not only how many people clicked on the story and then clicked on the ad but also how persuasively the ad performs. In most search engines, the number of clicks inside the advertisement also is measured. This allows the advertiser to determine the effectiveness of the ad by comparing the number of hits on the story to the number of hits on the ad site and the depth of entry into the Web site. Understanding an advertisement's effectiveness allows both the news source and the advertiser to set an appropriate value to the ad, i.e., how it will be priced.

Convergence Advertising and Journalism

Why should journalists even care? Journalists have been forced to care in both television and print because of the constraints of programming and the limitations of space. We have already described the influences on newspapers and how they may manage through change. For television, the revenue answers would be a bit different. Several questions need to be asked.

First, if on-demand television programming is available in real time via the Web or some computer-accessed hard drive, what form of advertising will be able to offset the costs of news and programming? Programming appears to have a few potential strategies, but embedding commercials or product codes in newscasts is a bit risky and *very* far afield of ethical consideration. Other approaches need to be found.

Fortunately for television, appointment TV is not dead yet. Although a great deal of time shifting already is underway by audiences, there doesn't seem to be a clear clamoring for some other access format. These formats are in development, but adoption is years away. In the meantime, television news needs to examine ways to protect its platform from further erosion in the marketing sense. As noted in Chapter 2, some media experts believe that convergence alone will help stop the bleeding of news revenues. Those results remain to be seen.

Internet Television and Advertising

Meanwhile, television may find a new home on the Internet. According to the *New York Times*, Internet users are flocking to high-speed broadband access. Only three years ago, some researchers were concerned that the promise of the Internet was dying because no one was interested in high-speed access. Again, it was more likely a question of price and capability than lack of desire on the part of the public. During the same time, computing capability has quadrupled while the prices for desktop machines have fallen to levels that allow nearly ubiquitous access. High-speed service costs have fallen as well, releasing pent-up demand for better services.

Emphasizing broadcasting requires accommodating streaming video. Video streaming is still slow but is facilitated through high-speed access. Motion often fails in large scale because the "pipe" isn't large enough to handle the size of the data packet required for real-time viewing. While solving this problem is still underway, the notion of online television is growing.[16]

From a marketing sense, full-screen video streaming could be available only through subscriptions. Those wanting to view the news over the Internet in real time would pay higher prices for the high-resolution pictures and stories. Lower-resolution small-screen viewing could be free with advertising placed around the screen.

Questions remain. For instance, how would potential viewers find the local news? Would we even need newscasts as they are currently configured? Some media managers have wanted to find ways to do away with high-priced anchors and put news back in the hands of reporters and producers. Perhaps the Internet is the way to do that. There would be substantial risks involved in this approach, however, because television audiences identify primarily with news, weather and sports anchors—not with reporters.

Newspapers are not burdened by the same packaging problems. The newspaper equivalent of a television anchor is a columnist, and columnist identities transfer readily to the Internet. They also have identities that are wrapped around specific perspectives and approaches to news events and issues. Anchors are more generic.

Conclusions

Convergence, advertising and public relations all will be tied together again, but how the new relationships will filter out is yet to be determined.

For now, we know that both advertising and public relations have the ability to succeed on the Internet.

How these successes will forge a new relationship with the public presents an interesting set of questions. Will public relations lose the traditional bonds of media relations and be capable of taking its messages directly to the public through game-based issue statements and interactive educational opportunities? Will advertising shift from needing traditional media to becoming an Internet-based tool where the public is in charge of the search and the marketers serve the will of some pluralistic audience?

Newsrooms must have funds to operate. For more than 150 years, those monies have come from traditional forms of advertising. How will convergence and the Internet change that relationship? Will news also become a subscription service? If so, what will prevent the public from further fracturing into groups bound not by idealistic issues but by common interests? Many questions remain.

Pavlik has said that because of the acceleration of new media technologies, "virtually every social institution is inexorably altered."[17] This is the case for more than just journalism, but also for the traditional agents that have fueled journalism both financially and through information delivery.

To say that convergence or new media technologies have little influence on the practices of either advertising or public relations is an unknowing approach. Everyone involved in media, regardless of his or her paradigm, needs to understand how dramatically technology is shifting the world. To understand that now is paramount to working practically in the future.

Exercises

1. Pick up your local newspaper. Select an advertisement at random. Using that advertisement as an example, go online to a search engine and type in the product advertised. Don't use the product name, only the product type (e.g., window cleaner, cell phone). How many hits did you receive in your search? Was the product from the newspaper one of the first on the Internet list? Was the newspaper product even on that list? Based on your readings in this chapter, why do you think that was the outcome?
2. Go to the Web site of a local television station. Are there many advertisements on the primary Web page? If not, is it loaded with promotions for the station? How do you think the Web site works as a marketing tool for the television station? Or for its news operation?

CHAPTER 10

The Media Management Frontier of the Future

Where will media management end up? Will regulators suddenly pull the plug on the media giants and reinstitute the firewalls that existed between print and broadcasters? Will the child called convergence be thrown out with the bathwater when owners get tired of trying to determine how to make the workplace efficient without losing its effectiveness? Just what is the future of news and information in an age of instant media?

According to *PC World*, "digitainment" is here. The technology brings the home PC and entertainment centers into one digital device.[1] Officials from the Yankee Group, a futurist think tank, report that by 2007, some 18.5 million American homes will own digital media receivers that wed entertainment and PC technology. Globally, the trend is expected to continue as well. According to Stephen Quinn, the U.S. already is behind the rest of the world in broadband adoption.[2]

In a recent issue of *PC Magazine*, Gateway Computers was advertising a new multimedia platform with the headline "Shhh. Don't tell it it's a computer."[3] Their version of a "Family Room Media Center" offered an integration of entertainment and computerized functions. It played CDs and DVDs, recorded television shows and functioned as a computer. It had a mouse, a keyboard and a remote. The integrated media center functioned at multiple levels, delivering entertainment and information on demand in the user's home, all of this while allowing the user to access and use any traditional computer programs. Rather than calling this a multimedia platform, perhaps Gateway should call it a single multi-platform media.

Gateway is a consumer-based company. The company needs volume sales to introduce and maintain products. It is clear that those who do not believe that television and other entertainment platforms will merge with information and task-specific platforms are wrong. The real test for most people will likely come in the form of organizing time—fun is almost always more attractive than work.

Several pages over, in an article in the same issue of *PC Magazine*, writers reported on recent nanotechnology and how researchers had attached micro-miniature carbon nanotubes to strands of DNA in a way that allowed the nanotube to further develop and complete itself, creating a nano-sized transistor.[4] The age of micro-machines is no longer in the distant future; it is next door. The implications for those of us in the information age are enormous.

This is evidence that technological convergence is finally taking place. Early adopters will flock to the new, technologically intriguing gadgets. Most of the rest of us will follow when we see usefulness for the technology in our lives, attractive prices and technology that is fully competitive with less-sophisticated technology.

Still, there are those who scoff at these developments. Michael Noll, a professor at the Annenberg School for Communication at the University of Southern California, believes that convergence is a myth.[5] His beliefs are based on the failed discussions and lost revenues of companies moving early to gather the tools of convergence technology to them.

Others believe that there is no place in the family home to integrate the platforms of news. They see these new technologies as fads. Noll correctly notes that convergence should not be a mantra for mass communication. That said, I believe the naysayers are wrong. The idea of convergence has certainly taken longer to reach fruition than many envisioned, but it is neither dead nor myth. It is simply the next step in the technological evolution that we have seen in media. One needs only to talk with a 14-year-old to discover how wrongheaded that thinking has become.

Part of the deception of new technologies is that there is a belief among those who create those technologies that they will be immediately interesting to the public. This is based on the expectation that because the technology will help people better organize their lives, it should be adopted. The truth is that most technologies are not adopted by the generation that creates them; they are adopted by the next generation.

Radio became a mainstay in homes once it appeared organized and provided people with easy-to-find entertainment; however, radio was available for more than 15 years before the surge in set sales. Those sales came along only when commercial enterprises—RCA and Westinghouse—in lcague with retail companies joined forces to make radio sets cheap with ready programming that was accessed easily.[6]

Television was invented in 1928. Many blame World War II for its slow adoption, but other factors kept it out of homes as well. Radio was just fine for most people. The younger families were the ones willing to look at the new technology. Adoption began with zest in the late 1940s.[7]

Personal computers, PDAs and cell phones all took time to see their technologies adopted into family life. One should not expect converged media to be any different. When the price meets demand and the technology meets its promise, it will be embraced.

The future is certainly fraught with more troublesome problems. Trying to negotiate through the maze of regulatory actions in the United States and the rest of the world is just one example of continuing troubles. The battle for the best form of delivery also remains unsettled. Convergence is still organizing.

Several years ago, the United States set its own parameters for satellite radio. The system, considered inferior in its technology to a system developed and adopted in Europe, was accepted because there were fewer marketing issues involved than with the system in Europe.[8]

Thousands of news operations have set up convergence activities, generally by creating multimedia Web sites. The content is unchanged from the material appearing in news pages or sent across airwaves. This is not convergence, but it is a step in that direction.

One hundred years from now, convergence likely will be an asterisk on the historical record of media development. It will have been fully supplanted by whatever technological revolution has come on the telecommunications scene. People will still hunger for information, but the instant news world we call the World Wide Web will likely have evolved into a wireless multi-level system of information delivery. The dot.coms and dot.orgs of today will have new iterations. News and information, suitably vetted, will be available on the dot.jous or the dot.nws of the time. The new versions of *Drudge Reports* will sit alongside the online version of *National Enquirer* and will be found at dot.tab or some similar iteration of access.

What we must realize is that the Web, coupled with its technology and our ability to use it properly, is still generally like a young child. It's there, and the intellect has been brought along, but it lacks organization. It will find itself, as will the next generation of journalism. News will still be news, and people will still be people.

Still, we must deal with the near future, a future likely to continue its current pace of change, and all of the ramifications of that change. For instance, according to KPMG Financial, about 83 percent of all mergers between 1980 and 2000 were unsuccessful in producing greater financial benefits for the companies that were merged.[9] In fact, most reports indicate that mergers have had a negative influence on all stakeholder groups except stockholders. The short-term financial benefits to those stockholders generally result in lost creativity, an exodus of good employees, often a loss in customer base and ultimately, harm to the acquiring company. So why bother? The expectations of convergence and its best use in presenting information remain elusive.

Convergence is a form of merger between previously competing news types, but that doesn't make it financially rewarding.[10] In fact, I believe that companies entering into convergence with efficiency and financial performance enhancement as their primary goals are misled by their consultants or are simply unaware of the true impact that converged news operations have on a community.

Convergence itself is not a bad thing. It is just—as the saying goes—the next thing. Robert Burns wrote that neither "tide nor time" wait for man.[11] Because we understand that times change and "wait for no man," we should also understand that what was once a reasonable explanation of the global media marketplace is no longer true. Bagdikian and McChesney have worried about the loss of voices as media concentration continues.[12] But as Demers rightly counters, the number of voices isn't going down, but up, because more information sources are available from which to gain information.[13]

Despite the concerns of those who would rail against the loss of voices or those who see it as monopoly creation, convergence has information delivery value. Part of that value comes from the very issue decried by diversity groups—that of delivering the same (or similar) message in multiple platforms. People today are inundated with information. The number of sources may actually be too large for most people to comprehend any source very well. Convergence creates a benefit by bringing more resources to important information and more platforms to the distribution of that information.

Thirty years ago, it took months for the public to even give a passing nod to what was considered one of the biggest stories of the time: the Watergate scandal. What began as an innocuous little burglary was revealed to be a conspiracy of national implications, ultimately toppling a president.[14] But even after the *Washington Post* broke the initial cover-up, many media outlets let the story pass for weeks . . . competition held them back from reporting someone else's story. This was the result of big media wanting to make every story its own, a premise that wafts through all news organizations even today. But how does adding converged operations to that equation change the likelihood that a number of voices will be stilled?

We must remember that society is locked in a neverending struggle for control from multiple sources. The expectation that democracy is anything other than an ongoing struggle is an oversimplified vision. Any good republic, whether masked as democracy or not, will be at odds with itself. For instance, McCarthyism took place in a post-war era when there were certainly adequate voices to put a stop to the red-baiting of the late '40s and early '50s, but the social consequences and potential risks kept people away from the issue but not the voices. Pacifica Broadcasting had called early on for the end of the hearings, but it took substantially more clout from the likes of Edward R. Murrow and major newspapers to end the witch hunt.[15]

American society, the source of much of the concern on convergence, prides itself on the tension between competing viewpoints. Capitalism and socialism generally represent two ends of a very long continuum on how many believe a society should act. Whether based on Adam Smith's notion of an "invisible hand" in the marketplace or Karl Marx's proletariat concept, people are allowed differing views. Still, the very expectation of difference creates change. How changes are valued, however, remains in the eye of the beholder. The struggle is ongoing, as it should be.[16]

The key to making convergence a powerful force for good is to require it to work for the public, not simply for the corporate shareholders. Those shareholders offer only one facet of the stakeholders group, and all stakeholders are best served when companies are willing to engage in convergence for news effectiveness' sake and not just to create short-term improvements to the bottom line.

Allowed to foster and grow, convergence could help redevelop public awareness of important issues. Today, television is overcrowded with news stories on crime, traffic accidents and fluff.

Recently, a reporter told me that he had trained for television news and worked diligently to make his mark in smaller television markets as a tough, no-nonsense reporter. When he reached the top 20, that all changed. He was told that the emphasis was on performance—not news, not good storytelling, only image. Although he lamented the situation, he readily admitted that he was being paid extremely well and still enjoyed most of the work—it just wasn't what he generally thought of as news.

Will convergence bring news reporting back to television? Some think so; others aren't so sure. As a method of news delivery, television is a powerful medium, still somewhat unfulfilled from the promise of its early days. As a journalistic venture, it sometimes has power, sometimes not.

Eighteenth-century English statesman Edmund Burke is credited with calling the printed press the "fourth estate."[17] He pointed to the press gallery in the House of Commons and said that the press was the most powerful group in the room, even more important than the Lords and the House of Commons. Now, 250 years later, one wonders how that power has continued.

Integrated Media: Convergence's Children

If convergence, as presently contrived, isn't working, what will? Several alternatives fill the landscape, but I would like to put forth a new method for developing integrated, rather than converged, media. Integrated media, as pointed out in earlier chapters, is the final genetic iteration in the evolution of convergence. It is a fully integrated news source with value at the local, national and international levels. It is news and information that is both compelling and offers near-immediate access to all who possess the appropriate technology.

To put forth a new model is somewhat daunting, but bear with the process. First, it is necessary that media owners recognize the impact of news and information on society. Second, it is absolutely essential that media owners are willing to invest in the futures of their currently non-converged or partially converged operations with the understanding that the changes that take place in those organizations will take time. It will also take money—money that may not be recouped for years.

With the preliminaries agreed to, media organizations will need to look at the platforms currently being groomed for integration and ensure that all are *equal* partners in any venture. Of the more than 60 converged news operations in the United States today, only a handful are truly converged or converging (see Chapter 3).[18] Having said that, it is necessary to understand that the venture is not aimed directly at current properties but at creating new and integrated properties from both the resources of those current properties and from new investment. From an organizational view, these operations will be entrepreneurial, non-aligned and independent from other information organizations in control of the parent company;

however, resources from existing operations will be made available to the newly integrated venues. Simply put, the organization forms an integrated media incubator.

More than 20 years ago, American businesses began the concept of incubator sites when technology and competition outran businesses' abilities to cope with their available material and personnel. Traditional, mature organizations were too weighted down with one set of expectations and cultures to branch out into new ventures. Today, media organizations face the same dilemma—move forward, die or at the least, retreat into minimalism. Create new products based on a new vision of the industry and do it with exceptional levels of excellence. This approach will create a series of doable entrepreneurial enterprises in targeted markets. It will also lead to increased flexibility in the marketplace and a strategic placement for future media products.

To get there, several activities need to be undertaken simultaneously on broadcasting, print and Internet platforms. Because of the regulatory climate, broadcasting should view the integrated opportunity as one of channel selection. As broadcasting moves from analog to digital transmission, media owners should assign one (and perhaps two) of the four digital channels to the integrated effort. This obviously creates a short-term loss of revenue, as the new mediated outlet will need to gain audience. Because appointment television is already in the throes of audience loss, however, the expectation is that the diversity of channel offerings will continue this overall erosion. Owners need to take risks. This means that stockholders need to be prepared for the coming changes. Risk is needed to break new ground.

Without convergence, information media will survive in a stilted fashion. Audiences will travel to other sources of information. Broadcast news will become a stepchild without portfolio—undervalued and underfunded. As pointed out earlier, media doesn't die, but it does change. Changes will take place whether they are supported by the old guard or not. Old rules and old thinking should be tossed out now rather than later. Fearing this, those perceptions should, at the very least, be reevaluated.

Incubators also would help converging partnerships in which the platforms were not owned by a single entity. Companies with major holdings in broadcasting and companies with major newspaper holdings could form joint ventures that operate independently of either parent company. These subsidiary news operations would then provide news content to the parents while also providing original content to their own platforms.

Without Frontiers

The concept that has brought us to this point is that of integrating existing technologies to provide information to the public through its venue of choice: print, broadcast or Internet. However, this is not the correct long-term view to be taken.

The future is different than it is conceived by convergence. Why should a family rely on standard communications systems to bring them news and information when new media are available and will soon become the mainstay of American information selection? For a time, we may need to access the Internet through existing telecommunications technology, but that doesn't mean people will have a long-term need to use those technologies in a converged atmosphere.

In 1980, most of the media world laughed at Ted Turner when he launched CNN as a 24-hour cable television news network. At the time, cable was a cheap entrée into the world of media programming.[19] Major companies already were buying up the broadcast media. Overvalued stations were cropping up throughout the United States and the rest of the globe. Turner took a risk. Although a great deal of disagreement exists about the outcome of Turner's venture, the need to take similar risks exists today on the Internet and World Wide Web.

It is possible today to create a combined media experience that will function with all of the interconnectivity sought by those who would converge. The upfront costs of creating Internet newsrooms around the country without the need for printing presses, broadcast facilities or licenses is much lower than attempting a startup in one of those industries alone. It comes back to risk. Who will take the risk?

What would a 24-hour newsroom that was built solely on the need for servers, graphics generators, digital imaging equipment, cameras and computers look like? Some of these newsrooms exist now, but their emphasis is primarily an extension of the print platform revamped to the Internet.

How would professionally trained news people function in cyberspace? Would they function differently than news people in any other platform? Would journalism refocus itself and use well-established ethical principles to gain viewers and readers? Would seeking "understanding and truth" of issues first rather than "what sells" reposition journalism? These are very interesting questions.

Without the tether of regulation, these newsrooms would operate freely. With low overhead and expenses, more investment could be utilized in creating exceptional products. Without ratings, reporters could (at least theoretically) take more time with important stories, knowing those stories could be posted to the Web organization immediately (at least until new deadline pressures were created) once completed.

These are interesting concepts, and they have been tossed around by a number of experts over the years. Startup costs, the need to train people into the system, and the marketing associated with drawing an audience would still exist. Still, the idea is tempting. Journalists tired of working through the restraints of inflexible organizations could bind together and form new information systems and frontiers. Once again, who will take the risks?

Regulatory indecisiveness today may actually lead to journalists adopting this path for the future of the field. Convergence makes sense. Universities are now training individuals in a multi-platform environment. Those who wish to move in that direction will have opportunities for cooperation that are not available in traditional media. Perhaps a new world journalism order is on its way simply because government is incapable of taking action. The Internet already is considered a bit of the Wild West, and the individuals willing to settle that Wild West from a journalistic standpoint will find value in their efforts.

Pavlik notes that the future characteristics of television may be such that it exists in multiple-access platforms.[20] Pavlik sees traditional terrestrial broadcast television providing the bulk of entertainment programming because it is not tethered to limits of bandwidth. Meanwhile, news will seek its own position on the technological spectrum.

Convergence Management Redux

The purpose of this book has been to explore the new frontier of managing media convergence. Through these pages, a great deal of discussion has taken place along with the positioning of a variety of ideas about the shape of future media. Still, it is important to bring the actions into focus.

Media is changing. Elements of change raise questions and fears among the heartiest of souls. Rolland writes that convergence is still in a pre-paradigmatic stage, similar to stages identified by Thomas Kuhn.[21] He calls for a search for clarification before diving into the confusing cacophony of ideas and issues that have not been resolved well enough to ensure profitability in the new sector.

Rolland therefore calls for creating value through the examination of the dimensions of convergence. He believes five or six convergence dimensions exist, based on the findings of the Norwegian Convergence Committee and the work of M. Fransman. The group created by the commission is most easily understood and includes service convergence, network convergence, terminal convergence and market convergence.[22]

Service convergence is defined as the interchange between forms, formats and interactivity. Network convergence includes the integration of all electronic services along the same transmission network (i.e., cable, telephony and Internet). Terminal convergence is the integration of terminals such as personal computers, televisions and telephones (as discussed earlier in this chapter). Market convergence refers to the infiltration of previously separate market economy segments into each other, resulting in larger and larger mergers and acquisitions. Rolland posits yet another convergence activity—that of value creation.

Each of these dimensions is interrelated. One sphere does not change without changes occurring to the other spheres. That premise is of utmost importance in understanding why defining convergence remains a daunting exercise. It is also why this book has attempted to work only from the perspectives of journalism and the influences of convergence on the field.

From the manager's view then, we must constantly be on the watch and understand that convergence, regardless of the component in which you are preparing strategies, is holistic in nature. Like molecular configuration, you cannot change one electron without influencing the element's entire atomic configuration.

If we think of management from a systems approach, we must understand that the nature of one part of the organism influences the entire organism. Changes in regulatory requirements will influence future development of the goods and service outputs of convergence. Changes in technology will influence the public's adoption of that technology. Changes in media size will influence government and non-government approaches to social reform in the name of convergence.

For managers, the task is to create balance in chaos. Earlier, we discussed some of those tasks, but it should be remembered that our goal is to improve the management of one unit of change—that of the journalist. Creating this balance requires first that we understand the complexities of the systems we are attempting to change. News managers must grasp the basics of electronic transmission systems, whether they are traditional broadcast, cable, Internet or satellite. Managers also must understand that various platforms will require employing various skill sets and will involve various levels of risk for both the manager and the journalist. In addition, market conditions and investors must be taken into account to ensure that the converged operation is profitable or moving toward profitability.

The art and competency of the media manager is in the individual's understanding of these issues and in his or her determination to see the organization through these issues to whatever outcome occurs for the converged news operation. Depending on the organization, the emphasis will shift. Some news operations may look like sophisticated multi-platform news services. Others may emphasize online story access coupled with traditional broadcast and print media.

Change is the currency; it is the arbiter of today's journalism. Management decisions will be made on how those changes take place. News managers should choose their courses of action wisely, but they also should be willing to encounter the risks necessary to create the new value opportunities inherent in convergence.

Society and Convergence

Society has changed dramatically in the United States in the past 50 years. Parking lots at high schools now take up more space than the schools themselves. In some locations, preschoolers have homework and grade school children are encountering back troubles from carrying packs of books to and from school each day.

At the same time, students play more video games, read fewer novels and enjoy online activities at a much higher level than their parents. Childhood obesity is at an all-time high, and social interaction seems more cumbersome and tied up in popularity at an ever-younger age. Some would blame the media for this.

Others blame the media for all sorts of things. Convergence is blamed for destroying voices that are already diminished by big media, but the evidence is unclear. In the distant past, voices were determined by who owned the press, but as new media formats were invented (radio, television, the Internet), developed and cast on the public landscape, the expectation of diverse voices became higher.

Innis argued that media technologies themselves change society. From stone tablets, to papyrus, to the moving press, to broadcasting and now the Internet, the argument is that when media change, people and societies change. Meyrowitz calls these scholars "medium theorists."[23]

As these mediums are introduced and embraced by cultures, the cultures are changed and somewhat reorganized around the new medium. If this is indeed true, then the introduction of the Internet, in and of itself, will change the nature of cultures. How-then-should society proceed?

Mankind has ways of adapting and adopting. Without going into the evolutionary aspects of each medium period, it is evident that adaptation takes place with adoption of these technologies. Change again will take place.

The challenge for managers, for journalists, for new technology gurus then, is to examine how these changes will help and hinder society. Where the technology advances the society in terms of richness in learning, understanding and embracing the ideas of others, it should be pointed out. Where the new medium fails society, as in the destruction of appropriate social values, the improper institution of a new political or information hierarchy, or the undermining of universal goals, these failings also should be pointed out. Yet all of these should be looked on with balance. Rarely does a society move forward without change.

Advancements in media-directed technology should therefore not be lamented by scholars and ne'er-do-wells as the destruction of society and the elimination of voices; rather, all of these individuals and groups need to understand that media is changed . . . not changing. The fundamental changes have taken place; we simply need to recognize those changes and turn to new ways of thinking.

In the end, we should remember what Cicero told us: "Time destroys the speculations of man, but it confirms the judgment of nature." What nature will bring, we await.

Exercises

1. Read about the influences of the invention of the movable type printing press. How did that change society? Then read about the history of radio. How did that change society? Based on these histories, what can we expect from new media and convergence?
2. What concerns should be raised by managers as they enter into the management of convergence? Is there one best way to assess the risks involved with converging media?
3. If journalism is to prosper in convergence, how do you suppose managers should work to find journalists willing to take the risks of working in the new medium?

Notes

Chapter 1

1 *Holy Bible.* (1972). Old Testament [King James Version]. p. 6. Thomas Nelson.
2 Bagdikian, B. (2000). *The media monopoly* (6th ed.). Boston, MA: Beacon Press.
3 McChesney, R. (2001, October 25). Policing the thinkable. Online debate at OpenDemocracy.net, available at http://www.opendemocracy.net/articles/ViewPopUpArticle.jsp?id=8&articleId=56
4 Ibid., 14th paragraph.
5 Rankings are available from a variety of sources, including but not limited to *Broadcasting and Cable Magazine*, annual Top 25 Media Companies report; others online at Media Information Center: http://www.mediainfocenter.org/top50Companies/ and http://www.thenation.com/special/bigten.html
6 Gibson, O. (2003, October 8). Vivendi finalises NBC Universal deal. *The Guardian.*
7 News Corporation Ltd. (2003, December 22). *News corporation, GM and Hughes complete Hughes transactions.* [News Release about DirectTV acquisition.] Available online at http://newscorp.com/index2.html
8 The *New York Times* wire service. (2004, February 12). Reprinted in *Tampa Tribune*, p. 1.
9 Benjamin Compaine notes that the ownership of the media in the United States is "extremely" democratic. See Compaine, B. (2001, August 11). The myths of encroaching global media ownership. Online debate at OpenDemocracy.net, available at http://www.opendemocracy.net/articles/ViewPopUpArticle.jsp?id=8&articleId=87
10 Demers, D. (2002). *Global media: Menace or messiah?* (Rev. ed.). Cresskill, NJ: Hampton Press.
11 Online NewsHour [Web site of *The NewsHour with Jim Lehrer*]. (2003, September 19). *AOL dropped from Time Warner name*. Retrieved from http://www.pbs.org/newshour/bb/business/aol_time_index.html
12 "Comcast makes hostile bid for Disney," The Associated Press. Retrieved 12 Feb. 2004 from http://www.msnbc.com
13 Compaine, B. (2001, August 11). The myths of encroaching global media ownership. Online debate at OpenDemocracy.net, available at http://www.opendemocracy.net/articles/ViewPopUpArticle.jsp?id=8&articleId=87

14 Ibid.

15 For instance, both WGN and WTBS (now TBS Superstation) have dropped their licenses for cable representation only.

16 Shi, M. (1995). *Sky TV.* Unpublished paper, University of Tennessee.

17 Demers.

18 Including 340,000 signatures collected by MoveOn.org through a massive Internet campaign. This was reported in a variety of publications, including *Columbia Journalism Review*, November/December, 2003, p. 20. *See also* Flint, M., & Flint, J. (2003, October 15). Station break: Behind media-ownership fight, an old power struggle is raging. Wall Street Journal, p. 1.

19 Epstein, E. (2003, October 14). Congress tries to put clamps on media mergers—Anger at FCC ruling brings calls for laws, but satisfying Bush, both houses difficult. *San Francisco Chronicle*, p. A6.

20 Houseley, W., Nicholls, T., & Southwell, R. (2001). *Managing in the media.* P. Block (Ed.). Oxford, England: Focal Press.

21 Williams, D. (2002, September). Synergy bias: Conglomerates and promotion in the news. *Journal of Broadcasting and Electronic Media.*

22 Ó Siochrú, S., & Girard, B. (2002). *Global media governance: A beginner's guide.* Lanham, MD: Rowman & Littlefield.

23 Popcorn, F., & Hanft, A. (2001). *A Dictionary of the future.* New York: Hyperion.

24 Information illustrated via the United Nations' organizational chart at http://unitednations.com

25 Freelance writer Stephanie Ragusso in interview in Tampa, FL, 2 February 2004.

26 Levin, J. (2003). Cross-media ownership: The debate continues. *Australian Screen Education*, 32, 39.

27 Selva, M. (2003, June 29). House of Lords wants communication bill to stop some media takeovers. *Knight Ridder Tribune Business News*, p. 1.

28 Waisbord, S. (2002, February 27). *Grandes gigantes:* Media concentration in Latin America. Online debate at OpenDemocracy.net, available at http://www.opendemocracy.net/articles/ViewPopUpArticle.jsp?id=8&articleId=64

29 Noll, A. M. (2003, Spring). The myth of convergence. *The International Journal on Media Management*, 5(1).

Chapter 2

1 Meeting on the campus of the University of South Florida, Tampa, FL, between School of Mass Communications faculty members and representatives of Media General, Inc.

2 Gorney, C. (2002). *The business of news: A challenge for journalism's next generation.* New York: Carnegie Corporation.

3 Networks not watching idly as viewing habits change. (2003, November 2002). *Wall Street Journal newswire*, via MoneySense, *Tampa Tribune*, p. 7.

4 Ibid.

5 More than twice as many magazine titles exist today than in 1975, and revenues are more than 10 times higher than for that period. See http://www.mediainfocenter.org/outlets/

6 *USA Today* is now the largest daily newspaper in the United States but was much maligned in its early years and took a substantial number of years to turn a profit. *Source:
Editor & Publisher*, Audit Bureau of Circulation MediaInfoCenter, 2002. http:medi-
ainfocenter.org/newspaper/data/top_20_daily_news.asp

7 Potter, D. (2002, July–August). The body count: Want to know why local TV news is
thin? Just look at the number of staffers. *American Journalism Review*, 24, 60.

8 Ibid.

9 The number of daily newspapers has fluctuated between 1400 and 1500 but is declining slowly. Daily average circulation is about 54,000. Source: E & P, NAA Market and
Business Analysis Department, 2002.

10 Pavlik, J. V. (2001). *Journalism and new media*. New York: Columbia University Press.

11 Hansell, S. (2003, December 23). Internet advertising thrives on targeted ads. *New York
Times*, p. C6. *See also* Industry hits ad spending target 12 months early. (2003, December 18). *NewMediaAge*, p. 1.

12 Bettig, R. V., & Hall, J. L. (2003). *Big media, big money: Cultural texts and political
economics*. Lanham, MD: Rowman & Littlefield.

13 Nace, T. (2002). *Gangs of America: The rise of corporate power and the disabling of
democracy*. San Francisco: Berrett-Koehler.

14 Bagdikian, B. (2000). *The media monopoly*. Boston, MA: Beacon Press. *See also* McChesney, R. (2001, October 25). Policing the thinkable. Online debate at OpenDemoc-
racy.net, available at http://www.opendemocracy.net/articles/ViewPopUpArticle
.jsp?id=8&articleId=56

15 Bolles, as president of the American Society of Newspaper Editors between 1924 and
1928, wrote a series of articles for *ASNE Reports* detailing the fears of small newspapers as chain ownership began to flourish throughout the United States' major cities.

16 Associated Press, The. (11 February 2004). Comcast makes hostile bid for Disney. Retrieved February 12, 2004, from http://www.msnbc.msn.com/id/42397/39/

17 Jennings, P. (2003, November). Remarks during town meeting at the University of
South Florida, Tampa, FL.

18 At the time of publication, the Federal Communications Commission was in the midst
of a series of hearings on "localism." The hearings were the result of the backlash from
its rescinding of cross-ownership rules in June 2003.

19 Miller, R. (2002, March). The Frankenstein syndrome: The creation of mega-media
conglomerates and ethical modeling in journalism. *Journal of Business Ethics*, 36(1/2),
105–110.

20 Williams, D. (2002, September). Synergy bias: Conglomerates and promotion in the
news. *Journal of Broadcasting and Electronic Media*.

21 Shoemaker, P. J., & Reese, S. D. (1996). *Mediating the message: Theories and influences on mass media content*. White Plains, NY: Longman.

22 Thelan, G. (2003, August). Remarks at retreat for School of Mass Communications,
University of South Florida.

23 Pavlik, J. (2001) Journalism and new media. New York: Columbia University Press.
See pp.106–109.

24 Potter.

25 Lehrer, J. (2002, September). *Returning to our roots*. The Red Smith Lecture in Journalism, John W. Gallivan Program in Journalism, Ethics and Democracy, University of
Notre Dame.

26 Pew Research Center for the People and the Press. (1999). *Striking the balance* [periodic review of the press]. See pp. 1–3.
27 In February 2004, 11-year-old Carlie Brucia was kidnapped and murdered in Sarasota, Florida. A security camera caught the abduction on videotape. The short and rather non-compelling video ran extensively on local, regional and national television for more than a month. On the upside, the extensive coverage did result in changes to the state's parole violation review system.
28 Cohen is essentially credited with wrapping together a variety of earlier research to produce one of the most quotable statements in mass communications research history. Cohen, B. (1963). *The press and foreign policy.* Princeton, NJ: Princeton University Press (see p. 13). *See also* McCombs, M., & Shaw, D. (1972). The agenda-setting function of mass media. *Public Opinion Quarterly*, 36, 176–187.
29 This is a general position taken as agenda-setting research pursues second-level agenda-setting factors. See (among others) McCombs, M., Shaw, D., & Weaver, D. (Eds.). (1997). *Communication and democracy: Exploring the intellectual frontiers of agenda-setting theory.* Mahwah, NJ: Lawrence Erlbaum.
30 Compaine, B. (2001, August 11). The myths of encroaching global media ownership. Online debate at OpenDemocracy.net, available at http://www.opendemocracy.net/articles/ViewPopUpArticle.jsp?id=8&articleId=87 (See paragraph 13.) A variety of other sources also have discussed what the next generation of journalists will look like. This book attempts to reflect somewhat on that issue.

Chapter 3

1 Shoemaker, P. J., & Reese, S. D. (1996). *Mediating the message: Theories and influences on mass media content.* White Plains, NY: Longman. See p. 145.
2 Of specific interest is Marca in Spain. Quinn points out that reporters at this operation focus on writing rather than on subjects, allowing them to work in various platforms. See Quinn, S. (2004, March 6). *Convergence's fundamental question.* Paper presented at the Southeast Colloquium of the Association for Education in Journalism and Mass Communications, Tampa, FL.
3 R. Gremillion. Remarks during personal interview in his office at the *Sun-Sentinel*, Fort Lauderdale, FL, October 2003.
4 Daily, L., Demo, L., & Spillman, M. (2003, July–August). *The convergence continuum: A model for studying collaboration between media newsrooms.* Paper presented at the annual convention of the Association for Education in Journalism and Mass Communication, Kansas City, MO.
5 Moses, L. (2003, June 30). Coming up for air. *Editor & Publisher*, 14–20.
6 Specifically, the *Sun-Sentinel* creates separate inside pages for promoting each partner station. These partnering promotions are then targeted to the particular DMA in which the television station broadcasts, using zip codes and targeted sections.
7 Larry Daily et al.
8 Ibid.
9 Ibid.
10 Thelan, G. (2003, August). Remarks at retreat for School of Mass Communications, University of South Florida.

11 R. Gremillion, personal interview.
12 Sohn, A., Wicks, J., Lacy, S., & Sylvie, G. (1999). *Media management: A casebook approach* (2nd ed.). Mahwah, NJ: Erlbaum.
13 Ibid.
14 Killebrew, K. C. (1993). *Management styles among mass media editors: A comparative study between SYMLOG and symbolic convergence theories.* Unpublished thesis, Illinois State University.
15 Redmond, J., & Trager, R. (2004). *Balancing on the wire: The art of media organizations* (2nd ed.). Boulder, CO: Coursewise. See p. 67.
16 Zavonia, S., & Reichert, T. (2000). Media convergence/management change: The evolving workflow of visual journalists. *The Journal of Media Economics*, 13(2), 143–151.
17 R. Gremillion, personal interview.

Chapter 4

1 Smith's work was based on economic philosophies developed by a variety of groups in Europe, including the notions of a group called Physiocrats, who believed that the economic system produced harmony even though each individual acted in his or her own selfish interest. In Lancaster, K. (1973). *Macroeconomics: Modern economics, principles and policy.* Chicago: Rand McNally & Company (p. 6).
2 Albarran, A. (1996). Media economics: *Understanding markets, industries and concepts.* Ames: Iowa State University Press.
3 Taylor, F. (1947). *Scientific Management.* New York: Harper.
4 Ibid.
5 Fayol, H. *General and industrial management.* (C. Storrs, Trans.). Sir Isaac Pitman and Sons, 1965. (Original work published 1949.)
6 Weber, M. *The theory of social and economic organization.* (A. M. Henderson & T. Parsons, Trans.). New York: The Free Press, 1947. (Original work published in 1921.)
7 Redmond, J., & Trager, R. (2004). *Balancing on the wire: The art of media organizations* (2nd ed.). Boulder, CO: Coursewise. See p. 43.
8 Ibid., pp. 45–46.
9 Ibid., p. 75.
10 Pringle, P., Starr, M., & McCavitt, W. (1999). *Electronic Media Management* (4th ed.). Woburn, MA: Focal Press. See p. 8.
11 Sohn, A., Wicks, J., Lacy, S., & Sylvie, G. (1999). *Media management: A casebook approach* (2nd ed.). Mahwah, NJ: Erlbaum. See pp. 93–94.
12 Ibid., pp. 94.
13 Redmond and Trager, pp. 129–130. Some have criticized management by objective for an over-emphasis on the outputs rather than the creative process, particularly in work environments such as those of journalists. This will be discussed further in Chapters 5 and 6.
14 Sohn et al. pp. 35–47.
15 Pringle et al. pp. 10–11.
16 Redmond & Trager, pp. 111–114

17 Ibid., pp. 53–54.
18 This is drawn from a number of sources including but not limited to Spitzberg, B. H., & Cupach, W. R. (1984). *Interpersonal communication competence.* Beverly Hills, CA: Sage. *Also see* Saral, T. B. (1979). Intercultural communication theory and research: An overview of challenges and opportunities. *Communication Yearbook 3.*
19 Eisenberg, E., & Goodall, H. L. (2004). *Organizational communication* (4th ed.). Boston: Bedford/St. Martins Press. Primarily pp. 168–170 for this discussion.
20 Redmond & Trager, pp. 73–74.
21 From Katz et al. *Writers on ethics: Classic and cultural*, pp. 174–178. Aristotle translated by F.W. Peters (no date given). 1962.
22 Ibid, p. 40, most notably expressed by St. Augustine (among others).
23 Among major philosophers not covered here, but a part of the early period of ethical system development and of note, are Seneca and Thomas Hobbes.
24 Katz et al., pp. 42–90.
25 Ibid., pp. 107–150.
26 Albarran, A. (2002). *Management of electronic media* (2nd ed.). Belmont, CA: Wadsworth.
27 Katz et al., pp. 573–614. *See* especially Dewey's "Continuum of ends-means."
28 Albarran, 2002.

Chapter 5

1 Bolman, L., & Deal, T. (2003). *Reframing organizations: Artistry, choice and leadership.* San Francisco: Jossey-Bass.
2 Etzioni, A. (1975). *A comparative analysis of complex organizations.* Free Press.
3 Bolman and Deal
4 Sohn, A., Wicks, J., Lacy, S., & Sylvie, G. (1999). *Media management: A casebook approach* (2nd ed.). Mahwah, NJ: Erlbaum. See pp. 62–66.
5 Powers, A., & Lacy, S. (1992). A model of job satisfaction in local television news. In S. Lacy, A. Sohn, & R. Giles (Eds.), *Readings in media management.* Columbia, SC: Association for Education in Journalism and Mass Communication.
6 Redmond, J., & Trager, R. (2004). *Balancing on the wire: The art of media organizations* (2nd ed.). Boulder, CO: Coursewise. See p. 67.
7 Zavonia, S., & Reichert, T. (2000). Media convergence/management change: The evolving workflow of visual journalists. *The Journal of Media Economics*, 13(2), 143–151.
8 Chan-Olmsted, S. (1998). Mergers, acquisitions, and convergence: The strategic alliances of broadcasting, cable television, and telephone services. *The Journal of Media Economics*, 11(3), 33–46.
9 Legare, T. L. (1998). The human side of mergers and acquisitions. *Human Resource Planning*, 21(1), 32–41.
10 Argyris, C. (1993). *Knowledge for action: A guide to overcoming barriers to organizational change.* San Francisco: Jossey-Bass.
11 Lewin, K. (1947). Group decision and social change. In T. N. Newcomb & E. L. Hartley (Eds.), *Readings In Social Psychology.* Troy, MO: Holt, Rinehart and Winston.
12 Nahavandi, A., & Malekzadeh, A. (1988). Acculturation in mergers and acquisitions. *Academy of Management Review*, 13, 79–90.

13 Ibid.
14 Weber, M. (1947). *The theory of economic and social organization* (A. M. Henderson & T. Parsons, Trans.). New York: Free Press. (Original work published 1921.)
15 Dose, J. J. (1997, September). Work Values: An Integrative framework and illustrative application to organizational socialization. *Journal of Occupational and Organizational Psychology*, 70(3), p. 227.
16 Rokeach, M. (1973). *The nature of human values.* New York: Free Press. *See* pp. 17–18.
17 Poole, S., & McPhee, R. D. (1983). A structurational analysis of organizational climate. In L. L. Putnam & M. E. Pacanowsky (Eds.), *Communication and organizations: An interpretive approach.* Newbury Park, CA: Sage. See p. 95.
18 Pavlik, J. (2001). *Journalism and new media.* New York: Columbia University Press. See p. 3.
19 Indeed, other research methods, including forced-choice approaches like Q-sorts, should prove valuable in identifying structures and various levels of structure.
20 Bolman and Deal, pp. 144–160.
21 R. Gremillion. Remarks during personal interview in his office at *Sun Sentinel*, Fort Lauderdale, FL. October 2003.

Chapter 6

1 Among others, *see* Jackson, D. (2000). *Becoming dynamic: Creating and sustaining a dynamic organisation.* New York: St. Martin's Press; Proctor, T. (1995). *The essence of management creativity* (A. Buckley, Series Ed.). London: Prentice Hall; and Gamache, R. D., & Kuhn, L. (1989). *The creativity infusion: How managers can start and sustain creativity and innovation.* New York: Harper & Row.
2 Pavlik, J. (2001). *Journalism and new media.* New York: Columbia University Press.
3 Gamache & Kuhn, p. *xi.*
4 Redmond, J., & Trager, R. (2004). *Balancing on the wire: The art of media organizations* (2nd ed.). Boulder, CO: Coursewise. See p. 128.
5 Coffey, S., III. (2003). *Best practices: The art of leadership in news organizations.* Arlington, VA: Freedom Forum. See p. 74.
6 Ibid., p. 73.
7 Eisenberg, E., & Goodall, H. L., Jr. (2004). *Organizational communication* (4th ed.). Boston: Bedford/St. Martin's Press. Primarily pp. 329–334 for this discussion.
8 Drazin, R., Glynn, M. A., & Kazanijian. (1999, April). Multilevel theorizing about creativity in organizations: A sensemaking perspective. *Academy of Management Review*, 24(2), 286–307.
9 Price Waterhouse Change Integration Team. (1996). *The paradox principles: How high performance companies manage chaos, complexity and contradiction to achieve superior results.* Price Waterhouse LLP. See pp. 69–79.
10 In most scenarios, change is a component to be accounted for in organizational learning methods. Several authors are presented here, and others should be noted, including
11 Schein, E. (1996, Fall). Three cultures of management: The key to organizational learning. *Sloan Management Review*, 38(1), 9–12.

12 Gherardi, S. (2002). Organizational leaning. In A. Sorge (Ed.), *Organization* (pp. 419–431). London: Thomson Learning.

13 Schein, E. (1997). *Organizational culture and leadership.* San Francisco: Jossey-Bass. See p. 363.

14 Burke, W. W. (2002). *Organization change: Theory and practice.* Thousand Oaks, CA: Sage (see pp. 28–32). See also Bussing, A. (2002). Motivation and satisfaction. In A. Sorge (Ed.), *Organization.* London: Thomson Learning.

15 The Paradox Principles, pp. 23–59.

Chapter 7

1 This discussion is based on a variety of sources, some specific and some less so. Among those that contribute to the conclusions set forth are Stephens, M. (1998). A history of news. New York: Penguin Books and Bogart, L. (1981). *Press and public: Who reads what, when, where, and why in American newspapers.* Hillsdale, NJ: Lawrence Erlbaum.

2 Fang, I. (1972). *Television news.* New York: Hastings House. Among the classics in the early teaching of broadcast news, Fang's book outlines the conditions of the industry at the time of its publication.

3 See notes 1 and 2. Additionally, my experience as both a print and broadcast journalist contribute to this assessment.

4 Mumby, D. (1987). The political function of narrative in organizations. *Communications Monographs, 54,* 113–127.

5 Foucault, M. (1977). *Discipline and punish: The birth of the prison.* Harmondsworth: Penguin. These notions are reiterated and clarified in several later works, including Foucault, M. (1986). Disciplinary power and subjugation. In S. Lukes (Ed.), *Power* (pp. 229–241). Oxford, England: Blackwell.

6 Bolman, L., & Deal, T. (2003). *Reframing organizations: Artistry, choice and leadership.* San Francisco: Jossey-Bass.

7 Ibid.

8 Alderfer, C. (1972). *Existence, relatedness and growth: Human needs in organizational settings.* New York: Free Press. This specifically relates to what is often termed "Alderfer's E-R-G theory" and creating coalitions within the organization.

9 Isolation is a time-honored philosophy in newsrooms. It is often used as form of control because of the levels of informal control that exist in news organizations.

10 Bolman & Deal, p. 377.

11 Gentry, James. Web site rating various news outlets in the country regarding their involvement in convergence activities. As of mid-February 2004, about 60 news organizations were listed as converged. Nearly 100 of their advertising and promotions activities were listed as converged. These would not meet the strict levels of convergence as defined in Chapter 3 but are still somewhat interconnected in nature.

12 Media General suffered the consequences of this when it encountered difficulty hiring new reporters for the *Tampa Tribune* and required them to become converged journalists. A number of vacancies remained open for more than a year until the organization abandoned the policy in favor of media partnering.

13 Gamache, R. D., & Kuhn, R. L. (1989). *The creativity infusion: How managers can start and sustain creativity and innovation.* New York: Harper & Row.

14 Jackson, D. (2000). *Becoming dynamic: Creating and sustaining a dynamic organisation.* New York: St. Martin's Press.

15 Eisenberg, E, & Goodall, H. L., Jr. (2004). *Organizational communication: Balancing creativity and constraint* (4th ed.). Boston: Bedford/St. Martin's Press.

16 Price Waterhouse Change Integration Team. (1996). *The paradox principles: How high performance companies manage chaos, complexity and contradiction to achieve superior results.* Price Waterhouse LLP.

17 Lewin, K. (1947). Group decision and social change. In T. N. Newcomb & E. L. Hartley (Eds.), *Readings In Social Psychology.* Troy, MO: Holt, Rinehart and Winston.

18 Argyris, C. (1993). *Knowledge for action: A guide to overcoming barriers to organizational change.* San Francisco: Jossey-Bass. Argyris has a significant body of work examining the forces that influence the workplace.

19 Schein, E. (1997). *Organizational culture and leadership.* San Francisco: Jossey-Bass. See p. 388.

20 Deetz, S. (1991). *Democracy in an age of corporate colonization.* Albany, NY: SUNY Press. Reported in Eisenberg and Goodall.

21. Eisenberg and Goodall.

Chapter 8

1 Congress has had an "awakening" of sorts regarding broadcast regulation. The Federal Communications Commission rescinding the cross-ownership rules was halted by Congress in September 2003, but President Bush had not taken action on the issue. Meanwhile, feeling the pressure from Congress, the FCC began holding hearings around the country on "localism" issues evolving out of cross-ownership issues. Those hearings were to conclude in June 2004.

2 Quinn, S. (2004, March 6). *Convergence's fundamental question.* Paper presented at the Southeast Colloquium of the Association for Journalism and Mass Communications, Tampa, FL. Quinn notes that the Scandinavian nations are most generally ahead of all other nations in creating a true convergence model. See Chapter 3 for more on the definitions of convergence.

3 Ibid.

4 Aufderheide, P. (1999). Communications policy and the public interest. New York: Guilford Press. *See also* Smith, F. L., Meeske, M., & Wright, J. W., II. (1995). Electronic media and government. White Plains, NY: Longman.

5 Smith et al.

6 Report of the Federal Communications Commission. Filings by Media General, Inc., December 2001 and February 2002. Also Federal Communications Roundtable on Media Ownership Policies, 2002.

7 Beckerman, G. (2003, November/December). Tripping up big media. *Columbia Journalism Review,* 15–20.

8 Van Cuilenburg, J., & McQuail, D. (2003). Media policy paradigm shifts. *European Journal of Communication,* 18(2), 181–207.

9 Baker, C. E. (2002). *Media, markets and democracy.* Cambridge, UK: Cambridge University Press.

10 Ibid.

11 Ibid., p. 146.

12 Easton, E. B. (2000, Fall). Annotating the news: Mitigating the effects of media convergence and consolidation . *University of Arkansas at Little Rock Law Review,* 23.

13 Van Cuilenburg, J., & Verhoest, P. (1998). Free and equal access: In search of models for converging communication systems. *Telecommunications Policy,* 22(3), 171–181.

14 Lancaster, K. (1973). Macroeconomics: *Modern economics, principles and policy.* Chicago: Rand McNally & Company. See p. 6.

15 Information available online at http://www.mediainfocenter.org

16 Ó Siochrú, S., & Girard, B. (2002). *Global media governance: A beginner's guide.* Lanham, MD: Rowman & Littlefield.

Chapter 9

1 Dr. Marie Curkan-Flanagan spent more than two decades in television news, primarily with the Gannett Company. Since joining the faculty at the University of South Florida, she has been working to help students diversify content toward the use of open-ended games as tools for the dissemination of news. She works closely with several others at the Pew Center for Journalism Excellence in the pursuit of journalism's next wave.

2 Pavlik, J. (1998). *New media technology: Cultural and commercial perspectives.* Boston: Allyn & Bacon. *See* 352–357. *See also* pp. 20–22, Straubhaar, J., & LaRose, R. (1996). *Communications media in the information society.* Belmont, CA: Wadsworth.

3 Schrage, M. (2002). Is advertising finally dead? In E. P. Bucy (Ed.), *Living in the information age.* Belmont, CA: Wadsworth.

4 Both the International Association of Business Communicators and the Public Relations Society of America have extensive codes relating to ethical means of practitioner behaviors. Because they are independent organizations, some bias toward objectivity would be expected.

5 Stein, N. (2002). Slate vs. Salon: The leading online magazines struggle to get the Net. In E. P. Bucy (Ed.), *Living in the information age.* Belmont, CA: Wadsworth.

6 Schrage, p. 114.

7 Hansell, S. (2003, December 23). Internet advertising thrives on targeted ads. *New York Times,* p. C6. *See also* Industry hits ad spending target 12 months early. (2003, December 18). *NewMediaAge,* p. 1.

8 Winter, C. (2003, November 30). Christine Winter column. *South Florida Sun-Sentinel,* via *Knight Ridder Tribune Business News,* p. 1. Winter describes recovery attempts of retailers through the use of online Web services for customers.

9 Hansell.

10 The Internet is Back. (2003, December 29). *Los Angeles Times,* p.

11 Rothenberg, R. (1998, June). Bye-bye: The Net's accountability will kill not only traditional advertising, but parasite, big media. *Wired Magazine.*

12 A variety of authors have discussed how the new programming media will look and work. Among others, *see* pp.352–357, Pavlik, J. (1998). *New media technology: Cultural and commercial perspectives.* Boston: Allyn & Bacon.

13 Using gaming techniques, however, the viewer could see alternative endings to the story or overall changes in the plotline just by following the advertising link built into the original story background.

14 Robert Gremillion, president and publisher of the *South Florida Sun-Sentinel*, works through a variety of options with staff to ensure branding efforts work in his newspaper's split television market. (R. Gremillion. Remarks during personal interview in his office at the *Sun-Sentinel*, Fort Lauderdale, FL. October 2003.)

15 Among others who give headlines only via email are *The New York Times* and *Broadcasting & Cable Magazine.* The headlines are delivered via email; full text is available only through subscriptions.

16 *See* Pavlik. *Also see* Bucy, E. P. (2002). *Living in the information age.* Belmont, CA: Wadsworth.

17 Pavlik , pp. 346–348.

Chapter 10

1 *PC World.* That's digitainment, p. 104. January 2004.

2 Quinn, S. (2004, March 6). *Convergence's fundamental question.* Paper presented at the Southeast Colloquium of the Association for Journalism and Mass Communications, Tampa, FL.

3 *See* Inside cover, *PC Magazine*, January 2004.

4 *PC Magazine.* Pipeline, p. 25. January 2004.

5 Noll, A. M. (2003, Spring). The myth of convergence. *The International Journal on Media Management*, 5(1).

6 Dominick, J., Sherman, B., & Messere, F. (2000). *Broadcasting, cable, the Internet and beyond.* Boston: McGraw-Hill.

7 Ibid.

8 Ó Siochrú, S., & Girard, B. (2002). *Global media governance: A beginner's guide.* Lanham, MD: Rowman & Littlefield.

9 Appelbaum, S., Gandell, J., Yortyis, H., Proper, S., & Jobin, F. (2000). Anatomy of a merger: Behavior of organizational factors and processes throughout the pre– during– post-stages (part 1). *Management Decision, 38*(9).

10 Pavlik.

11 Robert Burns. Quote taken from *Forty thousand quotations: Prose and poetical.* Charles Douglas (Ed.). (1917). George Sully and Company.

12 Bagdikian, B. (2000). *The media monopoly* (6th ed.). Boston, MA: Beacon Press. *See also* McChesney, R. (1997). *Corporate media and the threat to democracy.* Seven Stories Press: The Open Media Pamphlet Series.

13 Demers, D. (2002). *Global media: Menace or messiah?* (Rev. ed.). Cresskill, NJ: Hampton Press.

14 Halberstam, D. (1979). *The powers that be.* New York: A Laurel Book published by Dell.

15 History of Pacifica Broadcasting, Web site www:http//pacifica.org/

16 Adam Smith, quoted on p. 6 of Lancaster, K. (1973). *Macroeconomics: Modern economics, principles and policy.* Chicago: Rand McNally & Company. *See also* Karl Marx. (1848). *The communist manifesto.*

17 Burke, cited in Benet, W. R. (1969). *The reader's encyclopedia.* New York: Thomas A. Crowell. Benet lists Burke as the first individual to refer to the press as the Fourth Estate.

18 Gentry, James. Web site rating various news outlets in the country regarding their involvement in convergence activities. As of mid-February 2004, about 60 news organizations were listed as converged.

19 Dominick et al.

20 Convergence Tracker Web page: http://www.americanpressinstitute.org/convergencetracker

21 Rolland, A. (2003, Spring). Convergence as strategy for value creation. *The International Journal on Media Management,* 5(1).

22 Thomas Kuhn.

23 Innis.

24 Meyrowitz, J. (2002). Medium theory. In E.K. Bucy, *Living in the information age.* Belmont, CA: Wadsworth.

Bibliography

Albarran, A. (1996). *Media economics: Understanding markets, industries and concepts.* Ames: Iowa State University Press.

Albarran, A. (2002). *Management of electronic media* (2nd ed.). Belmont, CA: Wadsworth.

Albarran, A., & Arrese, A. (2003). *Time and media markets.* Mahwah, NJ: Lawrence Erlbaum.

Albarran, A., & Chan-Olmsted, S. (Eds.) (1998). *Global media economics.* Ames: Iowa State University Press.

Alderfer, C. (1972). *Existence, relatedness and growth: Human needs in organizational settings.* New York: Free Press.

Alexander, A., Owers, J., & Carveth, R. (1998). *Media economics: Theory and practice.* Malwah, NJ: Lawrence Erlbaum.

Allen, C. (2001). *News is people: The rise of local TV news and the fall of news from New York.* Ames: Iowa State Press.

Amabile, T., & Conti, R. (1999). Changes in the work environment for creativity during downsizing. *Academy of Management Journal, 42(6), 630–640.*

Anderson, S. L., & Betz, N.E. (2001). Sources of social self-efficacy expectations: Their measurement and relations to career development. *Journal of Vocational Behavior,* 58, 98–117.

Andriopoulos, C. (2001). Determinants of organizational creativity. *Management Decision,* 39(10), 834–840.

Appelbaum, S.H., Gandell, J., Yortis, H., Proer, S., & Jobin, F. (2001). Anatomy of a merger: Behavior of organizational factors and processes throughout the pre– during– post-stages (part 1). *Management Decision Journal,* 38(9), 649–661.

Argyris, C. (1990). *Overcoming organizational defenses.* Boston: Allyn & Bacon.

Argyris, C. (1993). *Knowledge for action: A guide to overcoming barriers to organizational change.* San Francisco: Jossey-Bass.

Associated Press, The. (February 2004, 11). Comcast makes hostile bid for Disney. Retrieved February 12, 2004, from http://www.msnbc.msn.com/id/42397/39/

Aufderheide, P. (1999). *Communications policy and the public interest.* New York: Guilford Press.

Bagdikian, B. (2000). *The media monopoly*. Boston, MA: Beacon Press.

Baker, C. E. (2002). *Media, markets and democracy*. Cambridge, UK: Cambridge University Press.

Bales, R. F. (1988). A new overview of the SYMLOG system: Measuring and changing behavior in groups. In R. B. Polley, A. P. Hare, & P. J. Stone (Eds.), *The SYMLOG practitioner: Applications in small group research*. New York: Praeger.

Ballve, M. (2004, January 30). The battle for Latino media. *Hispanic Business*.

Bandura, A., Pastorelli, C., Barbaranelli, C., & Capara, G. U. (1999). Self-efficacy pathways in depression. *Journal of Personality and Social Psychology, 76*, 258–269.

Beckerman, G. (2003, November/December). Tripping up big media. *Columbia Journalism Review*, 15–20.

Berry, J.W. (1983). Acculturation: A comparative analysis of alternative forms. In R. J. Samuda & L. S. Woods (Eds.), *Perspectives in immigrant and minority education* (pp. 66–77). Lanham, MD: University Press of America.

Bettig, R. V., & Hall, J. L. (2003). *Big media, big money: Cultural texts and political economics*. Lanham, MD: Rowman & Littlefield.

Bokeno, M. (2000, November). Dialogic mentoring. *Management Communication Quarterly, 14*(2), 237–270.

Bolman, L., & Deal, T. (2003). *Reframing organizations: Artistry, choice and leadership*. San Francisco: Jossey-Bass.

Brandenburger, A., & Nalebuff, B. (1998). *Co-opetition*. New York: Doubleday.

Breu, K. (2001, Summer). The role of relevance of management cultures in the organisational transformation process. *International Studies of Management and Organisation*.

Bucy, E. P. (Ed.). (2002). *Living in the information age: A new media reader*. Belmont, CA: Wadsworth Group.

Burke, E. (1969). Address before British Parliament circa 1780. In W. R. Benet, *The Reader's Encyclopedia* (2nd ed.). New York: Thomas Crowell.

Burke, W. W. (2002). *Organization change: Theory and practice*. Thousand Oaks, CA: Sage.

Burns, R. (1917). Quote in C. Douglas (Ed.), *Forty thousand quotations: Prose and poetical*. George Sully and Company.

Burston, J. (2001, December 20). Lullaby of broadway? Big media and the future of commercial theatre. Online debate at OpenDemocracy.net, available at http://www.opendemocracy.net/articles/ViewPopUpArticle.jsp?id=*&articleID=33

Bussing, A. (2002). Motivation and satisfaction. In A. Sorge (Ed.), *Organization*. London: Thomson Learning.

Cameron, K., & Whetten, D. (1983). *Organizational effectiveness: A comparison of multiple models*. San Diego, CA: Academic Press.

Champlin, D., & Knoedler, J. (2002, June). Operating in the public interest or in pursuit of private profits? News in the age of media consolidation. *Journal of Economic Issues,* 36(2), 459–469.

Chan-Olmsted, S. (1998). Mergers, acquisitions, and convergence: The strategic alliances of broadcasting, cable television, and telephone services. *The Journal of Media Economics,* 11(3), 33–46.

Clegg, S. R. (2002). Power. In A. Sorge, (Ed.). *Organization.* London: Thomson Learning.

Clymer, A. (2003). *Journalism, security and the public interest: Best practices for reporting in unpredictable times.* Washington, DC: The Aspen Institute.

Coffey, S., III. (2003). *Best practices: The art of leadership in news organizations.* Arlington, VA: Freedom Forum.

Cohen, B. C. (1963). *The press and foreign policy.* Princeton, NJ: Princeton University Press.

Comcast makes a move on Disney. (2004, February 12). *The Tampa Tribune,* p. 1.

Compaine, B. (2001, August 11). The myths of encroaching global media ownership. Online debate at OpenDemocracy.net, available at http://www.opendemocracy.net/articles/ViewPopUpArticle.jsp?id=8&articleId=87

Connor, P. E. (1997, November/December). Total quality management: A selective commentary on its human dimensions, with special reference to its downside. *Public Administration Review,* 501–509.

Conrad, C. (1983). Organizational power: Faces and symbolic forms. In L. L. Putnam & M. E. Pacanowsky (Eds.), *Communication and organizations: An interpretive approach* (pp. 173–194). Newbury Park, CA: Sage.

Cragan, J., & Shields, D. (1993). *Symbolic theories in applied communication research.* Cresskill, NJ: Hampton Press.

Criado, C. A., & Kraeplin, C. (2003, July–August). *The state of convergence journalism: United States media and university study.* Paper presented at the annual convention of the Association for Education in Journalism and Mass Communication, Kansas City, MO.

Cunningham, B. (2003, July 11). Rethinking objective journalism. *Columbia Journalism Review.*

Curran, J. (2002, May 23). Global media concentration: Shifting the argument. Online debate at OpenDemocracy.net, available at http://www.opendemocracy.net/articles/ViewPopUpArticle.jsp?id=*&articleId=37

Daily, L., Demo, L., & Spillman, M. (2003, July–August). *The convergence continuum: A model for studying collaboration between media newsrooms.* Paper presented at the annual convention of the Association for Education in Journalism and Mass Communication, Kansas City, MO.

Daniels, G. (2003, July–August). *Conceptualizing the convergence craze: A three-dimensional model of multi-media curriculum reform.* Paper presented at the annual convention of the Association for Education in Journalism and Mass Communication, Kansas City, MO.

Dash, J. (2003, October 17). More companies click on Internet advertising. *Baltimore Business Journal,* 21(22), 9.

Demers, D. (1993). Effect of corporate structure on autonomy of top editors at U.S. dailies. *Journalism Quarterly,* 70(3).

Demers, D. (2002). *Global media: Menace or messiah?* (Rev. ed.). Cresskill, NJ: Hampton Press.

Dennis, E. (1994, June 16–17). *Troubling trends or anomalous problems: Reflections on the field of communications.* Speech delivered as opening remarks at the University of Texas conference on the State of the Field of Communications, Austin, TX.

Dennis, E. E. (2003, Spring). Prospects for a big idea: Is there a future for convergence? *The International Journal on Media Management,* 5(1).

Dennis, E. E., & Merrill, J. C. (2002). *Media debates: Great issues for the digital age.* Belmont, CA: Wadsworth.

Dijkstra, J. J. (1999). User agreement with incorrect expert system advice. *Behavior and Information Technology,* 18(6), 399–411.

Dose, J. J. (1997, September). Work Values: An Integrative framework and illustrative application to organizational socialization. *Journal of Occupational and Organizational Psychology,* 70(3), pp 219-240.

Drake, W. (Ed.). (1995). *The new information infrastructure: Strategies for U.S. policy.* The Twentieth Century Fund, Inc.

Drazin, R., Glynn, M. A., & Kazanijian. (1999, April). Multilevel theorizing about creativity in organizations: A sensemaking perspective. *Academy of Management Review,* 24(2), 286–307.

Eisenberg, E., & Goodall, H. L. (2004). *Organizational communication* (4th ed.). Boston: Bedford/St. Martins Press.

Ekstrom, M. (2000). Information, storytelling and attractions, TV journalism in three modes of communication. *Media, Culture & Society, 22, 465–492.*

Epstein, E. (2003, October 14). Congress tries to put clamps on media mergers— Anger at FCC ruling brings calls for laws, but satisfying Bush, both houses difficult. *San Francisco Chronicle,* p. A6.

Etzioni, A. (1975). *A comparative analysis of complex organizations.* New York: Free Press.

Falbe, C. M., & Yuki, G. (1992). Consequences for managers using single influence tactics and combination of tactics. *Academy of Management Journal,* 35(3), 638–647.

Fayol, H. (1965). *General and industrial management* (C. Storrs, Trans.). Sir Isaac Pitman and Sons. (Original work published 1949.)

Federal Communications Commission (2002, September 13). *FCC initiates proceeding to review newspaper-broadcast cross-ownership rule.* [FCC press release].

Federal Communications Commission (2003, March 14). *In the matter of the 2002 biennial regulatory review.* (FCC Report No. 02-342).

Fee, F. (2002, August 7–10). *New(s) players and new(s) values? A test for convergence in the newsroom.* Paper presented at the annual convention of the Association for Education in Journalism and Mass Communication, Miami, FL.

Felkins, P. K., Chakiris, B. J., & Chakiris, K. (2001). *Change management: A model for effective organizational performance.* Portland, OR: Productivity Press.

Ferris, G., Perrewe, P., Anthony, W., & Gilmore, D. (2000, Spring). Political skill at work. *Organizational Dynamics, 28*(4), 23–37.

Fidler, R. (1997). *Mediamorphosis: Understanding new media.* Thousand Oaks, CA: Pine Forge Press.

Filak, V. (2003, August 6). *Cultural convergence: An examination of intergroup bias and journalism.* Paper presented to the annual convention of the Association for Education in Journalism and Mass Communication, Kansas City, MO.

Finegan, J. E. (2000). The Impact of person and organizational values on organizational commitment. *Journal of Occupational and Organizational Psychology, 73*(2), 149–170.

Fisher, D. (2002, November). *The editor's role in hypertext future: The journey from story generalist and media specialist.* Paper presented at the annual Newsplex conference on The Dynamics of Convergent Media, Columbia, SC.

Ford, C. (2000, April). Creative developments in creativity theory. *The Academy of Management Review, 25*(2), 284–285.

Ford, C. (2002). The futurity of decisions as a facilitator of organizational creativity and change. *Journal of Organizational Change Management, 15*(6), 635–646.

Foucault, M. (1977). *Discipline and punish: The birth of the prison.* Harmondsworth, England: Penguin.

Foucault, M. (1986). Disciplinary power and subjugation. In S. Lukes (Ed.), *Power* (pp. 229–241). Oxford, England: Blackwell.

Frieden, R. M. (2003, Spring). Fear and loathing in information and telecommunications industries: Reasons for and solutions to the current financial meltdown and regulatory quagmire. *The International Journal on Media Management, 5*(1).

Gamache, R. D., & Kuhn, R. L. (1989). *The creativity infusion: How managers can start and sustain creativity and innovation.* New York: Harper & Row.

Garcia-Murillo, M. (2003, Spring). The impact of technological convergence on the regulation of ICT industries. *The International Journal on Media Management, 5*(1).

Gherardi, S. (2002). Organizational leaning. In A. Sorge (Ed.), *Organization* (pp. 419–431). London: Thomson Learning.

Gibson, O. (2003, October 8). Vivendi finalises NBC Universal deal. *The Guardian.*

Gitlin, T. (1998). Not so fast. In N. Woodhull & R. Snyder (Eds.), *Media Mergers*. New Brunswick: Transaction Press.

Gorney, C. (2002). *The business of news: A challenge for journalism's next generation*. New York: Carnegie Corporation.

Haiman, R. J. (2002). *Best practices for newspaper journalists*. Arlington, VA: Freedom Forum.

Halberstam, D. (1979). *The powers that be*. New York: Dell.

Hansell, S. (2003, December 29). Internet advertising thrives on targeted ads. *New York Times*, p. c6.

Harrison, J. (2003, July 1). Pent-up demand for deals will spur media M&A as much as FCC rulings. *The Dealmaker's Journal*, p. 1.

Hesmondhalgh, D. (2001, November 29). Ownership is only part of the media picture. Online debate at OpenDemocracy.net, available at http://www.opendemocracy.net/articles/ViewPopUpArticle.jsp?id=8&articleId=46

Houseley, W., Nicholls, T., & Southwell, R. (2001). *Managing in the media*. (P. Block, Ed.). Oxford, England: Focal Press.

Howard, L. (1999). Mergers won't mesh without people plan. *National Underwriter (Property casualty/risk & benefits ed.)*, 103(34), 7–8.

Howard, P. (2004, March 6). Remarks during the 29th annual Southeast Regional Colloquium of the Association for Education in Journalism and Mass Communication, University of South Florida, Tampa, FL.

Hoynes, W. (2002, January 16). Why media mergers matter. Online debate at OpenDemocracy.net, available at http://www.opendemocracy.net/articles/ViewPopUpArticle.jsp?id=8&articleId=47

Inside cover. (2004, January). *PC Magazine*.

Jackson, D. (2000). *Becoming dynamic: Creating and sustaining a dynamic organisation*. New York: St. Martin's Press.

Jankowski, N. W. (2002). *Community media in the information age*. Cresskill, NJ: Hampton Press.

Jennings, P. (2003, November 19). Remarks during town hall meeting at the University of South Florida, Tampa, FL.

Kabanoff, B., Waldersee, R., & Cohen, M. (1995). Espoused values and organizational change themes. *Academy of Management Journal, 38*, 1075–1105.

Karnitsching, M., & Boston, W. (2002, February 6). German media firms try to save kirch—Aim is to block Murdoch from using the crisis to win dominance. *The Wall Street Journal*, p. A10.

Katz, J., Nochlin, P. & Stover, R. (1962). *Writers on Ethics: Classical and Contemporary*. Princeton, NJ: D. Van Nostrand Company, Inc.

Killebrew, K. C. (1993). *Management styles among mass media editors: A comparative study between SYMLOG and symbolic convergence theories*. Unpublished master's thesis, Illinois State University.

Killebrew, K. C. (2003). Culture, creativity and convergence: Managing journalists in a changing information workplace. *The International Journal on Media Management,* 5(1), 39–46.

Koncel, J. (1998). Managing in a time of uncertainty. *PIMA's Papermaker,* 80(10), 72–73.

Kunkel, T. (2002, March). Go slow on cross-ownership: It would be bad for news consumers. *American Journalism Review,* 24(2), 4.

LaBaton, S. (2004, February 9). Thorny issues await F.C.C. as it takes up Internet phones. *New York Times.*

Lancaster, K. (1973). *Macroeconomics: Modern economics, principles and policy.* Chicago: Rand McNally & Company.

Legare, T. L. (1998). The human side of mergers and acquisitions. *Human Resource Planning,* 21(1), 32–41.

Lehrer, J. (2002, September). *Returning to our roots.* The Red Smith Lecture in Journalism, John W. Gallivan Program in Journalism, Ethics and Democracy, University of Notre Dame, IN.

Levin, J. (2003). Cross-media ownership: The debate continues. *Australian Screen Education,* 32, 38–41.

Lewin, K. (1947). Group decision and social change. In T. N. Newcomb & E. L. Hartley (Eds.), *Readings in Social Psychology.* Troy, MO: Holt, Rinehart and Winston.

Li, J. (2000, August). *Looking for the right partners in the information era: A longitudinal study of acquisition strategies by the communications industries.* Paper presented to the annual convention of the Association for Education in Journalism and Mass Communication, Baltimore, MD.

Lim, V. (2004, March 6). Remarks during the 29th annual Southeast Regional Colloquium of the Association for Education in Journalism and Mass Communication, University of South Florida, Tampa, FL.

Liu, F. (2003, Spring). Partnerships between the old and new: Examining the strategic alliances between broadcast television networks and Internet firms in the context of convergence. *The International Journal on Media Management,* 5(1).

Lowe, A. (1998). Managing the post-merger aftermath by default remodelling. *Management Decision,* 36(2), 102–110.

Luna, C. (2003, October 20). The region: Internet upstarts savor victory in a big league. *Los Angeles Times,* p. B-4.

Mazzocco, D. (1994). *Networks of power: Corporate TV's threat to democracy.* Boston: South End Press.

McChesney, R. (1996). The Internet and U.S. communication policymaking in historical and critical perspective. *Journal of Communication,* 46(1), 98–124.

McChesney, R. (1997). *Corporate media and the threat to democracy.* Seven Stories Press.

McChesney, R. (2001, October 25). Policing the thinkable. Online debate at OpenDemocracy.net, available at http://www.opendemocracy.net/articles/ViewPopUpArticle.jsp?id=8&articleId=56

McCombs, M. E., & Shaw, D. L. (1972). The agenda-setting function of mass media. *Public Opinion Quarterly,* 36, 176–187.

Media and technology in 2004; as 2 powerful industries converge, change will abound. (2003, December 29). *The New York Times,* p. c1.

Media General 2000. (2000, December 8). Presentation and discussion on convergence with author at The News Center, Tampa, FL.

Mensing, D. (2003, July–August). *The economics of online newspapers.* Paper presented at the annual convention of the Association for Education in Journalism and Mass Communication, Kansas City, MO.

Merrill, J. C. (Ed.). (1995). *Global journalism: Survey of international communication* (3rd ed.). White Plains, NY: Longman Publishing.

Messmer, M. (1998). Managing and motivating during a merger. *Management Accounting,* 79, 10.

Meyrowitz, J. (2002). Medium theory. In E. K. Bucy (Ed.), *Living in the information age.* Belmont, CA: Wadsworth Publishing.

Miller, R. (2002, March). The Frankenstein syndrome: The creation of mega-media conglomerates and ethical modeling in journalism. *Journal of Business Ethics,* 36(1/2), 105–110.

Mills, T., Boylstein, C., & Lorean, S. (2001). "Doing" organizational culture in the Saturn corporation. *Organizational Studies,* 22(1), 117–143.

Mollison, T. (1998, Winter). Opening their window to the world. *Journal of Broadcasting,* 42(1), 128–142.

Morley, D. D., Shockley-Zalabak, P., & Cesario, R. (1997). Organizational communication and culture: A study of 10 Italian high-technology companies. *The Journal of Business Communication,* 34(3), 253–269.

Morris, M., & Ogan, C. (1996). The Internet as mass medium. *Journal of Communication,* 46(1), 39–51.

Mosco, V. (1999). New York.com: A political economy of the "informational" city. *Journal of Media Economics,* 12(2), 103–116.

Moses, L. (2003, June 30). Coming up for air. *Editor & Publisher,* 14–20.

Mumby, D. (1987). The political function of narrative in organizations. *Communications Monographs,* 54, 113–127.

Myrsiades, L. (2001). Looking to lead: A case in designing executive education from the inside. *Journal of Management Development,* 20(9), 795–812.

Nace, T. (2002). *Gangs of America: The rise of corporate power and the disabling of democracy.* San Francisco: Berrett-Koehler.

Nahavandi, A., & Malekzadeh, A. (1988). Acculturation in mergers and acquisitions. *Academy of Management Review,* 13, 79–90.

Napoli, P. M. (2001). *Foundations of communications policy: Principles and process in the regulation of electronic media.* Cresskill, NJ: Hampton Press.

News Corporation Ltd. (2003, December 22). *News corporation, GM and Hughes complete Hughes transactions*. [News Release about DirectTV acquisition.] Available online at http://newscorp.com/index2.html

Noll, A. M. (2003, Spring). The myth of convergence. *The International Journal on Media Management,* 5(1).

O'Keefe, D. J. (1990), *Persuasion: Theory and research*. Newbury Park, CA: Sage.

Online NewsHour [Web site of *The NewsHour with Jim Lehrer*]. (2003, September 19). *AOL dropped from Time Warner name*. Retrieved from http://www.pbs.org/newshour/bb/business/aol_time_index.html

Ó Siochrú, S., & Girard, B. (2002). *Global media governance: A beginner's guide*. Lanham, MD: Rowman & Littlefield.

Parsons, P. R., & Frieden, R. M. (1998). *The cable and satellite television industries*. Boston: Allyn & Bacon.

Pavlik, J. V. (1998). *New media technology: Cultural and commercial perspectives*. Boston: Allyn & Bacon.

Pavlik, J. V. (2001). *Journalism and new media*. New York: Columbia University Press.

Pearce, R. J. (2000). The general manager's perspective on how factionalism can impact the behaviors and effectiveness of top managers inside a shared management joint venture. *Journal of Management and Governance,* 4, 189–206.

Petty, R. E., & Cacioppo, J. T. (1986). *Communication and persuasion: Central and peripheral routes to attitude change*. New York: Springer-Verlag.

Pew Research Center for the People and the Press (1999). *Striking the balance* [periodic review of the press]. Washington, DC: Author.

Pipeline. (2004, January). *PC Magazine*, 25.

Poole, S., & McPhee, R. D. (1983). A structurational analysis of organizational climate. In L. L. Putnam & M. E. Pacanowsky (Eds.), *Communication and organizations: An interpretive approach* (pp. 195–219). Newbury Park, CA: Sage.

Popcorn, S., & Hanft, A. (2001). *Dictionary of the future: The words, terms and trends that define the way we'll live, work and talk*. New York: Hyperion.

Potter, D. (2002, July–August). The body count: Want to know why local TV news is thin? Just look at the number of staffers. *American Journalism Review,* 24, 60.

Powers, A., & Lacy, S. (1992). A model of job satisfaction in local television news. In S. Lacy, A. Sohn, & R. Giles (Eds.), *Readings in media management*. Columbia, SC: Association for Education in Journalism and Mass Communication.

Prasad, L. (1993, Summer). The etiology of organizational politics: Implications for the intrapreneur. *SAM Advanced Management Journal,* 35–41.

Pratkanis, A. R., & Greenwald, A. G. (1989). A sociocognitive model of attitude structure and function. In L. Berkowitz (Ed.), *Advances in experimental social psychology*, 22, 245–285. New York: Academic Press.

Price, V. (1992). *Communication concepts 4: Public opinion*. Newbury Park, CA: Sage.

Price Waterhouse Change Integration Team. (1996). *Paradox principles, the: How high performance companies manage chaos, complexity and contradiction to achieve superior results*. : Price Waterhouse LLP.

Pringle, P., Starr, M., & McCavitt, W. (1999). *Electronic Media Management* (4th ed.). Woburn, MA: Focal Press.

Proctor, T. (1995). *The essence of management creativity* (A. Buckley, Series Ed.). London: Prentice Hall.

Putnam, L. L. (1983). The interpretive perspective: An alternative to functionalism. In L. L. Putnam & M. E. Pacanowsky (Eds.), *Communication and organizations: An interpretive approach* (pp. 31–54). Newbury Park, CA: Sage.

Quinn, S. (2004, March 6). *Convergence's fundamental question*. Paper presented at the Southeast Colloquium of the Association for Education in Journalism and Mass Communication, Tampa, FL.

Ranieri, R. (2002, March 14). Can Berlusconi do no right? Online debate at OpenDemocracy.net, available at http://www.opendemocracy.net/articles/ViewPopUpArticle.jsp?id=8&articleId=63

Redmond, J., & Trager, R. (2004). *Balancing on the wire: The art of media organizations* (2nd ed.). Boulder, CO: Coursewise.

Rogers, M. (1998). Moguls, past and present. In N. Woodhull & R. Snyder (Eds.), *Media Mergers*. New Brunswick, NJ: Transaction Press.

Rokeach, M. (1973). *The nature of human values*. New York: Free Press.

Rolland, A. (2003, Spring). Convergence as strategy for value creation. *The International Journal on Media Management*, 5(1).

Rothenberg, R. (1998, June). Bye-bye: The net's accountability will kill not only traditional advertising, but parasite, big media. *Wired Magazine*, 72–76.

Roy, D. D., & Ghose, M. (1997, June). Awareness of hospital environment and organizational commitment. *The Journal of Social Psychology*, 137, 380–386.

Rushkoff, D. (2002). Public relations. In E. P. Bucy (Ed.), *Living in the information age*. Belmont, CA: Wadsworth Publishing.

Samoriski, J. (2002). *Issues in cyberspace: Communication, technology, law and society on the Internet frontier*. Boston: Allyn & Bacon.

Schein, E. (1993, Winter). How can organizations learn faster? The challenge of entering the green room. *Sloan Management Review*, 34(2), 85–96.

Schein, E. (1993). On dialogue, culture, and organizational learning. *Organizational Dynamics*, 22(22), 40–51.

Schein, E. (1996, Fall). Three cultures of management: The key to organizational learning. *Sloan Management Review*, 38(1), 9–12.

Schein, E. (1997). *Organizational culture and leadership*. San Francisco: Jossey-Bass.

Schein, E. (1999). *The corporate culture survival guide*. San Francisco: Jossey-Bass.

Schlesinger, P. (1993). Wishful thinking: Cultural politics, media and collective identities in Europe. *Journal of Communication,* 43(2), 6–17.

Schneider, W. H. (1994). *The reengineering alternative: A plan for making your current culture work*. Burr Ridge, IL: Irwin Professional.

Schrage, M. (2002). Is advertising finally dead? In E. P. Bucy (Ed.), *Living in the information age*. Belmont, CA: Wadsworth.

Sears, W., & Tamulionyte-Lentz, A. (2001). *Succeeding in business in Central and Eastern Europe*. Woburn, MA: Butterworth-Heinemann.

Sheler, M. (1961) *Man's place in nature* (H. Meyerhoff, Trans.). Boston: Beacon Press. (Original work published 1928.)

Shoemaker, P. J., & Reese, S. D. (1996). *Mediating the message: Theories and influences on mass media content*. White Plains, NY: Longman.

Singer, J. (2003, July). *The sociology of convergence: Challenges and change in newspaper news work*. Paper presented at the annual convention of the Association for Education in Journalism and Mass Communication, Kansas City, MO.

Smith, F. L., Meeske, M., & Wright, J. W., II. (1995). *Electronic media and government*. White Plains, NY: Longman.

Sohn, A., Wicks, J., Lacy, S., & Sylvie, G. (1999). *Media management: A casebook approach* (2nd ed.). Mahwah, NJ: Erlbaum.

Sorge, A. (Ed.). (2002). *Organization*. London: Thomson Learning.

Stamm, K., & Underwood, D. (1993, Autumn). The relationship of job satisfaction to newsroom policy changes. *Journalism Quarterly,* 70(3).

Stein, N. (2002). Slate vs. salon: The leading online magazines struggle to get the Net. In E. P. Bucy (Ed.), *Living in the information age*. Belmont, CA: Wadsworth.

Sullivan, W., Sullivan, R., & Buffton, B. (2002). Aligning individual and organisational values to support change. *Journal of Change Management*.

Taylor, F. (1947). *Scientific Management*. New York: Harper.

That's digitainment. (2004, January). *PC World, p. 104*.

Thelan, G. (2003, August). Remarks at retreat for School of Mass Communications, University of South Florida, Tampa, FL.

Timmereck, T. (2001, September). Managing motivation and developing job satisfaction in the health care work environment. *The Health Care Manager*, 20(1), 42–58.

Van Cuilenburg, J., & McQuail, D. (2003). Media policy paradigm shifts. *European Journal of Communication,* 18(2), 181–207.

Van Cuilenburg, J., & Verhoest, P. (1998). Free and equal access: In search of models for converging communication systems. *Telecommunications Policy,* 22(3), 171–181.

Vaughan, J. (2004, March 6). Remarks during the 29th annual Southeast Regional Colloquium of the Association for Education in Journalism and Mass Communication, University of South Florida, Tampa, FL.

Waisbord, S. (2002, February 27). *Grandes gigantes*: Media concentration in Latin America. Online debate at OpenDemocracy.net, available at http://www.opendemocracy.net/articles/ViewPopUpArticle.jsp?id=8&articleId=64

Watson, T., Libin, K., & Starr, R. (2003, March 3). What mergers will mean to you. *Canadian Business,* 76(4), 28–34.

Weber, M. (1947). *The theory of economic and social organization* (A. M. Henderson & T. Parsons, Trans.). New York: Free Press. (Original work published 1921.)

Weick, K. E. (1983). Organizational communication: Toward a research agenda. In L. L. Putnam & M. E. Pacanowsky (Eds.), *Communication and organizations: An interpretive approach* (pp. 13–29). Newbury Park, CA: Sage.

Williams, D. (2002, September). Synergy bias: Conglomerates and promotion in the news. *Journal of Broadcasting and Electronic Media.*

Williams, K. (2004, March 6). Remarks during the 29th annual Southeast Regional Colloquium of the Association for Education in Journalism and Mass Communication, University of South Florida, Tampa, FL.

Winter, C. (2003, November 30). Christine Winter column. *South Florida Sun-Sentinel*, via *Knight Ridder Tribune Business News*, p. 1.

Witkoski, M. (2002, November). *From Plato to Newsplex: Walter J. Ong and the convergences of the word*. Paper presented at the annual Newsplex conference on The Dynamics of Convergent Media, Columbia, SC.

Woodhull, N., & Snyder, R. (Eds.). (1998). *Media Mergers*. New Brunswick: Transaction Press.

Woodman, R., Sawyer, J., & Griffin, R. (1993, April). Toward a theory of organizational creativity. *The Academy of Management Review,* 18(2), 293–321.

Yang, C. (2003, June 9). Where media merger mania could strike first if the FCC eases its rules, look for local newspaper deals. *Business Week,* 96.

Zavonia, S., & Reichert, T. (2000). Media convergence/ management change: The evolving workflow of visual journalists. *The Journal of Media Economics,* 13(2), 143–151.

Index